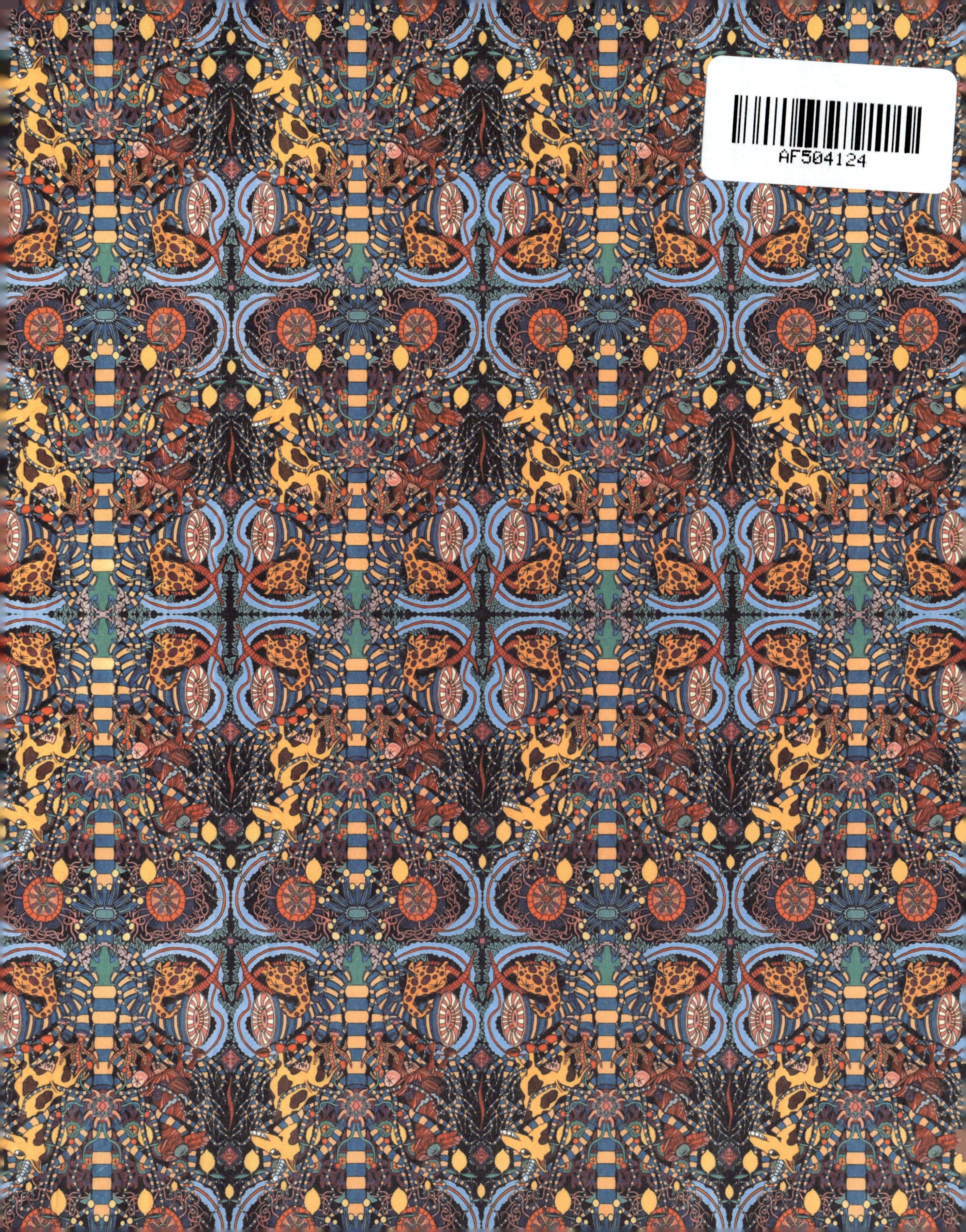
AF504124

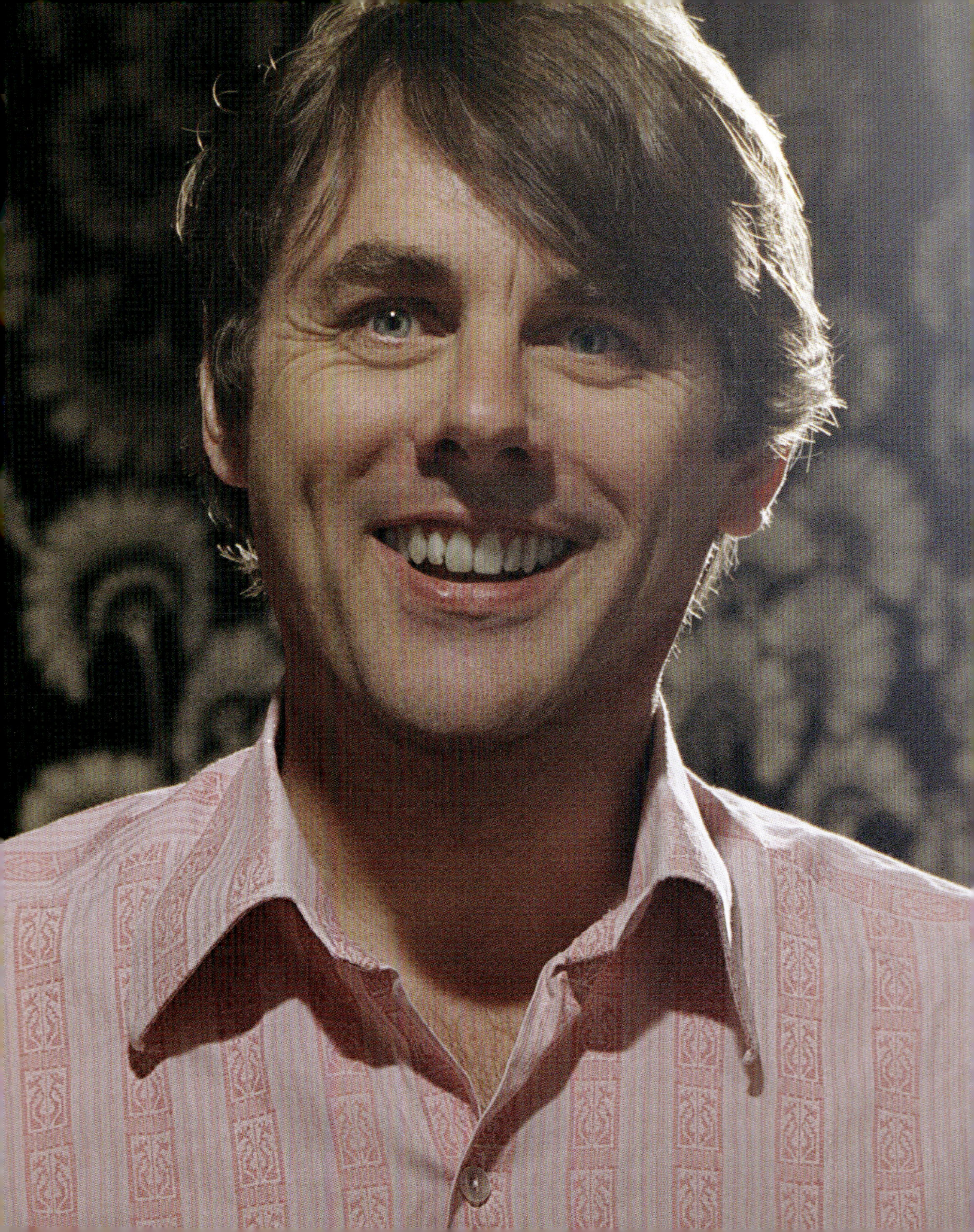

SIMON HENWOOD

Paintings and Films 1988 - 2008

Text
Charlotte Mullins
With additional contributions from
Christian Haye
Jullian Fuller
Roisin Murphy
Mario Testino
Makaito Saito

Editing
Samantha Hope

Design
David S. Blanco
originalblanco.com

Antoine Jean

Published by
Stephane Simoens Contemporary Fine Art
Golvenstraat 7
B - 8300 Knokke - Zoute
Tel. + 32 (0) 50 67 75 90
Fax + 32 (0) 50 67 75 90
stephanesimoens.com

Printed in Belgium

Adam Lucas, Adrian Sington, Alan James, Alex, Jasmin and Mel Kee, Alison Jaques, All at HSI London, Amelie De Andreis Angela McKalister, Anne Elizabeth Suter, Annie Philbin, Antoine Jean, Art Spiegleman, Balwant Adhir, Barry Adamson Beth Montague, Betsy Damon, Bob Petri (where are you now), Bronwyn Keenan, Carolyn Chrisov- Bakargiev, Charlie Inskip Charlotte Mullins, Charlotte Bavasso, Chris O'Reilly, Chris Webb, Christian Haye, Claire Luke, Dame Darcy, Dan Knight Daneil Aber, Dave and Francine Sumners, David O'Sullivan, David S. Blanco, Deryk Thomas, Devendra Banhart, Devon Dikeou, Dez Skin, Eddy Stevens, Edith Southwell, Edward Gorey RIP, Elaine Constantine, Emily Morley, Eric Pillault, Fernando Monoso, Fulvio Testa, Gareth McKewan, Gary Groth, Gerard Saint, Gerie Couture, Godfried Helnwien, Graham Fellows, Graham Peacock, Greg Burne, Henry Rollins, Imogen Heap, James Baker, James Elaine, Jason Gormley, Jeff Kinsel, Jennifer Heslin, Jesse Richards, Jim Coutrell, Jim Johnstone, Jimi Dams (and all at Envoy), Joe Lovett, Jon Adams John Canemaker, John Howard, Johnathan Attenborough, Jon Goldstein, Juliette Larthe, Kanye West, Karen Heard, Karvi Gupta, Kate Anderson, Koji Yoshida, Kylie Minogue, Larissa Harris, Larry Clarke, Lou Stathus (RIP), Luella Jane Wright M. Hennry Jones, Makaito Saito, Malcome Venvile, Mario Testino, Mark Freeland, Mark Procopio, Marshal Arisman Martin Carroll, Mary Barone, Matt Groening, Matt Law, Matt Maitland, Michael Gira, Michael Lavine, Mike Kieler, Mike McKenna, Monte Beauchant, Moritz Stieger, Mum and Dad, Nick Mayland, Nicola Doring, Noko, Ondrej Rudavsky, Page Paul Amer, Paul Cheshire, Paul Davis, Paul Hofner, Paul Smith, Paula Rego, Phil Bicker, Phil Miller, Phil Tidy, Polly Holt Rachael Amedeo, Raphiel Rubinstien, Richard, Richard Hell, Richard Heller, Richard Kern, Richard Mott, Richard Weager Ricky Gervais, Rob Manley, Robert Popper, Roisin Murphy, Sally Boon, Sam Hope, Sam Tidman, Sarha (Collete) , Sarha Staton, Stavros Merjos, Stephane McMillan, Stephane Siemons, Steve Gullick, Stu Mead, Stuart Spalding, Sue Tasky, Susie Jenkin Pearce, Tamzin Merchant, Ted McKeever, Theo Williams, Tom Hughes, Tony Thorne, Torch gallery, Tot Taylor

This book is dedicated to my Godsons, Kenneth, Atticus , Pedro, Herbie and to Mum, Dad and Roisin.

simonhenwood.com

Contents

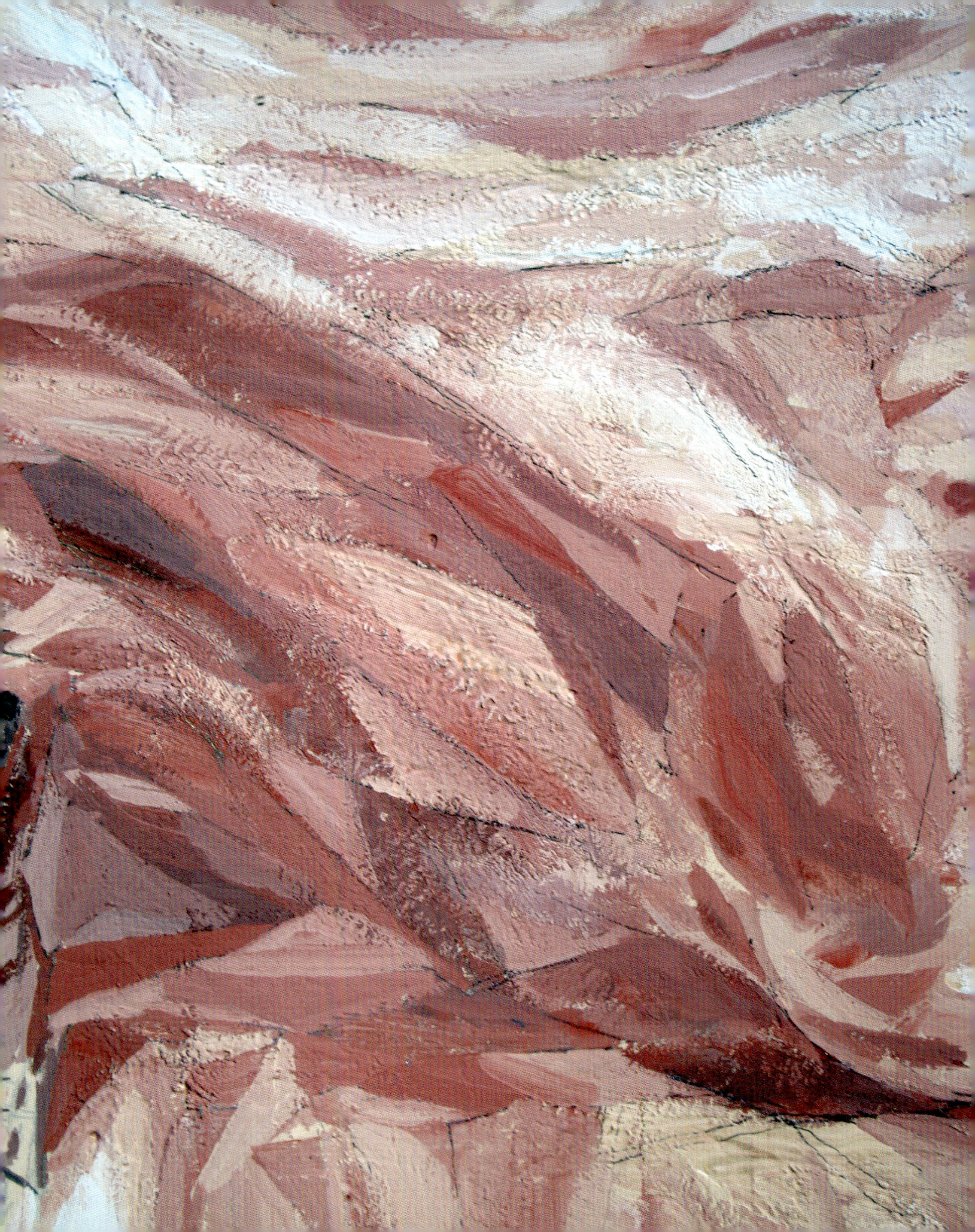

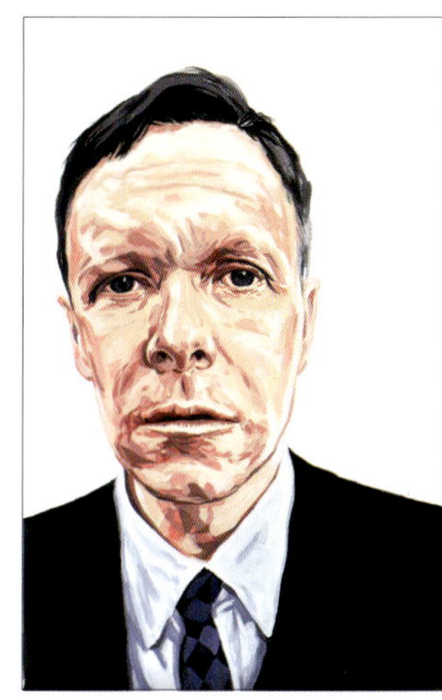

Introduction

Simon Henwood is a big hungry man with supernatural powers and a superhuman reserve of energy. He possesses an omnivorous appetite for all things visual and a seemingly omnipotent ability to transform what he devours into compelling visual talismans, whether in the medium of film, video, painting or graphics. One can only speculate (!) how he finds the time and personal stamina necessary to accomplish so many divergent tasks at once. With a Warholian dispassionate lust for popular culture, a natural affinity for the sybarite's approach to living and processing experience ala Francis Bacon, and the meticulous attention to detail and technique of Rossetti, he has somehow managed to make himself the true Master of the CRINGE. Particularly in his paintings of adolescents suffering at the cusp of their sexuality and the recent "Failed Actor" series, one can see the subjects of these pictures writhing in discomfort beneath his, and in turn, our gaze, like stunned insects feeling the precisely focused sun searing their shell beneath a well-directed magnifying glass. And that's how it should be. As I say, Simon's supernatural. In a way, he's looking down on all of us from behind a cloud. I pity those who fall subject to his visual scrutiny. I was one such victim myself, and barely survived.

Michael Gira 2008

Awkward Accoutrements

Charlotte Mullins

Alice! A childish story take,
*   And with a gentle hand*
Lay it where childhood's dreams are twined
*   In memory's mystic band,*
Like pilgrim's witherd   wreath of flowers
*   Plucked in a far-off land.*

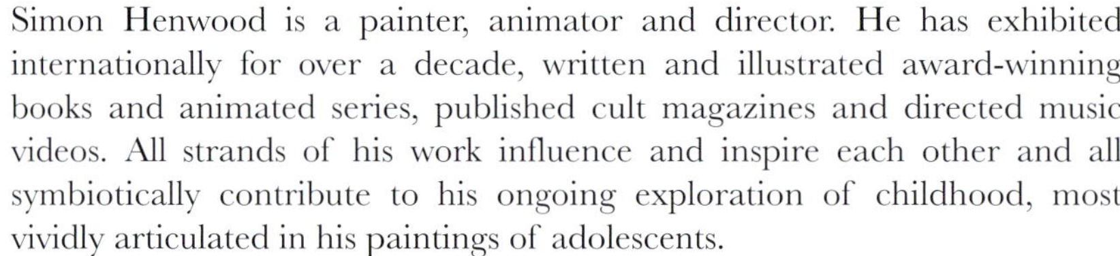

Simon Henwood is a painter, animator and director. He has exhibited internationally for over a decade, written and illustrated award-winning books and animated series, published cult magazines and directed music videos. All strands of his work influence and inspire each other and all symbiotically contribute to his ongoing exploration of childhood, most vividly articulated in his paintings of adolescents.

The childhood Henwood is interested in is not one of candy-coated innocence. It is the surreal territory of Alice as she ventures into Wonderland, the purity of childhood at all times threatened by the onslaught of maturity and an understanding of the capricious and bleak workings of the adult world. His inspiration is drawn from the films of Jean Cocteau and David Lynch as much as Disney, and he is attracted to the reworked fairytales of Paula Rego and the fantasies of Mervyn Peake. The uncanny, as explored by Sigmund Freud and typified by Edgar Allen Poe, Diane Arbus and Stanley Kubrick, laces his work. In his paintings, his teenage protagonists squint and squirm, their bed-head hair mussed up, their experimental make-up starting to run, their braces and spots awkward accoutrements. His children's books deal with greed, envy and quarrelsome relations; his animations feature a dystopic universe in which adults are hell-bent on destroying the world and only a group of children from the fringes of society can stop them.

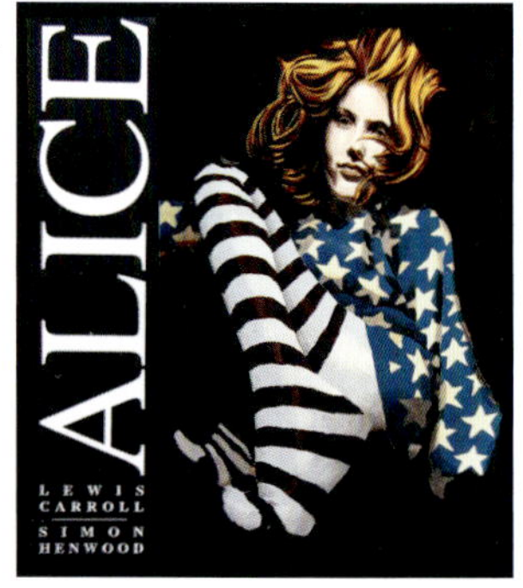

Cover for Alice in Wonderland
Artist edition, London 1991.

Given the range of Henwood's work, it is perhaps not surprising to discover that he graduated with a mixed arts degree from Exeter University. Following a peripatetic childhood he took a foundation course in Salisbury before enrolling at Exeter on a Fine Arts degree. But the limitations of the course frustrated him. One of the reasons for wanting to study at Exeter was its strong commitment to life drawing, and he spent two days a week, for three years, drawing and painting directly from the figure. But he also wanted to experiment with other media. He longingly eyed the old-fashioned typography department with its impressive array of metal fonts and the animation department where he was keen to explore hand-drawn animation. Henwood eventually persuaded the governors at Exeter to allow him to study these additional areas in his own time, and in 1986 he graduated with a degree in painting, animation and illustration.

Henwood moved to London after graduating and concentrated on illustration, visiting endless publishers' offices pitching his ideas for children's books. Both his illustrative style and his artwork at this point were largely graphic, a form of sketchy realism.

But by the time his first book, The King Who Sneezed, was published in 1988, his visual language was already changing. By the following year, with the publication of A Piece of Luck, he had pared his style down to feature simple, rotund characters with minimal props set against a generic townscape. "It was all about very simple expression," he says, 'getting a pose down, an idea simply communicated. My whole drawing had to be a slave to that, and it has informed everything else I have done since then."

His life drawing training, where he learnt to study and appreciate form, was combined with his own representational language, and in a little over two years he wrote and illustrated eleven children's books. They allowed him to finance a studio and his paintings at the time took their lead from ideas developed in the books. Each book was illustrated with flat planes of colour delineating sky, rocks, dresses, hands, faces. And while form was much reduced, Henwood still managed to communicate a wide range of emotions on the faces of his snub-nosed characters. In A Piece of Luck, a disturbing and fantastical tale about a greedy man who won't share the luck he finds, we see his face express glumness, surprise, happiness, avarice, pride, arrogance, worry, concentration, effort and misery. In the angle of an eyebrow or the downturn of his mouth the greedy man lets the reader know exactly how he is feeling at any given moment.

The emotions recorded in A Piece of Luck are not those traditionally associated with children's books, and in these early publications Henwood's interest in the darker side of childhood can be seen. Much stems from his memories of his own upbringing. An only child, he attended eleven schools the length of England and Scotland as his family repeatedly moved to follow his father's job as a meteorologist. As a teenager, Henwood was placed in a school just outside Glasgow where he was endlessly bullied for being English. He remembers always feeling like an outsider, having to build relationships with other children to try to fit in, only to be told that he was moving schools yet again. (JM Barrie's maxim, "To be born is to be wrecked on an island", seems sadly appropriate .)

After two years in London Henwood decided to move to New York, and in 1989 took a room at the Chelsea Hotel for six months. His books were already being published in America, and he went on to produce more books from his new base. The late 1980s were a good time to live in the city as a figurative painter. In London, figuration had long been sidelined – Tony Cragg won the 1988 Turner Prize; sculptors such as Richard Deacon and Bill Woodrow were riding high – and those who were painting the figure all fell under the tenebrous shadow of Francis Bacon. For young artists, Goldsmiths College and quick-hit multi-media artworks made from vitrines,

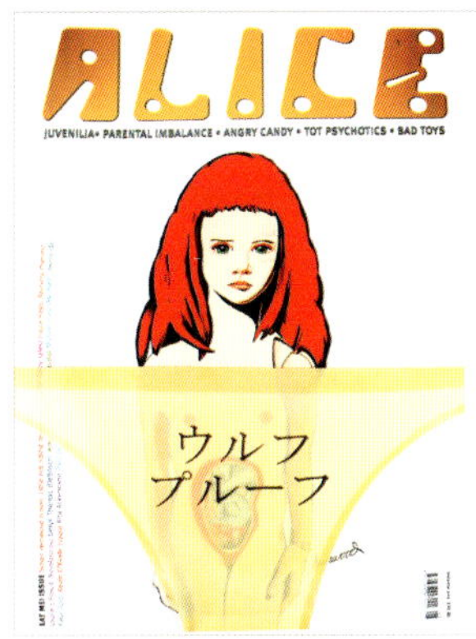

Cover of Alice magazine number one. Painting copyright Simon Henwood. Special Limited Japanese edition to the regular Format. (Featuring wrap round rubber pants – inscribed in Japanese - loose translation. "Wolf proof". 1997.

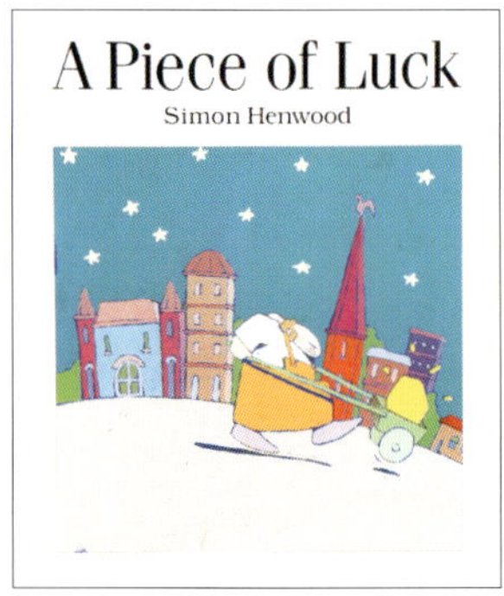

*Cover to A Piece of Luck
Published by Farrar, Straus
& Giroux, New York 1989.*

kebabs and concrete were starting to make the headlines. But in New York, artists such as John Currin were making an impact, and figurative artists such as Rita Ackerman and Elizabeth Peyton found it a sympathetic home.

As an artist who had already found success in other areas, Henwood also felt more at home in New York than London. In London, he recalls, the prevailing belief (excluding Goldsmiths and its revolutionary new teaching practices) was still that you had to earn Your dues as an artist by serving a long and penniless apprenticeship tucked away in a remote studio.Henwood had always had to earn a living and chose to fund his painting by publishing books, but such polymathic behaviour was frowned upon. In New York however he felt that it was more acceptable, and that if someone liked your work they gave you an opportunity without scrutinizing the rest of your CV. And so he moved out of the Chelsea Hotel into an apartment and spent three years in the city, increasingly spending his time painting.

Henwood returned to London in 1992 and established the multimedia arts company Blue Eyed Dog Ltd. The company was built on relationships he had fostered in New York. It had its own record label, Kennel Club, which issued recordings by artists including Iggy Pop and Sonic Youth, as well as functioning as a television and film production house. It was also a publishing studio. Its first title was PURR, a quarterly magazine edited and in-part illustrated by Henwood and launched as a vehicle for articles and artworks for which there was currently no outlet in the UK. PURR featured writing by Hubert Selby Jr, erotic photographs by Richard Kern and an interview (conducted by Henwood) with reclusive US illustrator Edward Gorey.

Gorey had long been a hero of Henwood's. By the time he interviewed him, Gorey was 70 but was still publishing a book or more a year. His work has been described as sinister little tales about haunted, pale-featured characters living in a world of bleak, clouded landscapes and gloomy shadow-filled interior's and he has been dubbed the master of American Gothic . His pen-and-ink stories are set in claustrophobic Edwardian rooms filled with aspidistras and flock wallpaper, and often feature children coming to grizzly ends as in The Gashlycrumb Tinies (1963). Henwood first interviewed him when he lived in New York after seeing an exhibition of his work and being excited that illustration was being shown in a gallery. He went on to publish a version of Gorey's The Beastly Baby (1962) in 1995, and still talks fondly of him .

PURR came out at around the time of Dazed & Confused, and for a time shared the same distributor. Both had small print runs (PURR's was marginally larger) and served a loyal audience. But, for Henwood, the magazine took up an increasing amount of his time, and he decided to call an end to it. He continued for a while with the PURR gallery he had opened next to the Lisson on Bell Street in London where he exhibited artists featured in the magazine and published artist's books, including those by Kern and Gorey. But by 1997 he had closed this too to make way for a new exhibition and publishing programme: Alice.

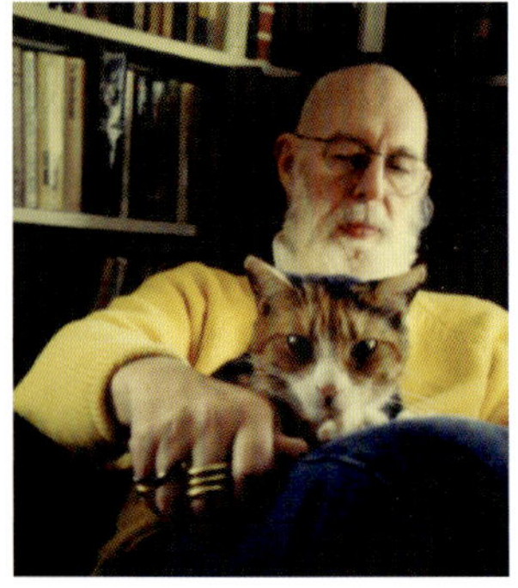

*Edward Gorey at home,
Cape Cod. Photograph
Copyright Simon Henwood 1995.*

Long before the first issue of Alice was published, shortly after his return from New York, Henwood met Paula Rego for the first time. She had just completed her year-long residency at the National Gallery, London where she had responded to the collection by producing a series of paintings based on the lives of saints.

At the time she was in the middle of looking at children's stories for inspiration. In 1988-89 she had completed a series of etchings based on the dark side of nursery rhymes , all satanic spiders and deranged farmer's wives and in 1992 she was commissioned by the Folio Society to produce fifteen prints in response to Peter Pan. She would go on to respond to the dancing animals in Fantasia and the fairy tales "Snow White" and "Pinocchio"

Henwood and Rego met several times at the National Gallery and her studio in Camden. She owned several copies of his children's books; he admired her passion for storytelling and her love of the figure, and saw in her work a validation of his own interest in children and their stories. While Rego was drawing inspiration from Peter Pan, the world-famous tale by JM Barrie, and etching the darkness embedded in the story, Wendy sewing on Peter's shadow; Captain Hook pinning a lost boy to his thigh with his hook , Henwood was responding to another children's book, Alice's Adventures in Wonderland.

In 1993 Henwood made a short film called Alice, with a score by Barry Adamson. The five minute film concentrates on the moment before the white rabbit appears in Alice's Adventures in Wonderland where Alice Liddell, having been taken on a boat trip by Lewis Caroll, sits on the riverbank with her sister. Using reverse film techniques and applying strategic colour to black-and-white footage he creates a visual wonderland that precedes the imagined story that follows. At college, Henwood had been deeply influenced by the work of Jean Cocteau, in particular his 1946 film Beauty and the Beast, and elements of it can be seen in Alice. Both Alice's Adventures in Wonderland and the fairy-tale "Beauty and the Beast" revolve around metamorphosis. In Alice's case this manifests itself in her regular bouts of shrinking and growing and the anthropomorphosis in the books of normally static objects such as the chess set . In Cocteau's film there are similar incidences of objects springing to life , the candelabras on the wall are living arms and hands, for example , and the film's denouement is the transformation of the Beast himself. Children's stories, from "Beauty and the Beast" to Alice, have an intensity and magic to them that is supplied by the transformative current that runs through them. They are dreamlike, surreal, and gain power from the story's ability to effect a great change in its protagonists.

Henwood's interest in fairy tales stretched to "Little Red Riding Hood" in 1997, and his cover illustration for the first issue of his new magazine Alice was called Little Red Ridding Hood. Under the strapline "Juvenalia, Parental Imbalance, Angry Candy, Tot Psychotics , Bad Toys" a naked

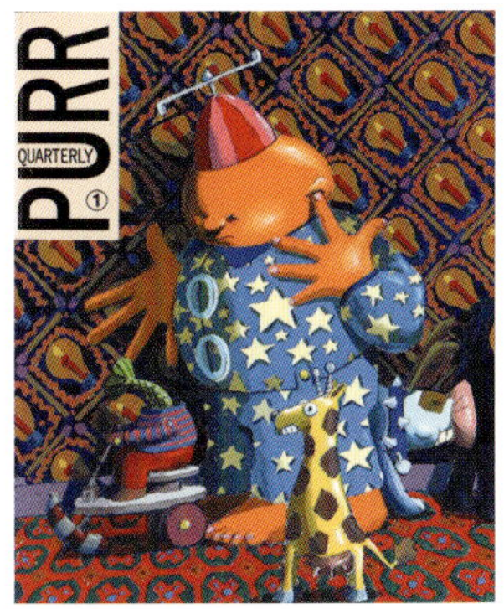

Cover to Purr magazine number one. Cover painting copyright Simon Henwood. Published by Blue Eyed Dog publishing 1992.

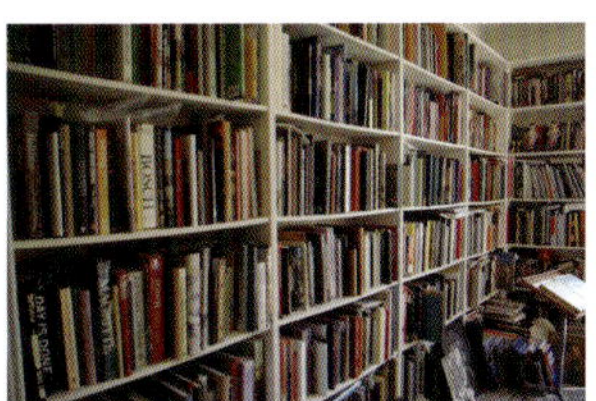

Detail of Henwood's own Library. Containing over Twenty thousand books, But still a fraction of what Edward Gorey's House Contained.

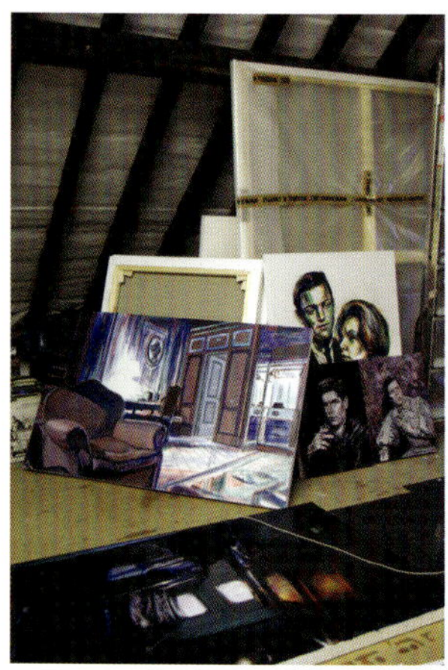

The Artists studio (detail) 2008
Works in progress.

Phil, London 2005
30 x 40 cm Gouache on paper
Portrait of one of the artist friends
From an ongoing series.
Private collection, London.

pre-pubescent girl with a mannequin's arm stands staring out from under a thick head of red hair, her stomach cut away to show a wolf growing in her tiny womb. Is she an automaton come to life, or a vision of a dystopic future where humans are part-machine? The font of the title looks like it is made from pieces of Meccano - or razor blades - and there's a fusion of life and mechanics about the entire cover that is futuristic yet disturbing. (In another work with the same title, Henwood shows a girl in a skimpy bikini appear to devour the grandmother of the "Little Red Riding Hood" story, a Regoesque emancipation of the girl's passivity in the original tale.)

The magazine Alice was published to explore how childhood is recycled in art and the media and as a way to focus ideas that had surfaced in Henwood's own work. And in the same year as the first issue of Alice was published he exhibited his first paintings publicly. They increasingly focused on teenage life as captured through portraiture. Three works were included in a group show (coincidentally also called "Alice"), which looked at childhood through the works of several artists, including Henwood and James Rielly.

Rielly paints siblings with matching black eyes; fathers and sons smoking together or with their trousers round their ankles; twin men in underpants holding hands. His work often leaves the viewer uncomfortable, but, as Emma Anderson has questioned, is this because of what we read into the work rather than something explicitly expressed by Rielly himself? A similar question could be asked of Henwood's early portraits. If we feel uncomfortable looking at scaled-up portraits of boys with pimples and braces or plump girls dressed by their mothers, is it because it takes us back to our own childhoods, to the awkward moment of metamorphosis when we started our own transformation into adulthood?

Henwood's first solo show was at the Institute of Contemporary Arts in London in September 1998. It accompanied a two-day conference called "Spoilt Children" and included seven large-scale portraits of children ranging in age from ten to fifteen. The works are painted in thick layers of gouache, each oversized head and shoulders framed against a white paper background. They are like giant passport photographs rejected by officials the bleary-eyed Daniel, age 14 from Manchester; Joey, age 14 from Las Vegas, who has no shirt on and has his index finger jammed in his mouth. In reproduction these works can look flat, causing early critics to erroneously compare them to the work of Alex Katz, and in parts the children's clothing and hair does seem startlingly two-dimensional. But in the areas of flesh they have chosen to expose the surface is richly textured and layered. They are like cartoon portraits - all sharp shadows and stylized hair - that have been worked over by a painterly colourist. The paint squirms and stretches over the teenager's skulls and around their eyes, lips, spots, as they contort their faces to look out at us.

With the exception of Johnny, age 10 Las Vegas 1997, and Sarah, age 15 Isle of Wight 1998, both of which have coloured backgrounds, the paintings in the ICA show point to a direction that Henwood has been exploring ever since. They are stripped of all superfluous detail such as background settings, props and even a coloured ground, and present each

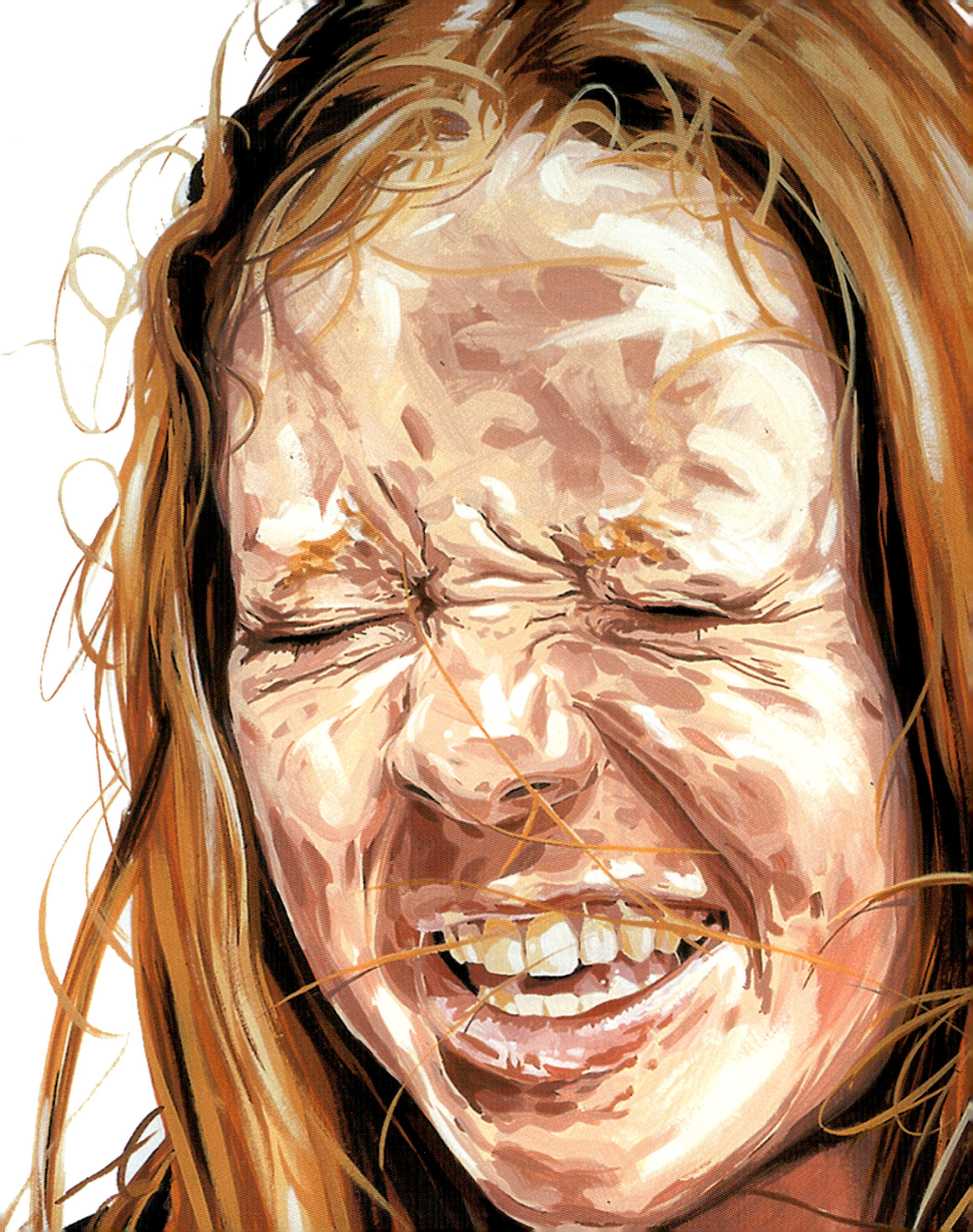

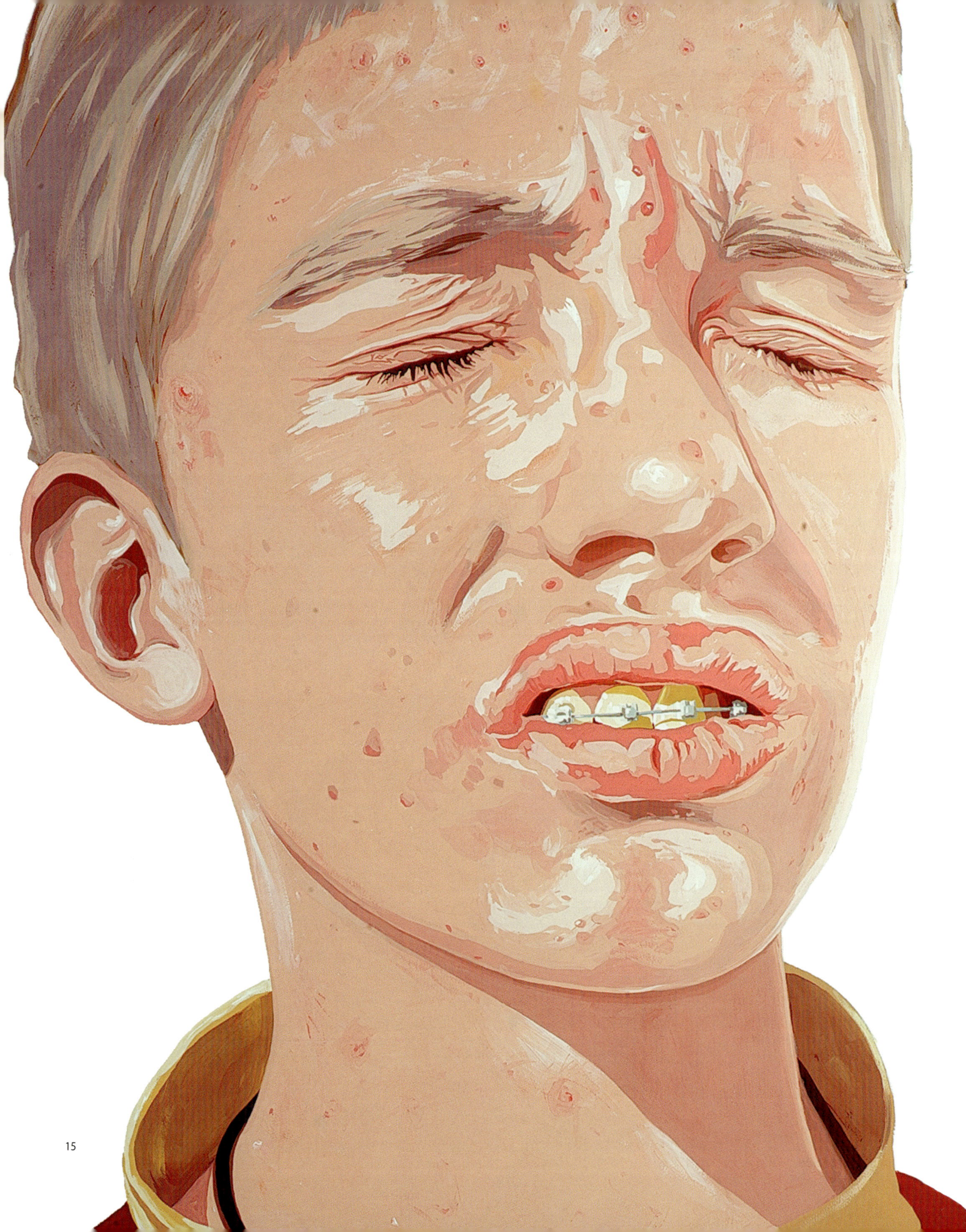

child as a close-up study of the rapidly changing emotions experienced as a teenager. Sophie stands, shoulders slightly turned away from us, looking out hesitantly, meeting our gaze with guarded eyes. Her mouth gives nothing away; it is set against us defensively. Joey (Joey, aged 14 Las Vegas, 1998) on the other hand is showing off, with his bare torso, his grimace, his attitude. There's something aggressive about the way he has rammed his finger between his teeth and now stares out, full frontal, confronting us with his entire body. As with the illustrations in his children's books, Henwood may have pared down the superfluous detail in these portraits but he has lost none of the emotional impact, and his subjects in the ICA show appeared variously arrogant, guarded, worried, serene, aggressive, embarrassed and uncaring.

Henwood says he has been drawn to paint youth because it is the quintessential transitional period of life, with so many things happening both on and under the surface. When children and teenagers sit for him he anticipates the moment in which they close down and switch off, retreating into their own minds. In the finished paintings he gives us their names, ages and the cities in which he encountered them. This is the intimate information that defines you as you are growing up. But, most importantly, Henwood distances himself from each adolescent in terms of styling and shaping the portrait. He likens the experience of painting them to visiting the dentist, "intimate, but sort of clinical." He paints them in whatever they choose to wear, and however they choose to appear. Unlike traditional portraits, where carefully selected clothes and accessories point to wealth or power or position, these children will be in tomorrow's fashions by the time the paint is dry. These are not images designed to halt the march of time but to record how fleeting it is, and to try and capture the mercurial essence of adolescence.

By returning to the same model, which Henwood frequently does, and painting them at regular intervals he records what has changed about them and what has stayed the same. But by doing this he also creates doppelgangers for each child, uncanny likenesses who look the same yet different every time. Henwood's models are already doppelgangers in a way, reminding him of children he remembers or aspects of his younger self. Doubling or dividing, an aspect of metamorphosis is something that repeatedly occurs in Carroll's Alice books, both as she talks to herself (a verbal double) and by her encounter with identical twins Tweedledum and Tweedledee. Henwood enjoys the films of David Lynch and Stanley Kubrick and the photography of Diane Arbus, all of whom have utilised the unnerving affects of duplication to disturb the viewer. From the twin girls in the hotel corridor in Kubrick's The Shining to Lynch's repeated casting of one actress in contrasting roles in the same film, the uncanny doppelganger regularly appears. Michael Bracewell has compared Arbus's unsettling photographs to the Gothic strangeness of David Lynch, and her picture of identical twins, taken in Roselle, New Jersey, in 1967 (surely the inspiration for Kubrick's mesmeric twins) has the uncanny power to completely unnerve the viewer.

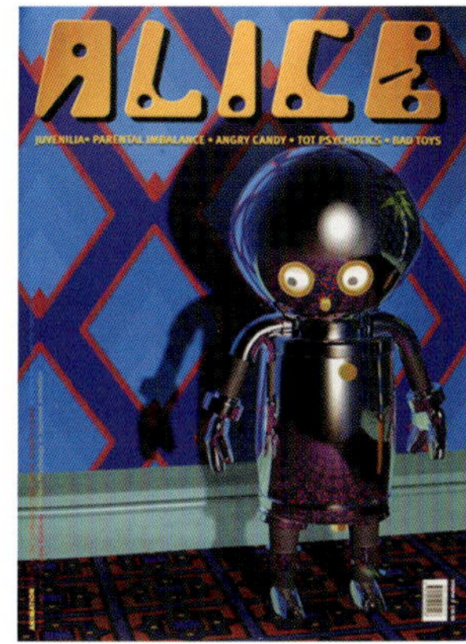

Cover to Alice magazine number two. Cover image. CGI still. The tin platted toddler -Johnny Pumpkin.

Left. Joey age 13 - Las Vegas 1998 100 x 139 cm gouache on paper.

Sigmund Freud, in his essay on "The Uncanny" (1922) includes doubling or repetition in his analysis: telepathically linked twins, characters who have split personalities, recurring events or numbers. He also includes everything "that ought to have remained secret and hidden but has come to light", and cites instances of inanimate objects coming to life as uncanny. In Henwood's works such as Real Girl, Real Doll (1999) and Little Red Ridding Hood (1997) he evokes this sense of the uncanny by softening the boundaries between the real and the imagined, the fusion of mannequin and living child.

Lewis Carroll riddled his books with uncanny happenings, not least the repeated size changes for Alice. Henwood also plays with scale. Following his early portraits where faces appeared too big to fit a paper size measuring 139x100cm, Henwood started to draw back and float certain figures in their entirety on the same white ground. As we see Sophie age in his repeated portraits of her, for example, we also see her appear to shrink, from a close-up of her face aged 14 to a half-portrait two years later and a full portrait shortly afterwards. Henwood gives us her age with each portrait, so we know she is growing, developing. But in the portraits she is shrinking, in direct contrast to a regular teenager's rapid physical growth.

Henwood's ICA exhibition led to two solo shows the following year in Tokyo and New York. The New York show was called "White Kitten" a reference to the kitten - one of a pair - at the beginning of Carroll's Through the Looking Glass. Carroll often wrote in his diaries of his interest in dreams and the subconscious; Alice's whole adventure in Wonderland takes place in a dream. The surrealists, gathering strength at the time Freud wrote "The Uncanny", were also interested in dreams (as of course was Freud) and signified their commitment to the subconscious and the world of dreams in a group photograph printed in La Révolution Surréaliste in 1929. In it, photo-booth portraits of sixteen of the key players - including André Breton, Max Ernst and Luis Buouel - surround a painting of a naked woman by Magritte, each with their eyes firmly shut. They have closed their eyes on the real world as if they are collectively dreaming the woman in their midst.

For Carroll, the surrealists and many teenagers, the interior world is more challenging and exciting than anything the "real" world can offer. Henwood's portraits allude to this. Many of his teenagers have their eyes shut, either screwed up against the sun, held firmly closed like the surrealists or caught in a blink as if a photograph has been taken at an inopportune moment. It is a physical trait that reminds us of the moment Henwood has described when he witnesses a child shutting down, switching off, entering their own imaginary, private world, the eyelids signifying that a far greater metaphysical barrier has descended.

Cartoons often occupy dream worlds, and Henwood's ongoing fascination with animation led him to develop Johnny Pumpkin, a character who lives in a dystopic fantasy world where children have to fight to save the planet from developers. Pumpkin is allergic to UV light and so lives his life in the shadows, a dark existence with other children from the edges of society.

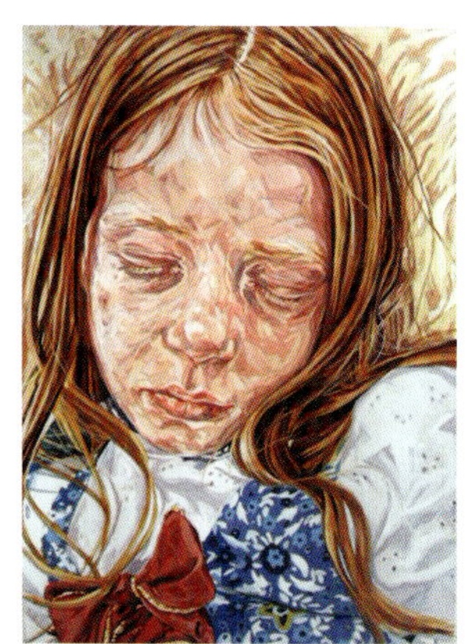

Study for Alice, 2006
20 x 40cm gouache on paper.

Henwood started working on Johnny Pumpkin in the mid-1990s, creating hundreds of paintings that professional animators then transformed into a CGI film. In many ways the cartoon is an extension of his children's books, the central character Johnny Pumpkin having the same rounded head and body as the greedy man in A Piece of Luck. Pumpkin sports blue pyjamas and a small red-and-white striped cap that is part dunce's hat, part skullcap. He goes barefoot, accompanied by an etiolated blond girl, a small boy in a motorcycle helmet and various reflective robots and invented animals. The battle is set to save the world from environmental chaos and commercial exploitation caused by adult tycoons. There are elements of Edward Gorey's diabolical tales in Johnny Pumpkin, as well as outsider-artist Henry Darger's The Story of the Vivian Girls. Johnny Pumpkin is a fairy story for contemporary society, full of "good guys" and "bad guys" all living in a fantastical, strange, grotesque world that has unnervingly similar parallels to our own.

As Henwood was completing Johnny Pumpkin he was also producing a body of paintings that were shown between 2003-05 in his "Kido" exhibition. "Kido" brought together paintings of many of his regular sitters. Sophie went from 14-year-old girl-next-door to nascent goth, her eyes now averted from the viewer, her lips stained near-black. A later work shows her a year on again, in headscarf and bomber jacket, eyes to the floor. Many of the later portraits in the show were half-length figures, and all offered more surface detail. The bright sunlight captured in many of the paintings still gave a look of surface flatness and cartoon shadow – in Helen, age 18 London, 2000, for example – linked them back to early paintings such as Johnny, age 10 Las Vegas, 2000, but the flesh was now more substantial and nuanced, the characters more life like if less forgiving.

Henwood is a great admirer of Ingres, and seeks to paint what he sees in a similar way. In Ingres' Comtesse de Tournon (1812) for example, we are initially seduced by the surfaces Ingres recreates: the bottle-green velvet of her empire-line dress, the fine woollen stole, the sheer net headdress. Then we register that she is not a beautiful woman, and Ingres has in no way tried to prettify her. He simply paints what he sees: her sumptuous dress, her prominent nose, her smooth skin, the start of a double chin not quite hidden by her ruff. For Henwood, he wants to paint the reality of adolescence – hairstyles, jewellery, fashions – but above all he wants to capture the internal emotion of his sitters. Like Ingres, Henwood is not trying to beautify or misrepresent them, but to paint them honestly.

In Henry, aged 20, London, 2002, we sense Henry's wariness as he stands naked to the waist clutching his skateboard as if it were a trophy or a protective shield. The skateboard, his closely cropped head and the designer underwear visible above his low-slung jeans form the identity he presents to the world. But Henwood, while painting these signifiers of Henry's, also paints what is signified by them. There's a sadness to Henry's pale eyes, reinforced by the slight tilt of his head and body. His bare chest is an outward sign of bravado, of maleness, but his hairless body and slim build point to his youth and inexperience. (Although, at 20, he is a relatively old subject for Henwood.)

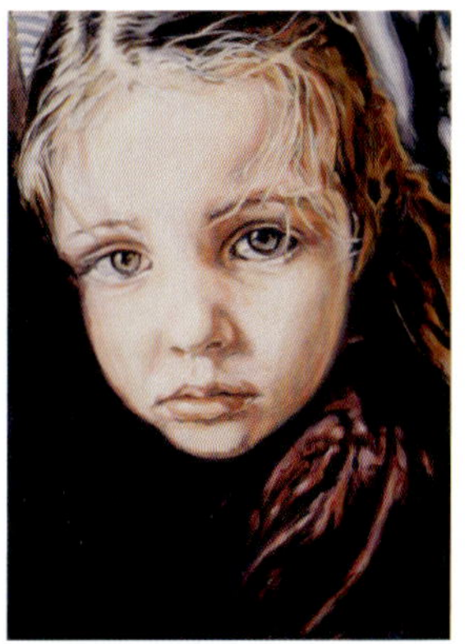

Saoirse, 2006
10 x 14 inch Oil on canvas
Private collection London.

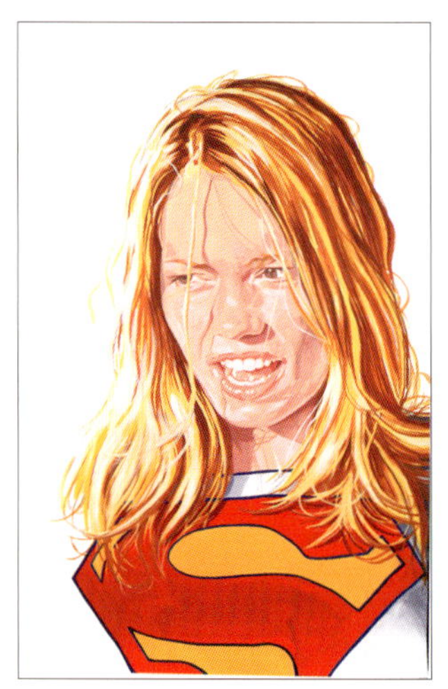

*Super girl, 50 x 90 cm Gouache on paper
2003, Special project for Interview magazine
New York.*

While from afar Henry, aged 20, London appears quite graphic, his form of Henry flattened against an anonymous white background, as you approach, the flesh breaks down and you see the quick brushstrokes ranging from dark crimson to near white that delineate his body. There's a delicacy to Henwood's treatment of the face – facets of colour not unlike those built up by Cézanne record the once-broken nose, the sheen of ginger hair. The strokes over the body are bolder. At times, in Henwood's paintings, the brushstrokes suggest the deft touch of Hals, but here, particularly under the armpit, they bring to mind the meat paintings of Soutine or the layers of unflinching realism of a Lucian Freud.

If Larry Clark were British, you would expect someone like Henry to appear in one of his films. Clark – a US film director, photographer and writer – immerses himself in the pre-adult world in a similar way to Henwood. He started out photographing his friends as they all grew up in Tulsa, Oklahoma in the 1960s, and has continued to look at youth culture ever since. His film Kids (1985) documented adolescent boys having sex, drinking and taking drugs, and his recent film, Wassup Rockers (2007), featured twenty-four hours in the life of a gang of Latino skateboarders in Los Angeles. Clark's comments on why he focuses on this period of life could well be Henwood's. In a recent interview he said, "My films are about different ways of growing up." In another he expanded on this: "I think [youth's] a real important time of our life when things that happen to us dictate who we're going to be like as adults. It is this time where I find that kids can be so open and honest. I'm trying to show the reality of being that age and I'm making a social comment… I let the kids bring themselves to the work. I try to show that."

While there is much in Henwood's work that connects it to the long traditions of figurative painting, there is an undeniable mood that seems to stem from photography. With Clark there's the inevitable link of the subject matter – children on the cusp or undergoing metamorphosis. But Henwood's whole approach to portraiture seems to come as much from photography as from painting. This is not to say there are any clear photographic influences in his work, but more that there's a shared sensibility as to what a portrait can and should offer.

In On Photography (1977), Susan Sontag wrote that photographs provide "knowledge dissociated from and independent of experience". While all but Henwood's most recent series of paintings are based on life sittings as well as photographs of his subjects, he also seems to take a step back and present each sitter objectively. He has previously compared painting portraits to a trip to the dentist – something that requires human contact, but no or little exchange of emotion. Because of this, his work seems to possess an observational quality that we see elsewhere in the photographs of Philip Lorca diCorcia, Rineke Dijkstra and Thomas Ruff. In diCorcia's Streetwork series (1993-97), he photographed pedestrians as they passed in front of his lens. He rigged remote flashlights and set the camera some way away, so he was able to photograph them without them knowing. The resulting images are therefore not posed but record the individual as they negotiate a busy street unaware they are being watched, recorded, preserved. Each person is surrounded by people and yet appear quite alone, closed off from the world. DiCorcia's Heads series (2000) isolated each figure even more, resulting in photographs where the individual appears removed from the street and framed by a black background. They are captured in a natural state by the camera, in much the same way as Henwood's ongoing relationships with his sitters allow him to observe and paint them at ease rather than work from a stiff, formal studio pose.

This connection with the sitter is something that could also be said of Clark or Richard Avedon. Henwood has a well-thumbed copy of Avedon's In the American West, a seminal book that documents 125 American people and was published in 1985. In it, the people – teenagers, miners, the unemployed – stand against plain white backgrounds, the focus squarely on them. When individual portraits from this series were printed and framed by Avedon they would measure over a metre tall, giving each sitter a presence and authority beyond that of their everyday lives. Henwood also works on a similar scale, demanding we take his subjects seriously despite our lack of recognition of each sitter. Thomas Ruff gives a similar gravity to his subjects in his ongoing photographic series of passport-style mugshots, printed at a scale of 3:1. The scale helps remove the individual from the work, and takes them into the realm of the archetype.

Rineke Dijkstra's works are life size, showing the full figure of her subjects who are often teenagers. Her Beach series (1992-96), taken across America and Europe, shows adolescent boys and girls in their swimwear, alternatively posing awkwardly for the camera or mugging, showing off to their peers. Her work connects both to August Sander's People of the Twentieth Century (1920-27) in its interest in archetypes and attention to detail in recording names, dates and locations – as does Henwood's – as well as to Diane Arbus. Dijkstra has often quoted Arbus's well-known statement about "the gap between the intention and effect" and it is in this area that her work comes closest to Henwood's. With Henry, aged 20, London, for example, what Henry thinks he is presenting to the world and to the artist is not all we see in the final portrait.

Diane Arbus crops up repeatedly when considering the various facets of Henwood's work. In his music videos we can also see the ghost of her presence. In the last few years Henwood has directed videos for, among others, Badly Drawn Boy, Roisin Murphy, Devendra Banhart and Apollo 440 . It is in his video for indie-folk singer Devendra Banhart (Heard Somebody Say, 2005) that Arbus's presence is most strongly felt as Henwood chose to set the film on Coney Island, New York, a favourite haunt of Arbus's. In it we see snatched footage of ticket booths and fun fairs, locals dancing for the camera, Devendra rolling a fob watch in his hands and holding it above his head, a girl sitting with a melon on the sidewalk, the beach at sunset. Yet although the subject matter of the film is reminiscent of Arbus's work, the flavour of the video points towards another American photographer, William Eggleston. Henwood admires Eggleston's understanding of colour and form. "There is a tone running

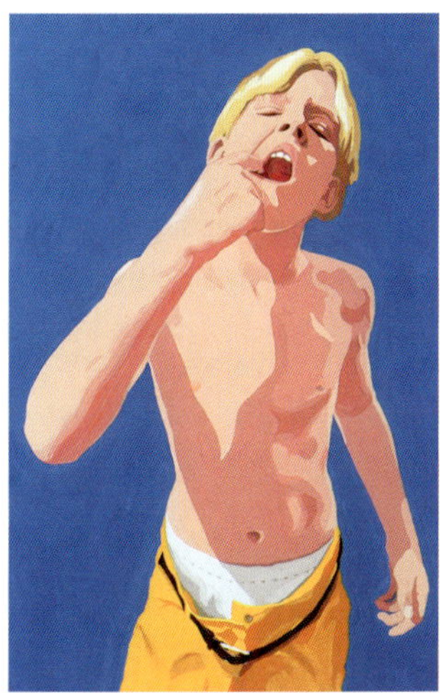

(Detail) Johnny age 10, Las Vegas 1997
Collection of Larry Clark, New York.

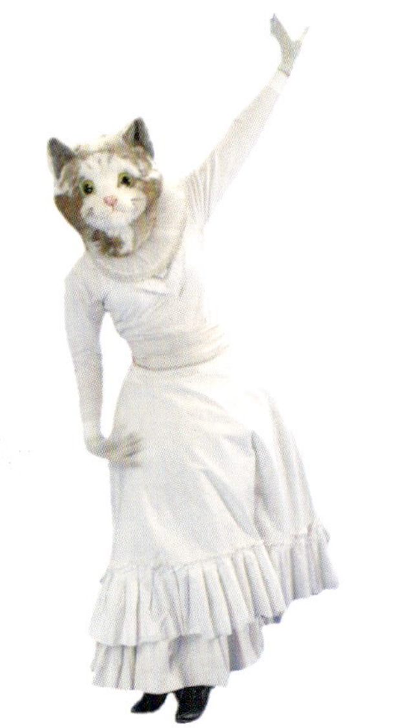

*Film stills, 35mm – You were right,
The Badly Drawn Boy, London 2002.*

through his work," Henwood says, "it is always there. If you see a photograph by him you know it is his."

As one of the first art photographers to work in colour, Eggleston managed to make certain hues seem particularly saturated, notably blood red as in the Red Ceiling (1973), with its red walls and off-centre naked lightbulb, and Untitled (Boy in Red Cardigan) (1971). In the video for Banhart's Heard Somebody Say, there's a 1970s feel to the shaky camerawork and bleached sunshine, and the film is punctuated by rich red accents, a tattered flag, shop lettering, a kilt, a neckerchief, the toy cars Devendra and his friends race. But beyond the subject matter and the tonal qualities of the video there's a sense of a hidden story buried in each vignette that seems the greatest connection to the work of Arbus and Eggleston. Both photographers conveyed drama and suggested a deeper narrative while shooting subjects as mundane as a family sunbathing on a lawn or an abandoned tricycle .

Henwood brings an artist's eye to music videos and frequently references not only photographers but painters as well. In The Delays' Hideaway (2006) there's a beauty to the enchanted light that emanates from an open bag that is reminiscent of Caravaggio, and Badly Drawn Boy's You Were Right (2003) draws on the 1960s collages of Peter Blake such as his 1967 Sgt Pepper's Lonely Hearts Club Band album cover for The Beatles. You Were Right also suggests the rapid-segue surreality of Terry Gilliam's Monty Python animations. And, yet again, we see Alice return, this time as a large-scale cut-out of John Tenniel's original engraving, hand-coloured in her trademark blue dress with red trim. Towards the beginning of the video Alice holds out her hand for a much smaller man to dance on, setting the tone for the arbitrarily scaled events that are staged on Badly Drawn Boy's wonderland aeroplane.

Many of Henwood's videos are wholly animated, from Badly Drawn Boy's You Were Right to Apollo 440's hallucinogenic Dude Descending a Staircase (2003). But in other instances he fuses animation with studio footage of the singer. Imogen Heap's Headlock (2006) features stuffed and animated animals accompanying her on a bicycle journey, and Roisin Murphy's Sow Into You (2005) has her wearing a variety of masks and costumes some of which become threateningly animate, suggesting Little Miss Muffet's long-legged spider seen through the eyes of Paula Rego. Both the videos for Heap and Murphy feature layered identities and enchanted objects, from music boxes to puppet theatres. Henwood creates magical environments for the singers through which they navigate as if walking through dreams.

Working with Henwood to create these three-minute films must have been as intense as sitting for a portrait by him, something both Roisin Murphy and Devendra Banhart have also done. Through working with them on the videos Henwood discovered things about each singer that he wanted to explore further in paint. He painted three portraits of Roisin variously

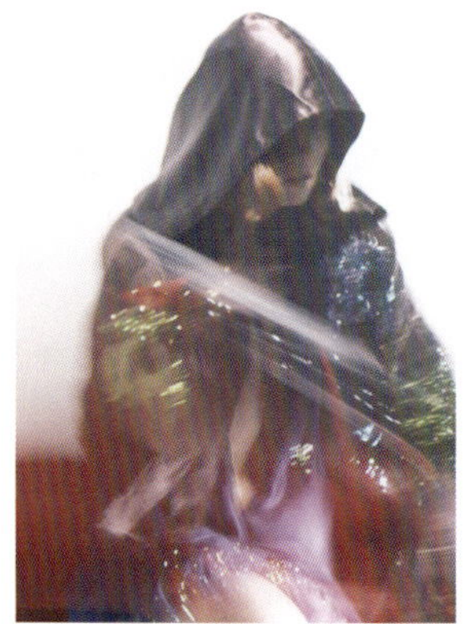

*Film still - Sow into you -
Roisin Murphy 16mm and
CGI animation, 2005.*

dressed in a multi-coloured sequin jumper, an ornate black-and-orange feathered headdress and a black sequinned catsuit. They were used by her for the artwork for her debut album Ruby Blue, and shown in Paris at Collette gallery in 2005 along with a selection of "Kido" portraits.

Shortly after his show at Collette opened, Henwood started to experiment in oils. Up to this point he had painted in gouache on paper, working quickly and layering the paint over itself as it dried. But he wanted to add more light into the works themselves, and found slow-drying oil paint the way to do this. His 2006 portrait of Devendra Banhart, when compared to the 2004 portrait completed in gouache, shows what a difference the material makes. Both based on photographs taken at the same sitting, we see 22-year-old Devendra in two different poses. In the 2004 portrait he looks out at the camera, his hair and clothes stylized and two-dimensional, his striped jersey resolutely flat. Only in his face do we see the modulated colouration that gives Henwood's models life and emotion. But the 2006 portrait has an overall depth and luminosity to it far beyond the earlier work. The bright sunlight now seems to illuminate his face and hair rather than bounce off it, and the focus on his face is thrown into contrast by the soft treatment of his clothes, rather like a photograph where the surrounding elements are slightly out of focus. Painting in oils has allowed Henwood to light his subjects from within, to give them a life of their own.

Henwood further explored this in a painting of actress Tamzin Merchant. A comparison can be made between Henwood's 2006 portrait of Tamzin Merchant, in oil on linen, and a gouache of the same year called Girl with an Orange. Both works are of Merchant – she is wearing the same distinctive patterned sundress – but whereas the gouache suggests the story is in the accessories (why is she holding an orange?), in the oil the story is within her. Her hair has a preternatural brightness, a fairytale blondness that suggests the light is coming from behind her, emphasized by the dark background. But there's also a secondary light source in front of her, highlighting her right eye, cheek and an area of her neck. It casts her left cheek and chin into shadow, a shadow made up of tessellations of yellow, lime, orange, red, purple and grey. Only her turquoise eyes shine out (mirrored by the trim of her dress) as they stare at something far away and out of sight. She is Alice all grown up, in contrast to the child who appears in the books who also makes an appearance in a painting from the same year as the little girl in the blue dress with red trim in The Vale of Avoca (2006).

The 2006 painting of Devendra Banhart and the two paintings of Tamzin Merchant were included in Henwood's 2006 exhibition "Cricklewood" at his New York gallery Envoy. Cricklewood is the area of north London where Henwood lives. It defines a territory, in much the same way as the works in the exhibition all shared a mood. All the sitters appear contemplative, looking up to the heavens or eyes shut as if dreaming. Only the two portraits of little girls – The Vale of Avoca and Saoirse (2006) – stare out at us, but their eyes are filled with melancholy secrets. Even the portrait of

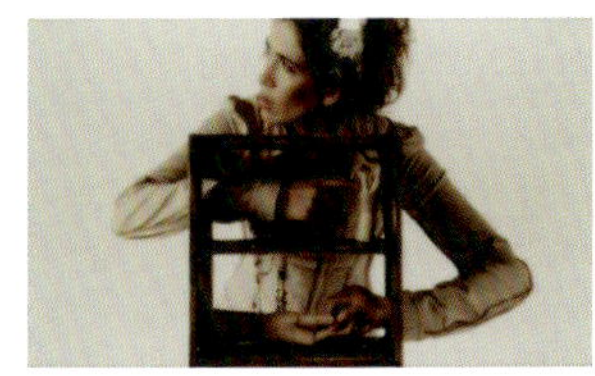

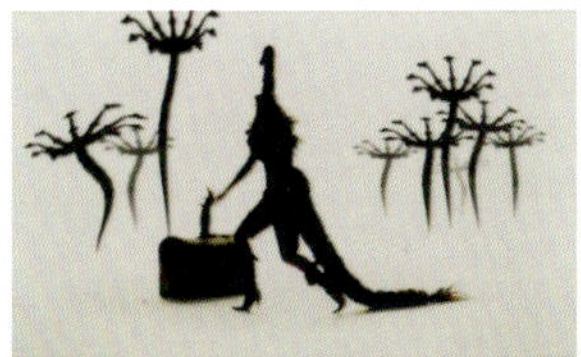

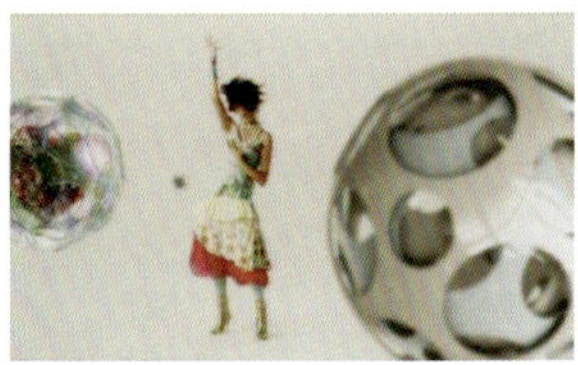

Film stills, 16mm – Headlock, Imogen Heap, London 2005.

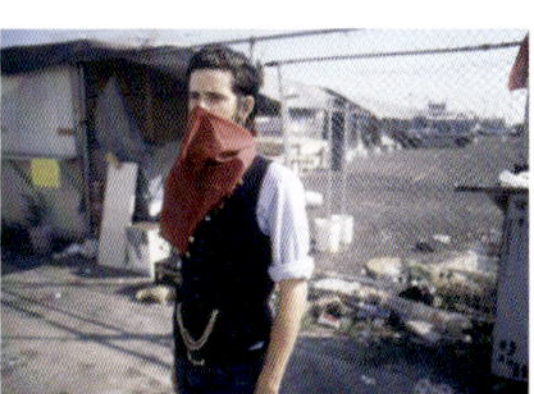

Film still, 16mm - Heard somebody say - Devendra Banhart, New York 2005.

Joey from Las Vegas, Medusa (2006), shows him eyes cast down, his face made gaunt by deep shadows, his hair an unruly mop of ginger snakes. It's a contrast to the earlier 2000 portrait of him aged 14, where he stands in bright sunlight against a flat ultramarine ground, eyes and lip wrinkled against the glare of the sun.

On the basis of his portraits of actresses and musicians such as Tamzin Merchant and Devendra Banhart, Henwood was asked to take part in a group show on the theme of celebrity. But he was loathe to submit these portraits and preferred to explore the theme of fame in a new body of work, several of which he exhibited in the group show and all of which were exhibited together at envoy in "There for the Grace of God".

Ever since Warhol subjected iconic images of Marilyn and Elvis to his printing presses at the Factory, celebrity images have been quick to become devoid of meaning and personality. They are icons in the traditional sense of the word, to be worshipped for what they stand for, not for what (or who) they really are. Several years ago, Henwood started collecting 1960s and 1970s studio photographs of would-be celebrities, actors photographed in three-quarter poses who hoped that their "look" would bring them fame and fortune. While they seem familiar, none of them became household names and without Henwood immortalizing them on canvas would have continued their slide into obscurity. Using photographs as a base in this way – he has never met any of those photographed – gives him an increased distance from his sitter that he has never previously experienced. In a similar way to Gerhard Richter, an artist he greatly admires, using photographs has allowed him to start with a subject that is depersonalized. If the subjects are still alive, they will no longer resemble the photographs Henwood possesses. It is as if they have left behind a hollow ghost from which he can construct a new, more lifelike reality.

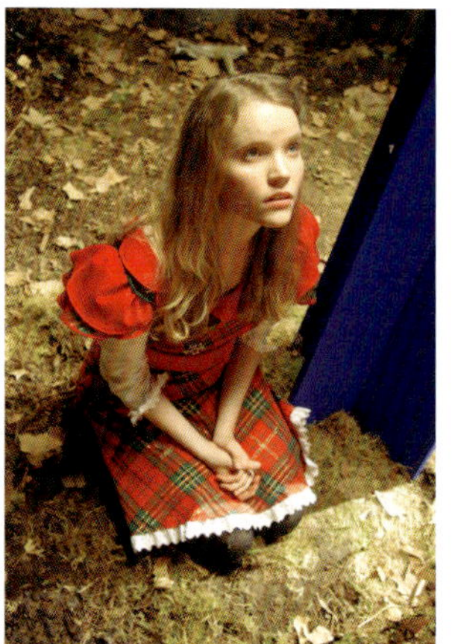

Film stills, 35mm –The Fallen Eye,
Tamzin Merchant on set, London 2007.

Henwood became fascinated with these characters and their yearning for fame. Not unlike the teenagers he paints, or the everyday characters in the work of Richard Avedon or August Sander, his portraits of these men impose gravity and longevity on those who otherwise would remain unknown. Yet in the case of the actors, well-turned out in suit and tie, hair brushed back, eyes scanning the horizon for fame, there's a deep sense of melancholy to them. For they want to be better known, they crave public recognition. They are actors who without an audience have no purpose. For Henwood they link back to his images of children and teenagers in the sense that they too are dreaming about their future. They too wear clothes that they hope makes them appear or be "read" in a certain way. Their dream gives them hope, keeps them alive. And yet at the same time, by painting actors in grisaille like black-and-white portraits of a long-gone era, Henwood suggests that their dreams came to nothing. These are not paintings of Cary Grant or Marlon Brando but of people who styled themselves on their heroes, hoping for a similar leg up to the big time. As if to emphasize the hopeless dreams of the would-be actors, Henwood

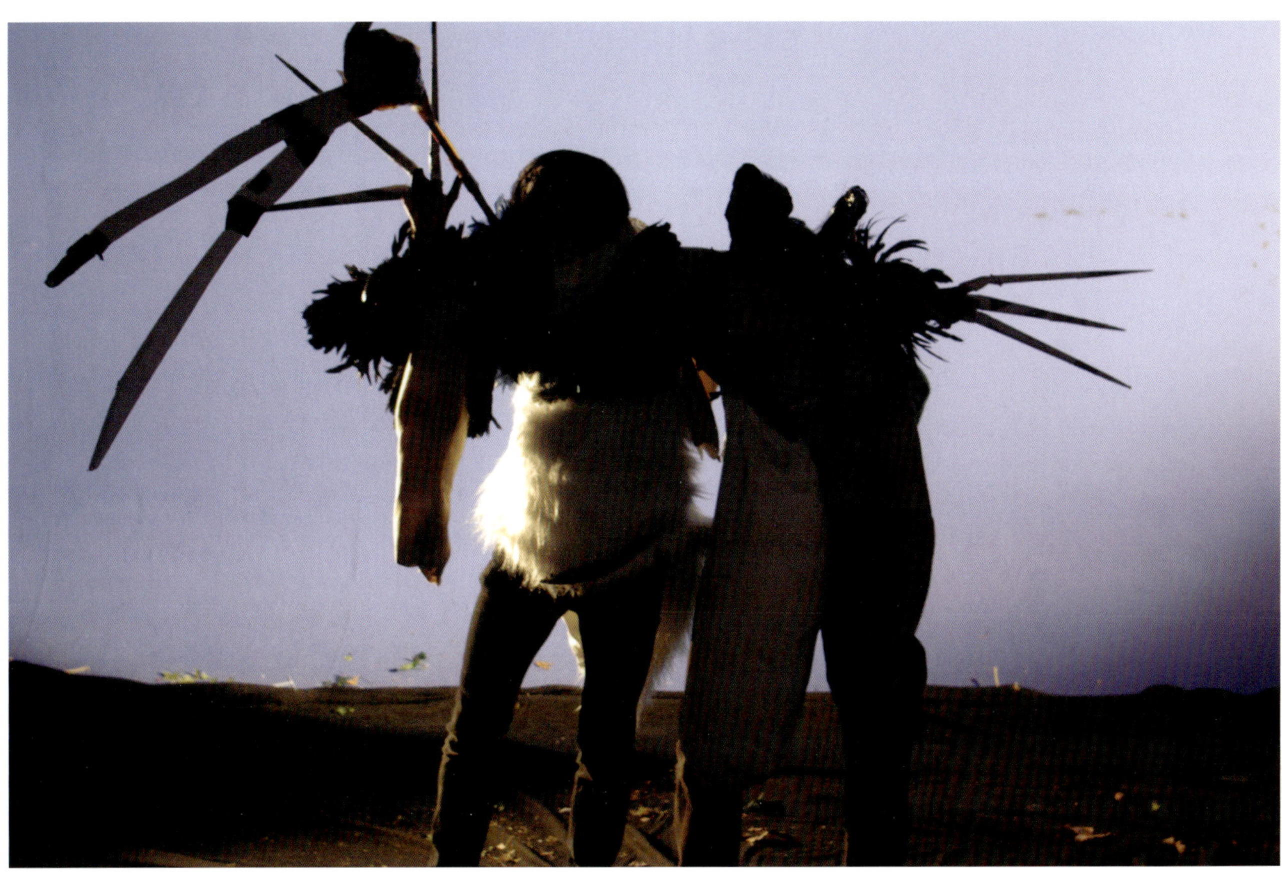

supplemented them in "There for the Grace of God" with paintings of dying flowers. These browning, entropic still lives still have a surprising beauty to them, and yet we know that soon the petals will fall and the stalks will rot.

While the flower paintings link to the series of actor's portraits by emphasising the time lag between when the original photographs were taken and the reality of the actors now, the unstoppable march of time, in fact they stem from an ongoing film project that Henwood has been working on called The Fallen Eye. In it he recreates the birth of the first flower on earth, the beginning of creation. In an Odilon Redon-inspired set he explores what someone (played by Tamzin Merchant) would do if confronted with a vision of their future. Would they be excited or apathetic? Would they retreat to an existential position of fate having already been decided or fight against it? The film is currently in post-production, and is destined for both cinematic and gallery release. And, unlike the film's protaganist, we will have to wait to see what the final film, and Henwood's future, holds. But if Henwood's past is anything to go by, it will be rich, varied, strange and luminous.

Charlotte Mullins
8 September 2007

Early Paintings
Makaito Saito

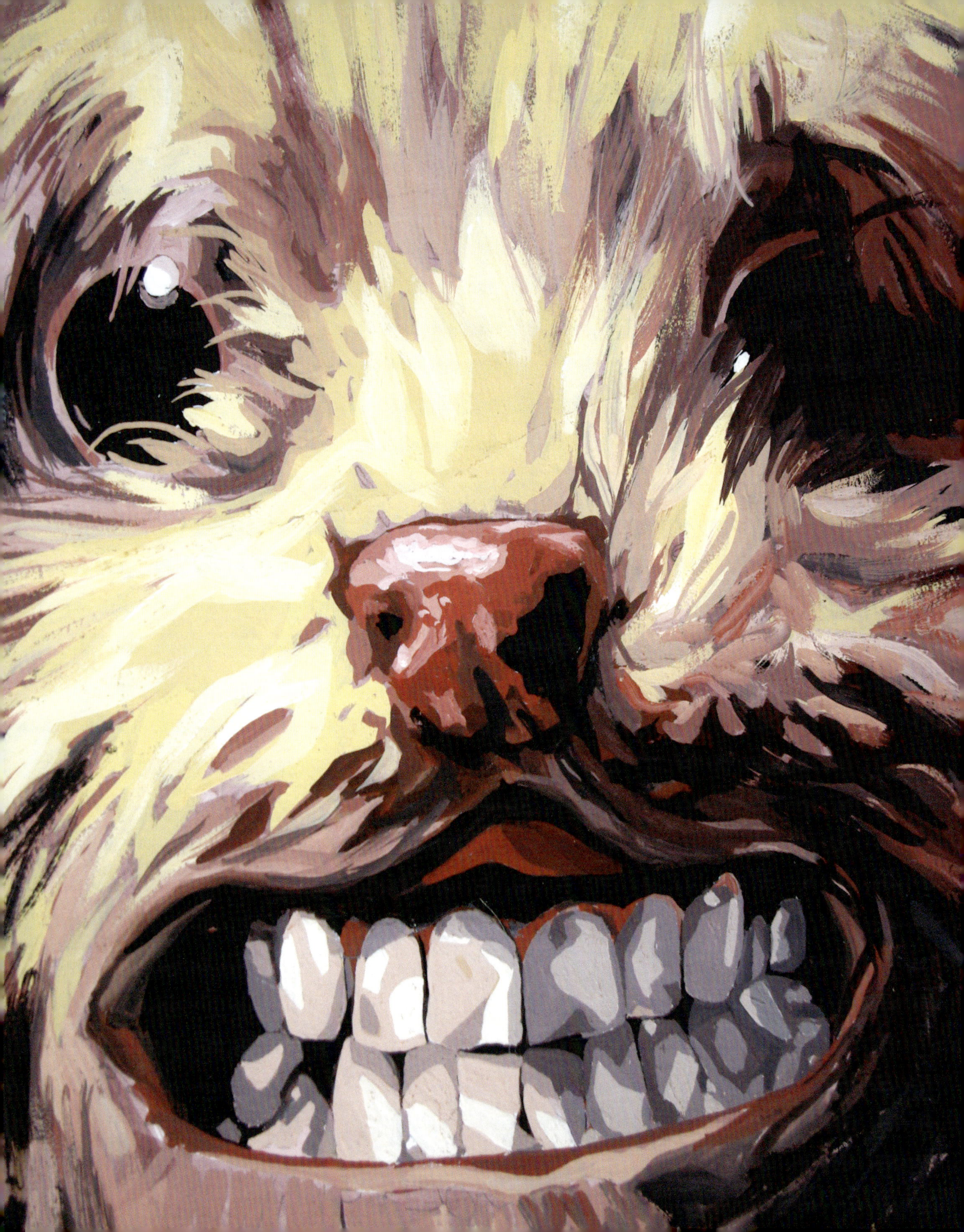

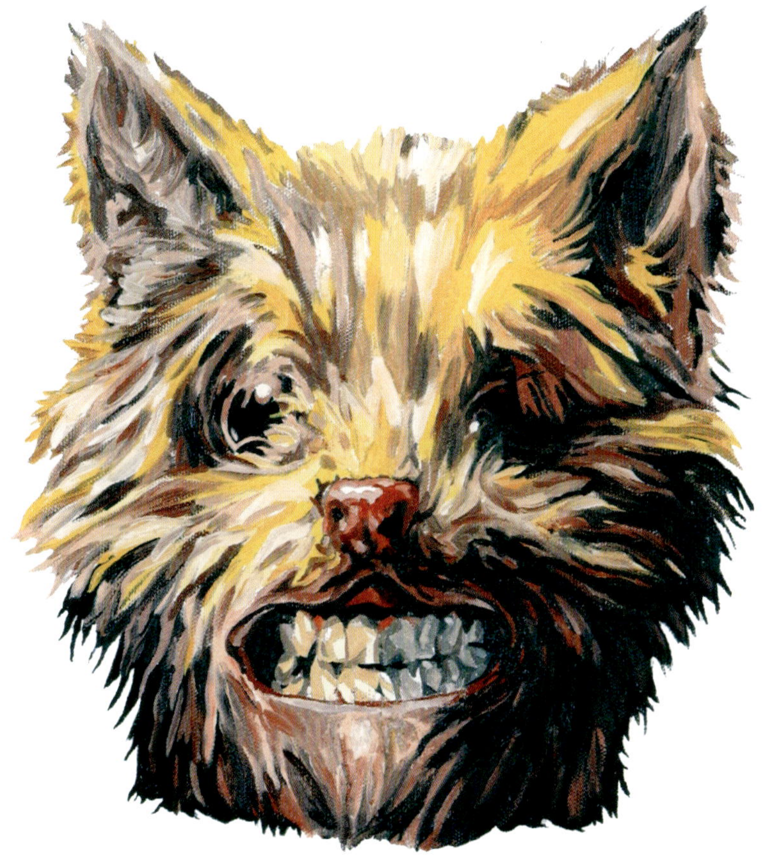

One girl's group made a million in the music industry with their commercial pop-movie - it went on a road show last spring, and next season, it was sold as a video in the shops. This year, however, they had already stopped working as a group and started on their own solo careers. When an important person dies, the world has a moment to express its grief, though after a month the death will be forgotten in society as if nothing has happened before. The newest blockbuster SFX movies are made and flooded everywhere by the rapid endless development in technology that consists of perfectly analysed data from the past. The most brutal crime ever is frequently reported all over the world, and it is like the creation of world records won by athletes.

On the other hand, the world has now started compressing the history of human beings which is almost 2000 years too much. The Cyberspace environment, for example, the Internet, eventually turns an individuals brain into an Internet terminal. Information has become accessible in an instant anywhere in the world, and when it is not necessary any more you can get rid of it at the push of a button. Everything becomes compact and pragmatic in Cyberspace, and because of that we find it difficult to dream in out world. Digital technology has plundered mystery in the world and all events are categorised like data in a library. Through that step the world is decreasing more and more. It does not even miss capturing and dissolving the expanding history

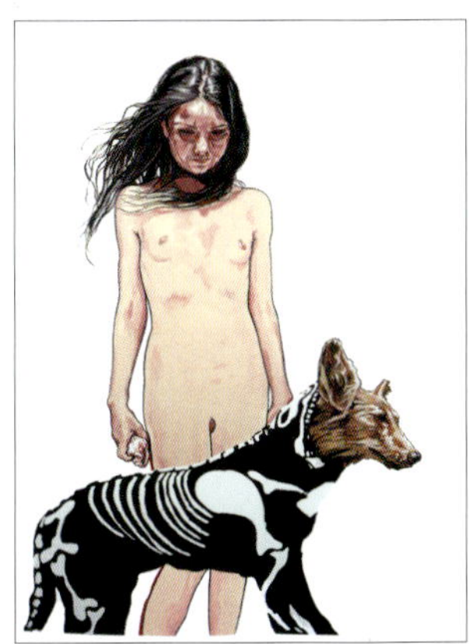

Skellydog, 2003 100 x 139 cm Gouache on paper.

Pussy Tooth, 2005 30 x 30cm Oil on canvas Private collection, London.

Left *(detail) (Gouache study)*
Pussy Tooth, 2005.

Darkness and Hip Together...
Fuck, Death and more Pop,
These words, his internal slogan

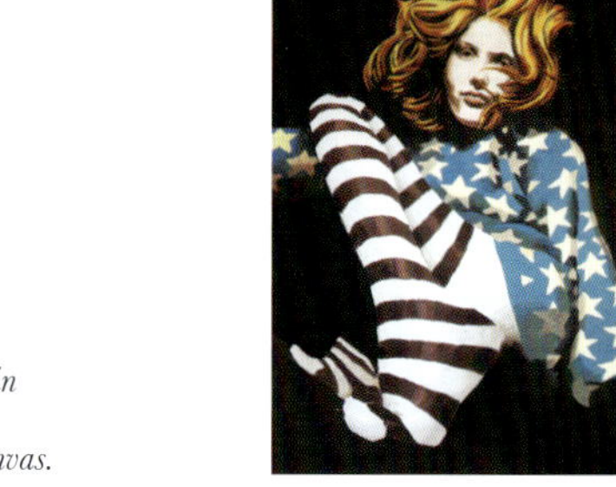

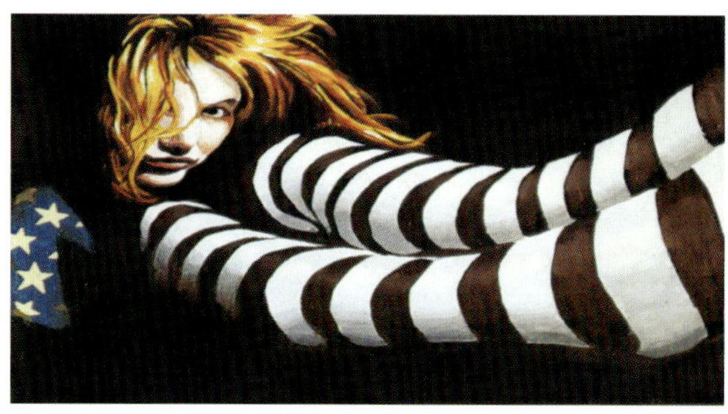

*Study number one for Alice in
Wonderland 1991
80 x 120 cm Acrylic on canvas.*

*Study number two for Alice in
Wonderland 1991
60 x 120 cm Acrylic on canvas.*

*Right (Left side) Alice in the world
of Cornell, 1991
140 x 200 cm Acrylic on canvas.*

*Right (Right side) Stretch Alice,
1991 80 x 240 cm Acrylic on canvas.*

You are the media - it is the only one way of not being sunk or disappearing amongst the digital age but to live as vivid individuals. It is important not to fit yourself into a stereotype but to make yourself as media which is not anyone or anyone else.

Simon Henwood is a good example of a talented artist who keeps creating work ideally in the idea of self-media art. His works are very much related to something very dark and black. Alice - is the art comic magazine that decodes life and death - icons in children' s picture books understood from a subcultural context. Poor Johnny Pumpkin - the story of a boy called Johnny Pumpkin whose skin is not strong enough against the UV light and so he only can play with his friends in the shadows. Purr - is a visual magazine that defines crime as a pop culture as if it is the same as pop music.

Yet, what makes Simon's ideas in his art new is that because he does not used disliked images of life and death. He successfully combines the darkness and hip together. Fuck, death and more pop! - these words, his internal slogan, are distinguishing Simon Henwood from hundreds of other underground artists. The sensitivity in his memory of his childhood also has an inevitable effect on his art world.

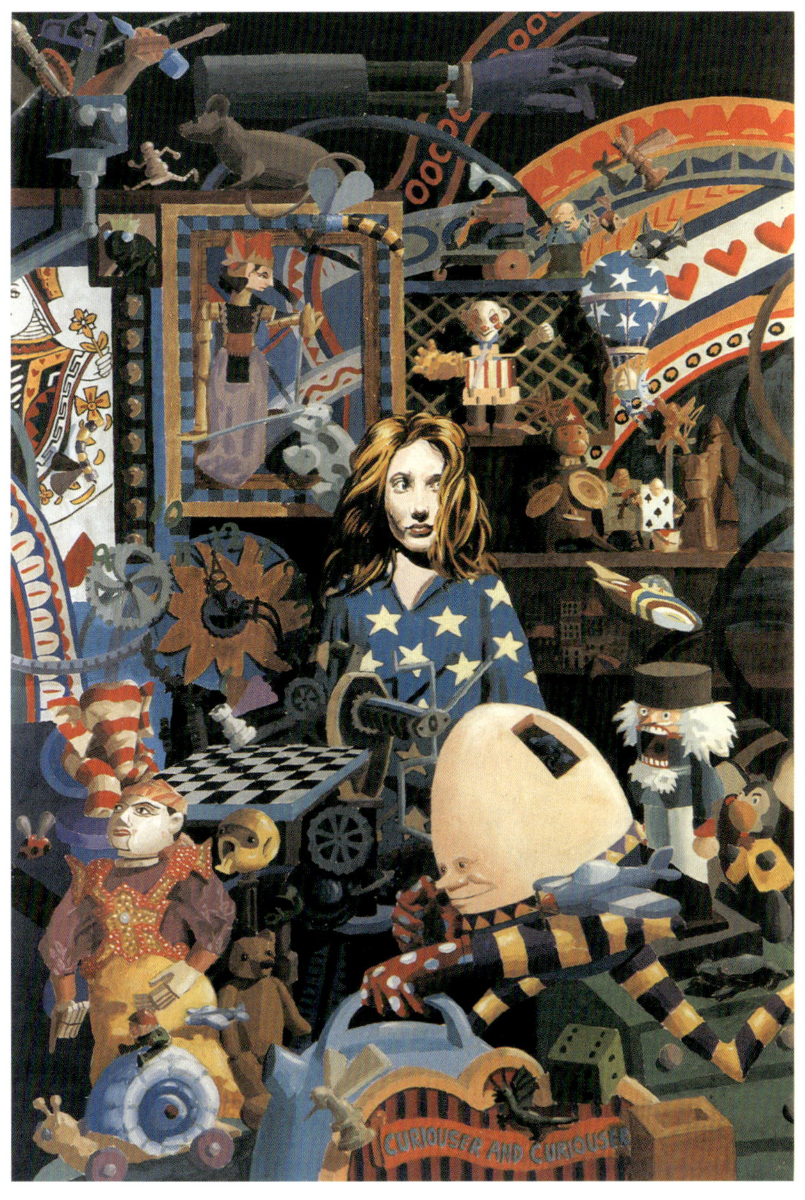

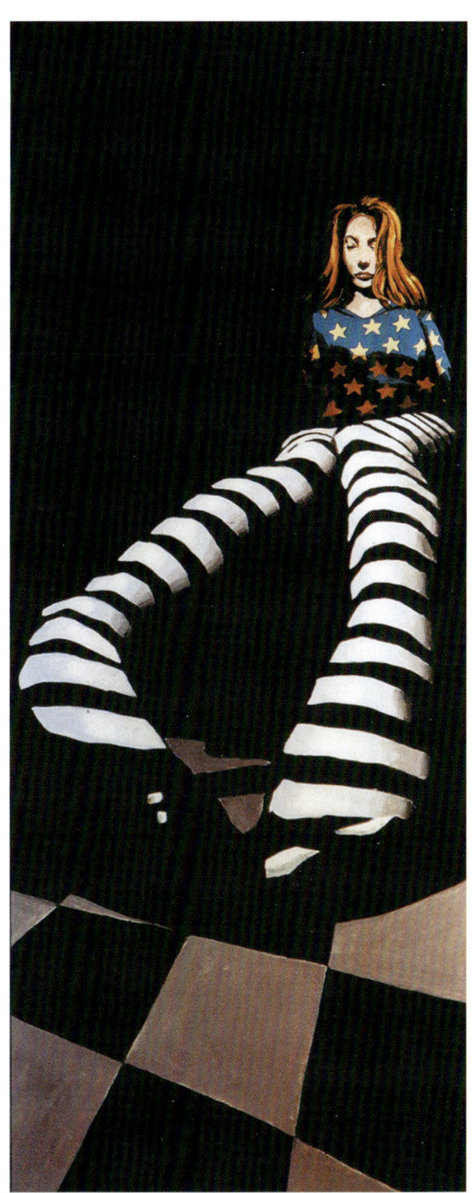
CURIOUSER AND CURIOUSER

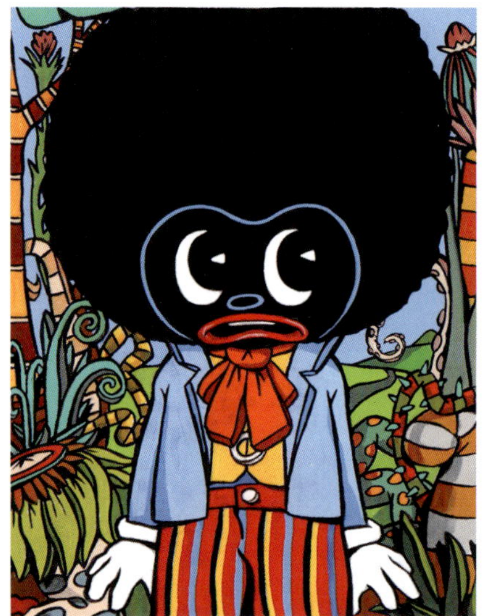 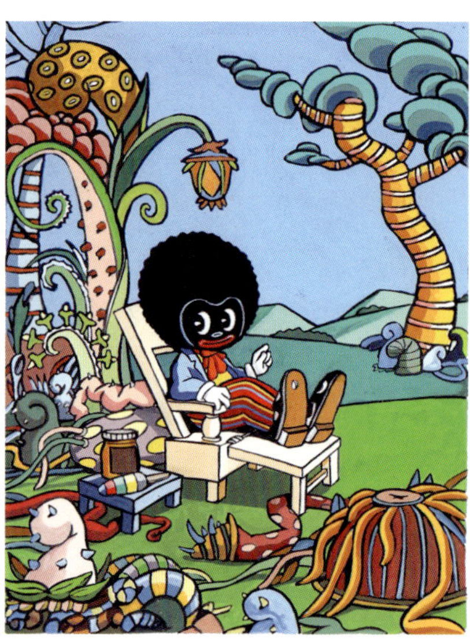

Good Golly, 2003
30 x 40 cm Gouache on paper.

Golly Garden, 2003
30 x 40 cm Gouache on paper.

Giant Golly, 2003
150 x 220 cm Oil on canvas.

In the last three to four years, creators from my generation, tend to look back at their own childhood. For example, Hero from the children's TV programme in the '70s has become a popular character for TV commercials now. By looking at them, we can experience the same emotion and feeling. It is because what we already have in our memory that it gives us a stronger message/impact. (Excerpt from H magazine, March 1998 Japan).

This phenomenon is not only in the UK but also in the USA and Japan. For example, the fact that the young audience for Austin Powers all over the world, can share, understand and enjoy the humour of a parody of 007. This shows the fact of a common memory amongst young people whose experiences have been created by the media. It is a typical phenomenon in the decreasing world. This art book, White Kitten, describes/shows the portraits of these mediarised young people captured in cool-downed brush strokes. It's still the models who have an uneasy expression and anxiety in their eyes towards the world. We won't be absorbed by the media! - young models' silent message, it is the best concept of the self-media artist, Simon Henwood.

Mikato Saito
Editor-in-chief 'H' magazine.
Tokyo, 30th July 1999.

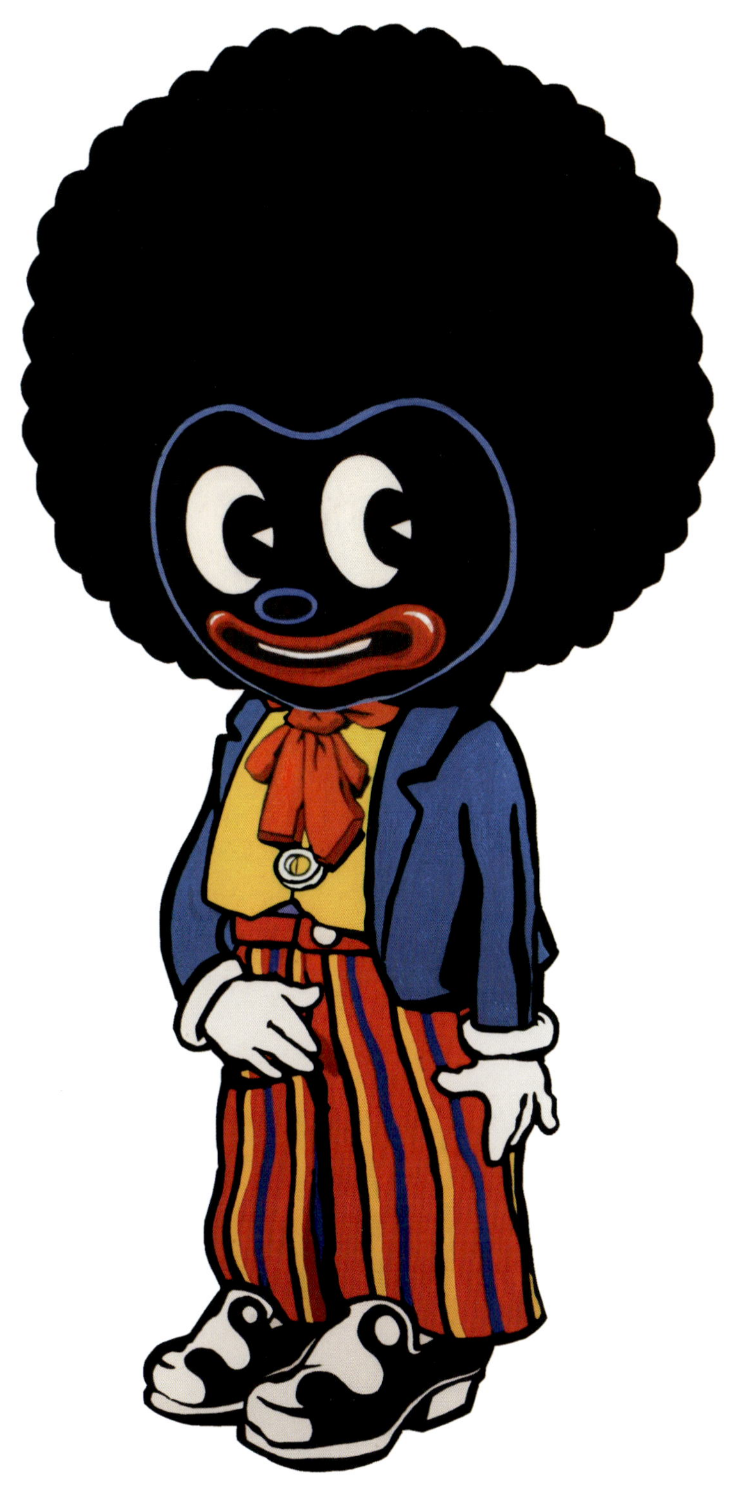

Real girl, real doll - 1999
100 x 139 cm Gouache on paper
The West collection, Philadelphia.

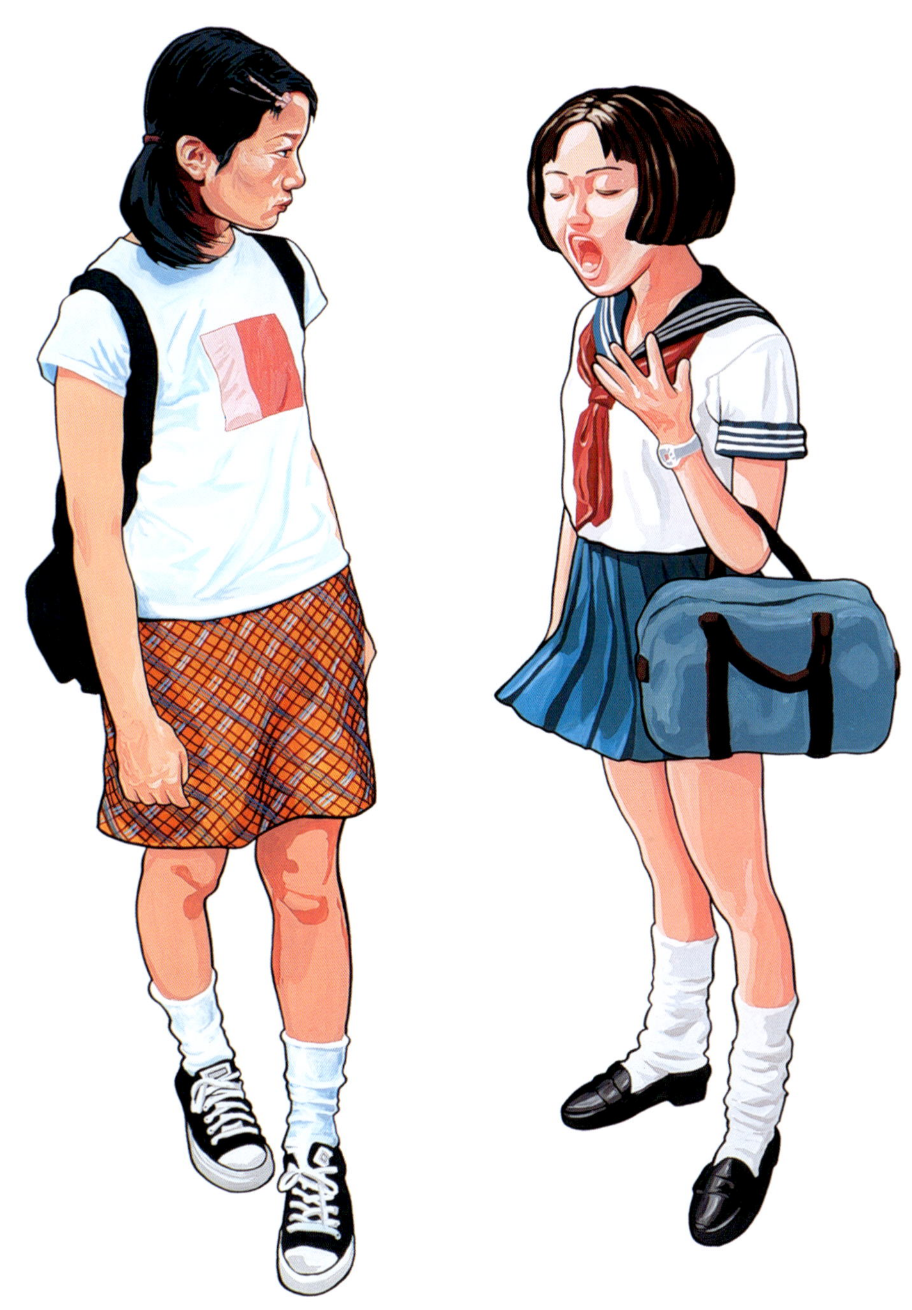

Kylie 11 - 1999
100 x 139 cm gouache on paper
Private collection, Australia.

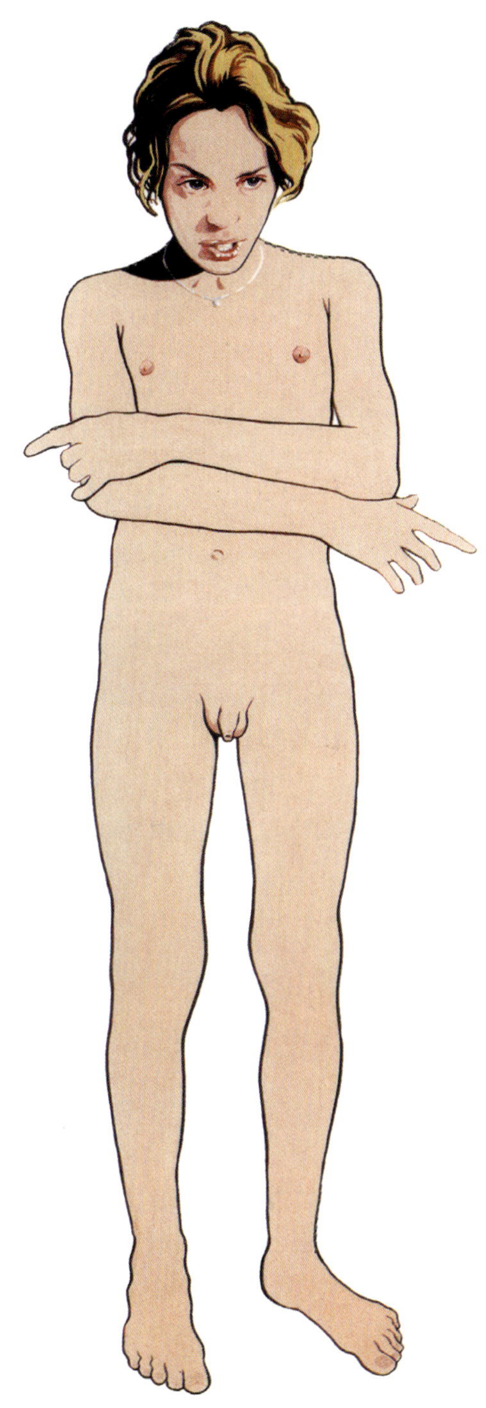

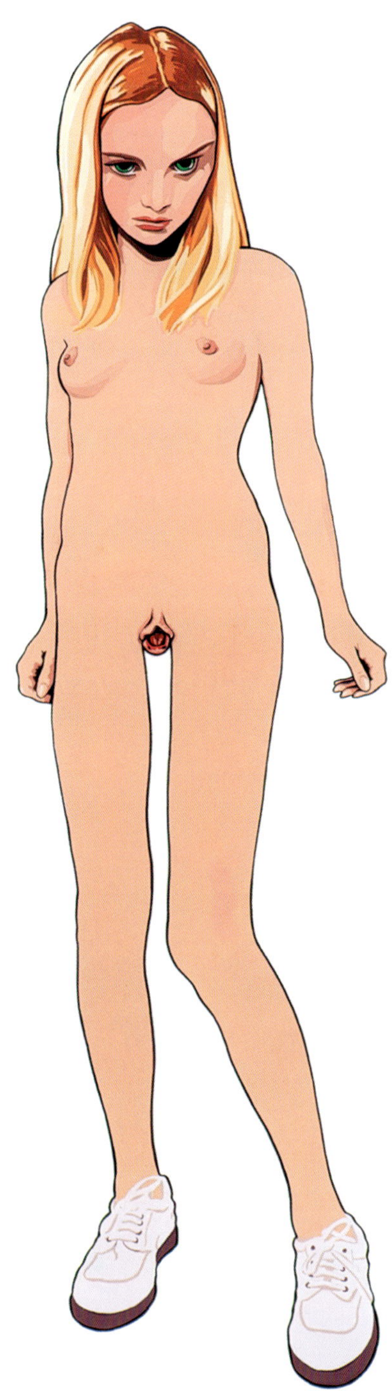

Little Red Riding Hood - 1997
30 x 50 cm Gouache on paper
Collection of Mary Barone and Neil Manson, New York.

Following page

Little Red Ridding Hood - 1997
Loves little lessons one and two.
100 x 139 cm Gouache on paper.

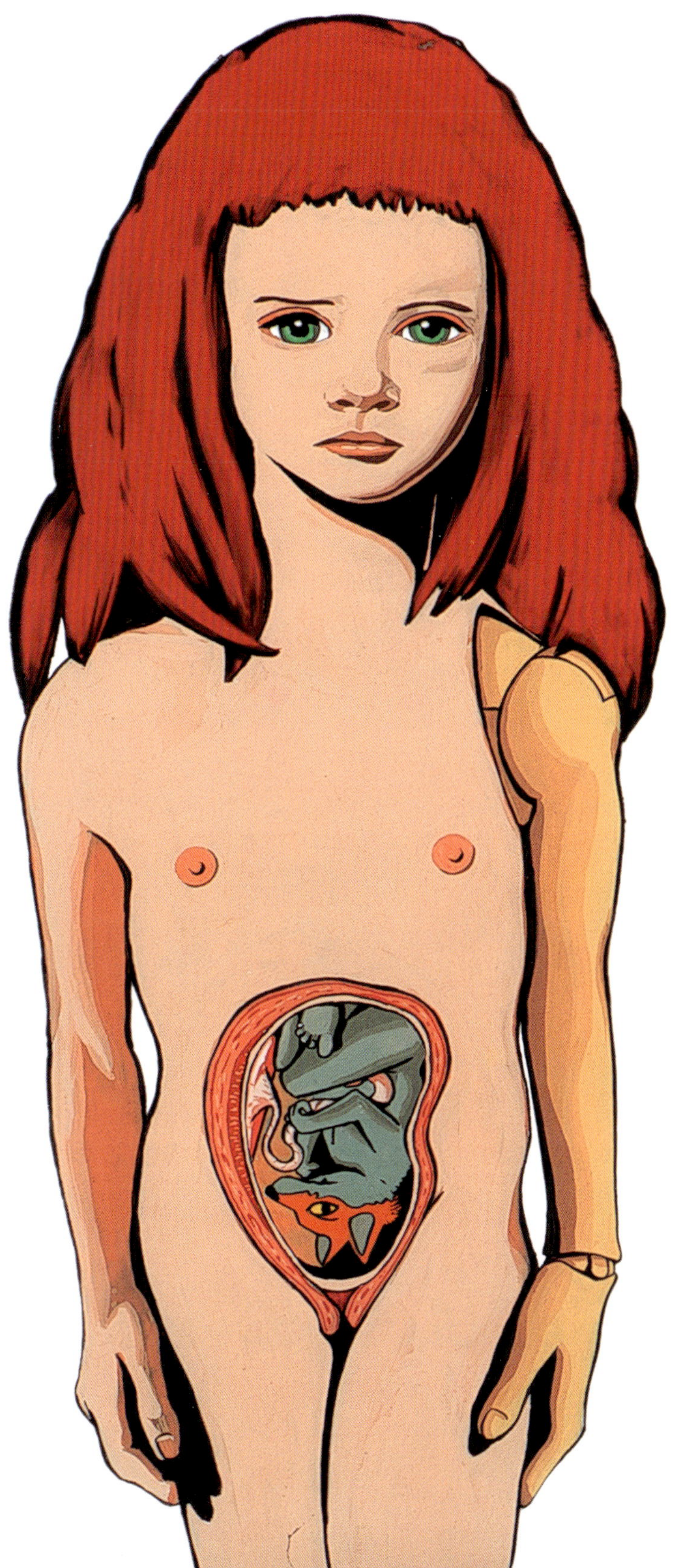

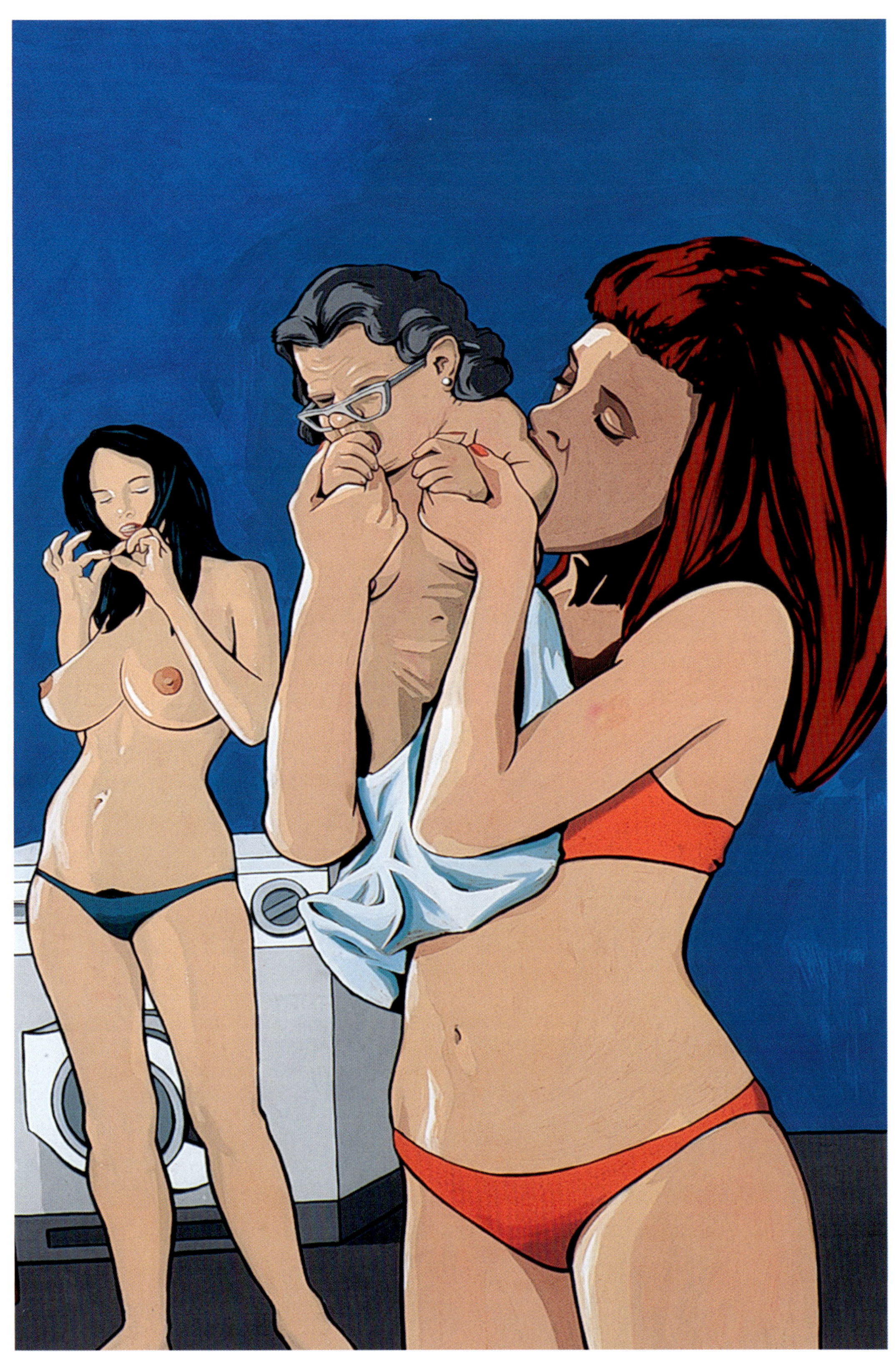

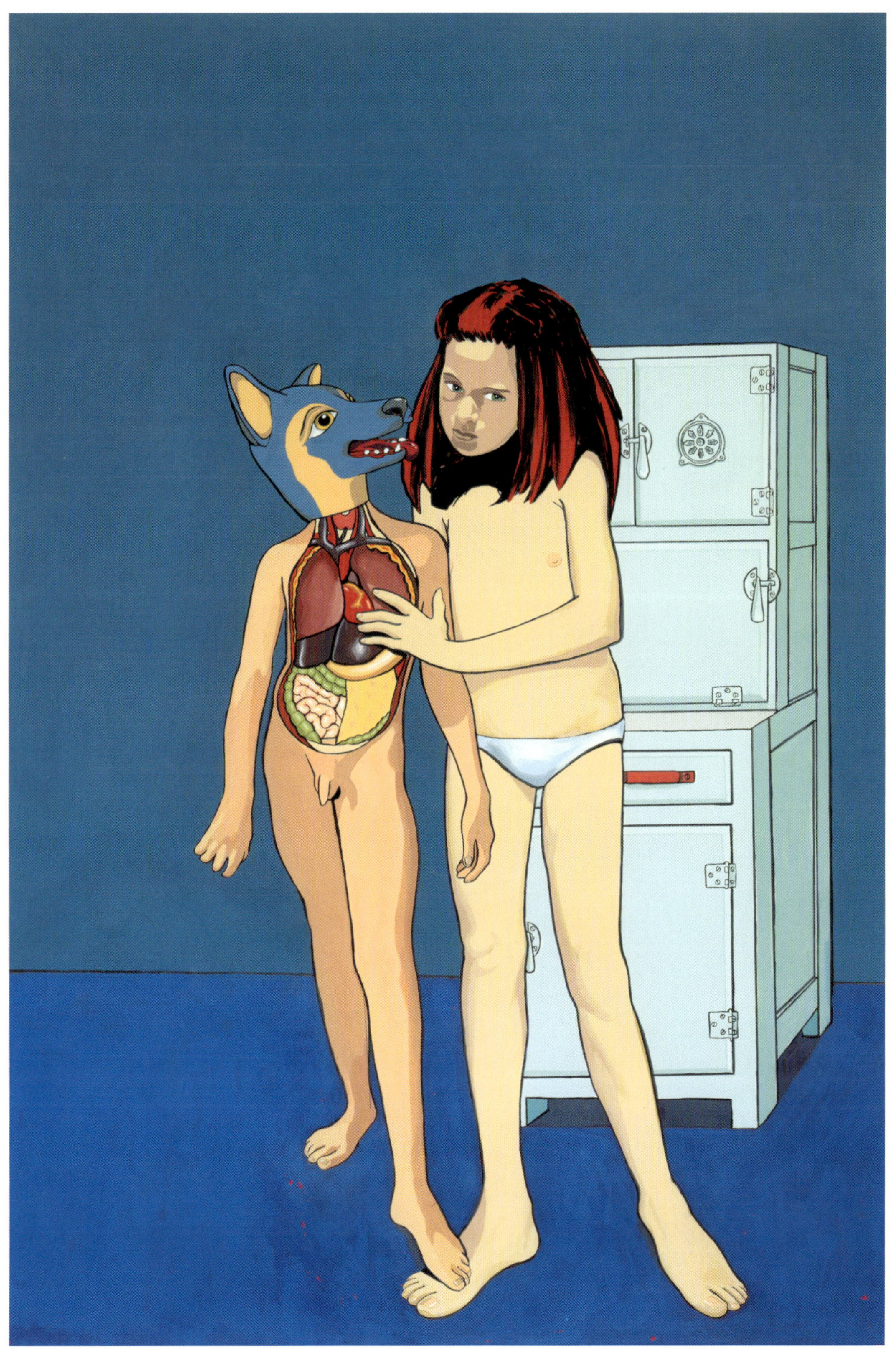

Teenage Portraits
Mario Testino

A record of an individuals life

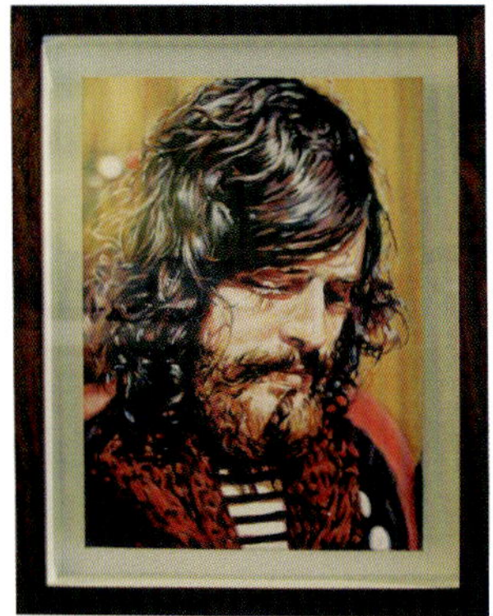

Devendra Installation Shot, New York 2006
10 x 14 inch Oil on canvas
Private collection, Antwerp Belgium.

Simon Henwood's painting appropriates a particular photographic style with which I am familiar - a street wise sense of "styling" to use a term from commercial photography, set against a stark background: in fact an absent background, that pushes the subjects appearance forward. The eye has nowhere to travel except across the foreground to study a certain gaze, a choice of accessories, a combination of personal choices that help us determine a character. My objective in using this technique is to sell these choices - but I find Simon's work interesting because I am curious about how such a technique can be transferred across to a very different medium and take o a different meaning.

I believe that the key to understanding this appropriation must lie in the selection of the subjects being presented. Visually speaking, such a composition is easily interpreted, it is direct and of course relates back to the influence that advertising has in creating our personal choices, how we present ourselves to the world. Simon's characters are ordinary people, that is to say, non-professional models, people that you or I may cross on any given day on any street without casting a second glance. Yet presented on canvas through paintings- a formal medium, these people in painting appear elevated to a permanent document of their character. These portraits separate them from the random street acquaintances we experience and transform them into a record of an individual's life.

Mario Testino

Joey age 15, Las Vegas 2000
100 x 139cm Gouache on paper
Private collection New York.

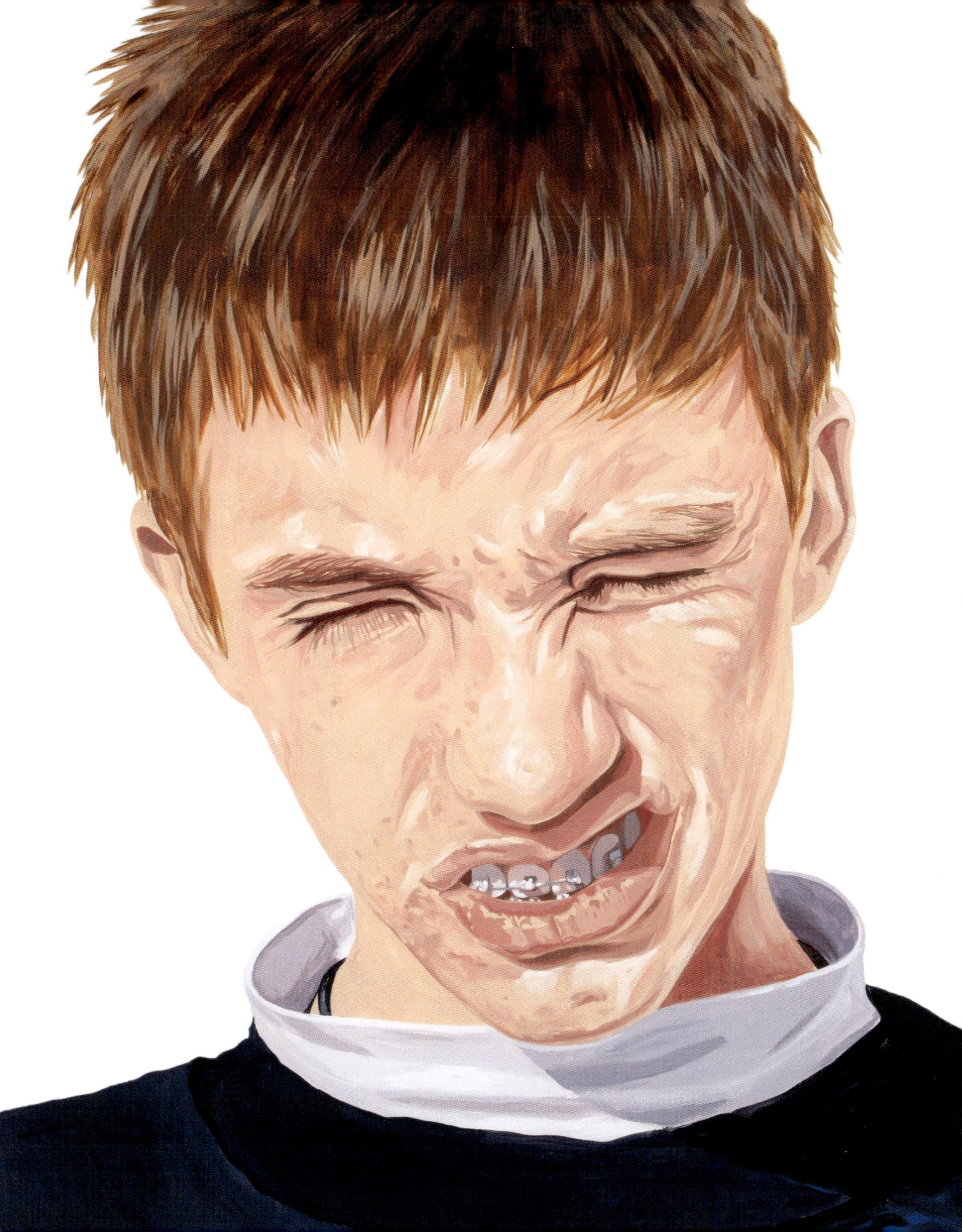

Johnny age 10, Las Vegas 1997
100 x 139cm Gouache on paper
Collection of Larry Clark, New York.

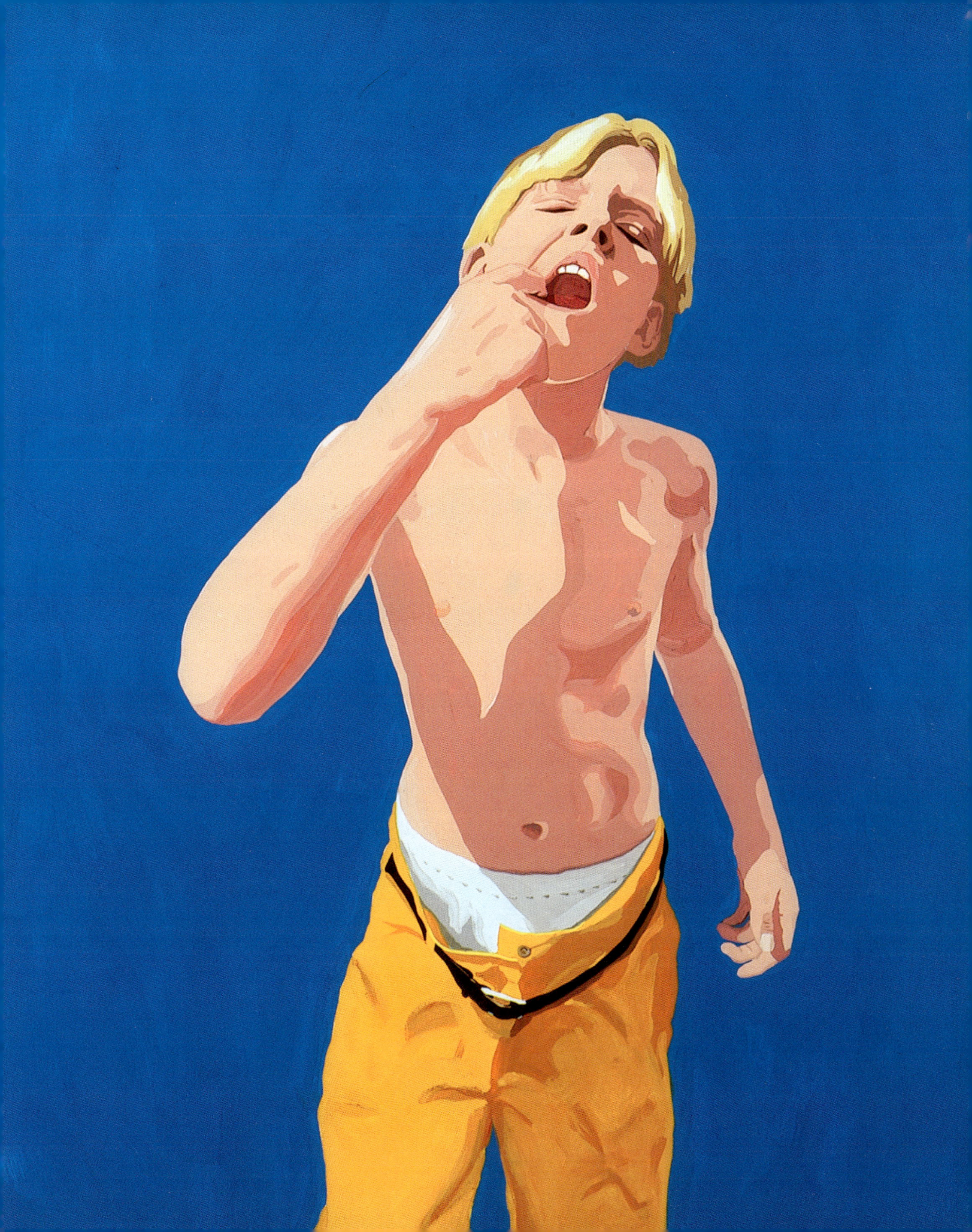

Sophie age 14, London 1998
100 x 139cm Gouache on paper
Private Collection, New York.

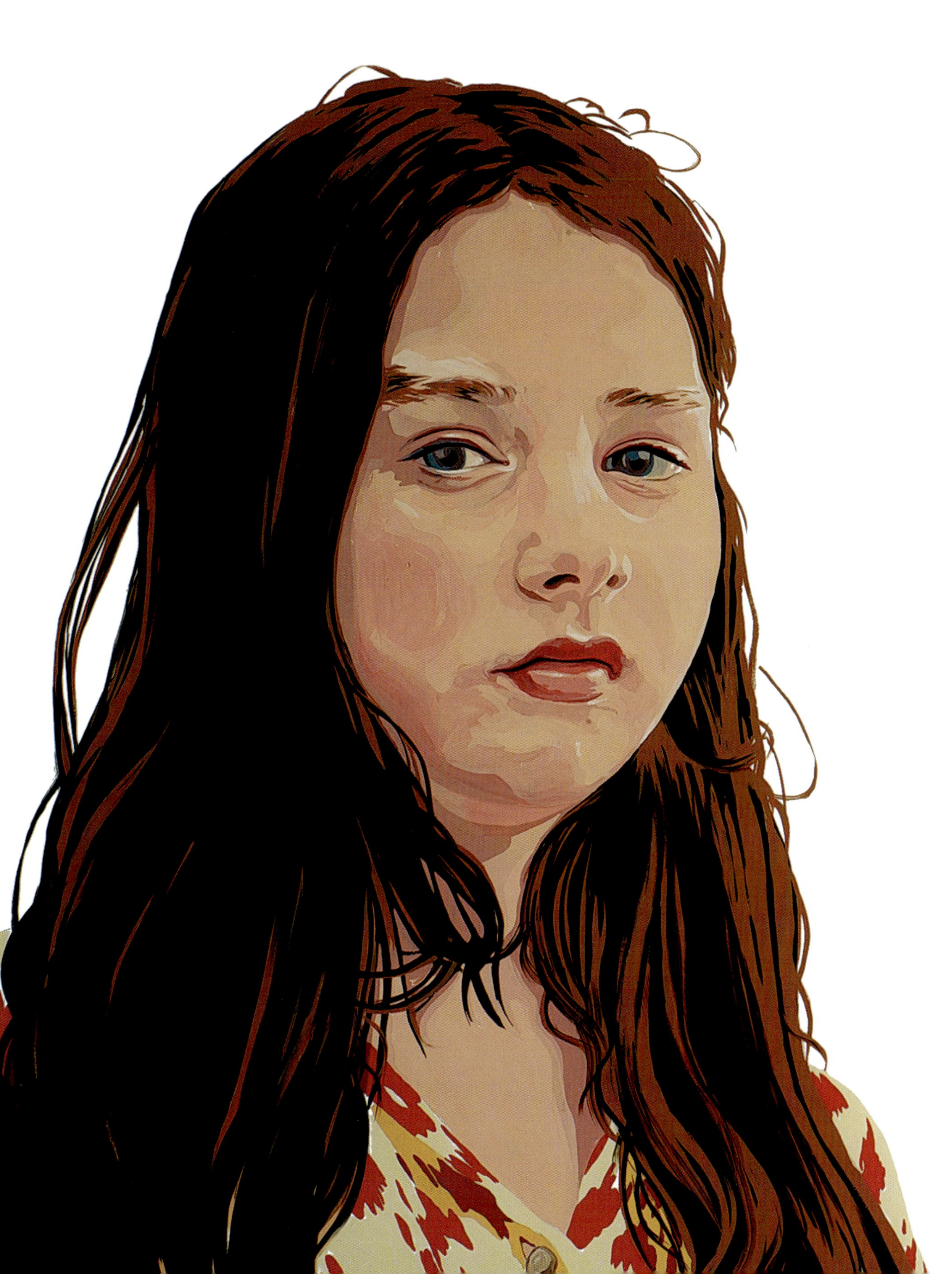

Guy age 10, Manchester 1998
100 x 139cm Gouache on paper
The West Collection, Philadelphia.

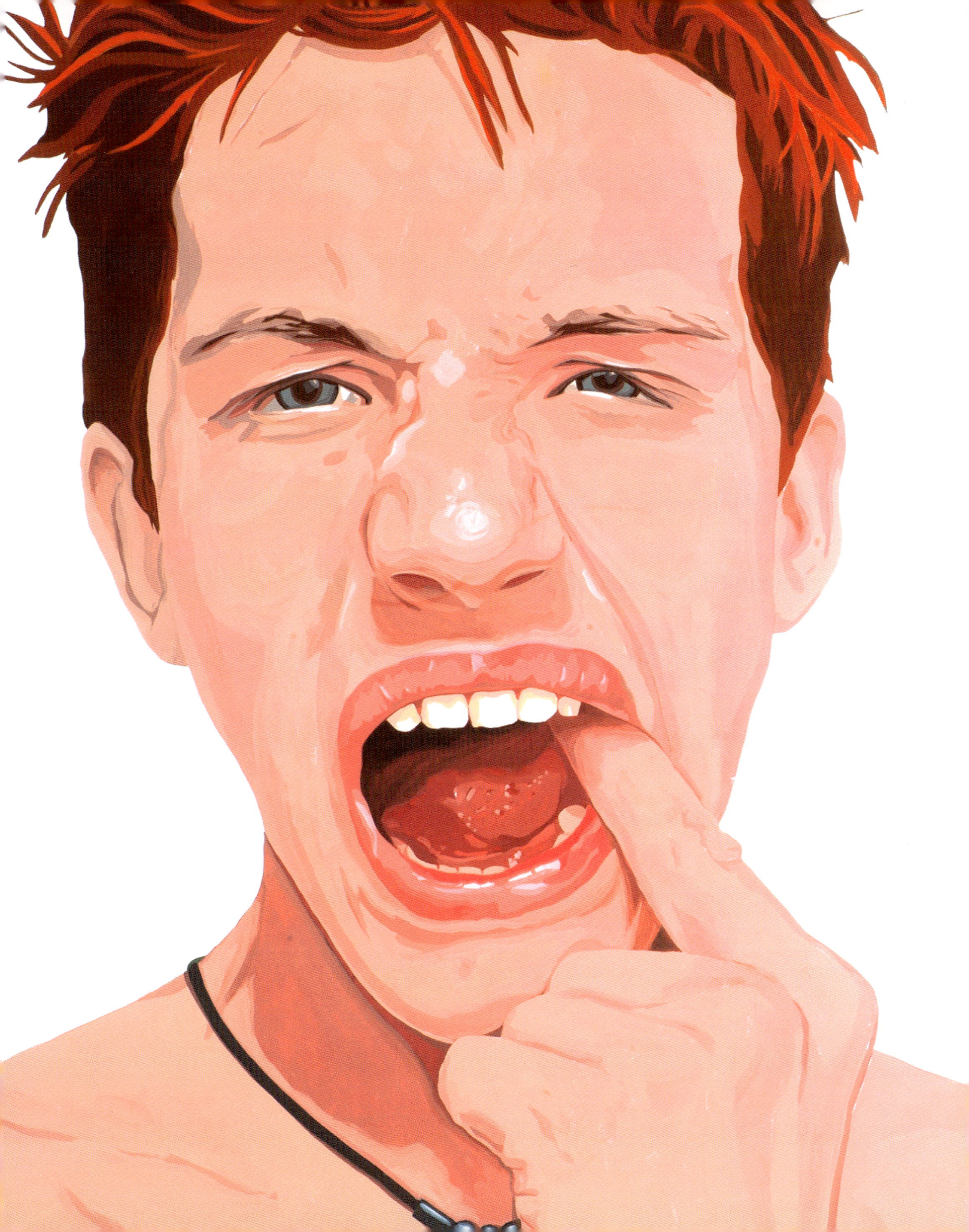

Jasmin age 8, London 2000
100 x 139cm Gouache on paper.

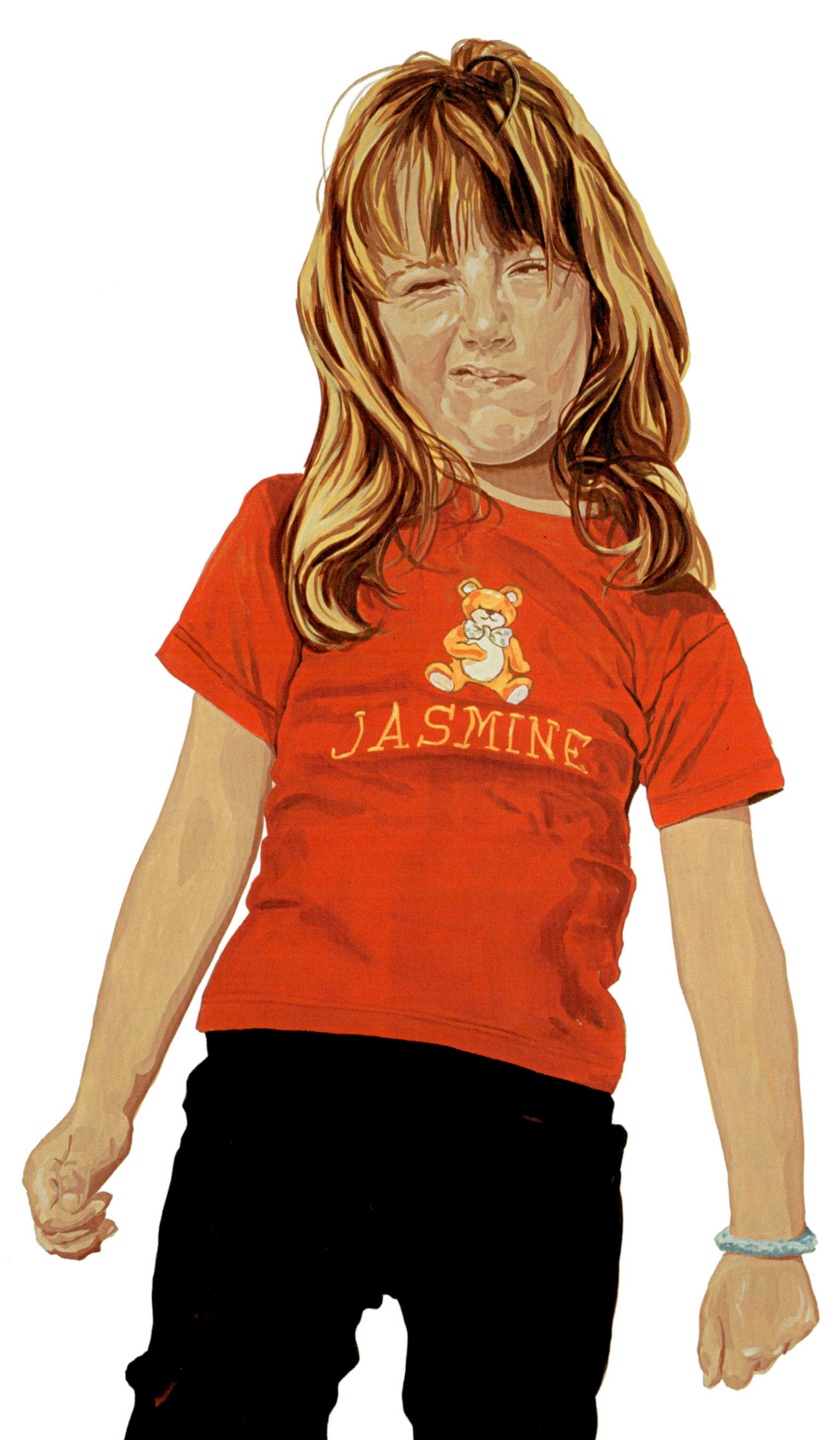
JASMINE

Following Page

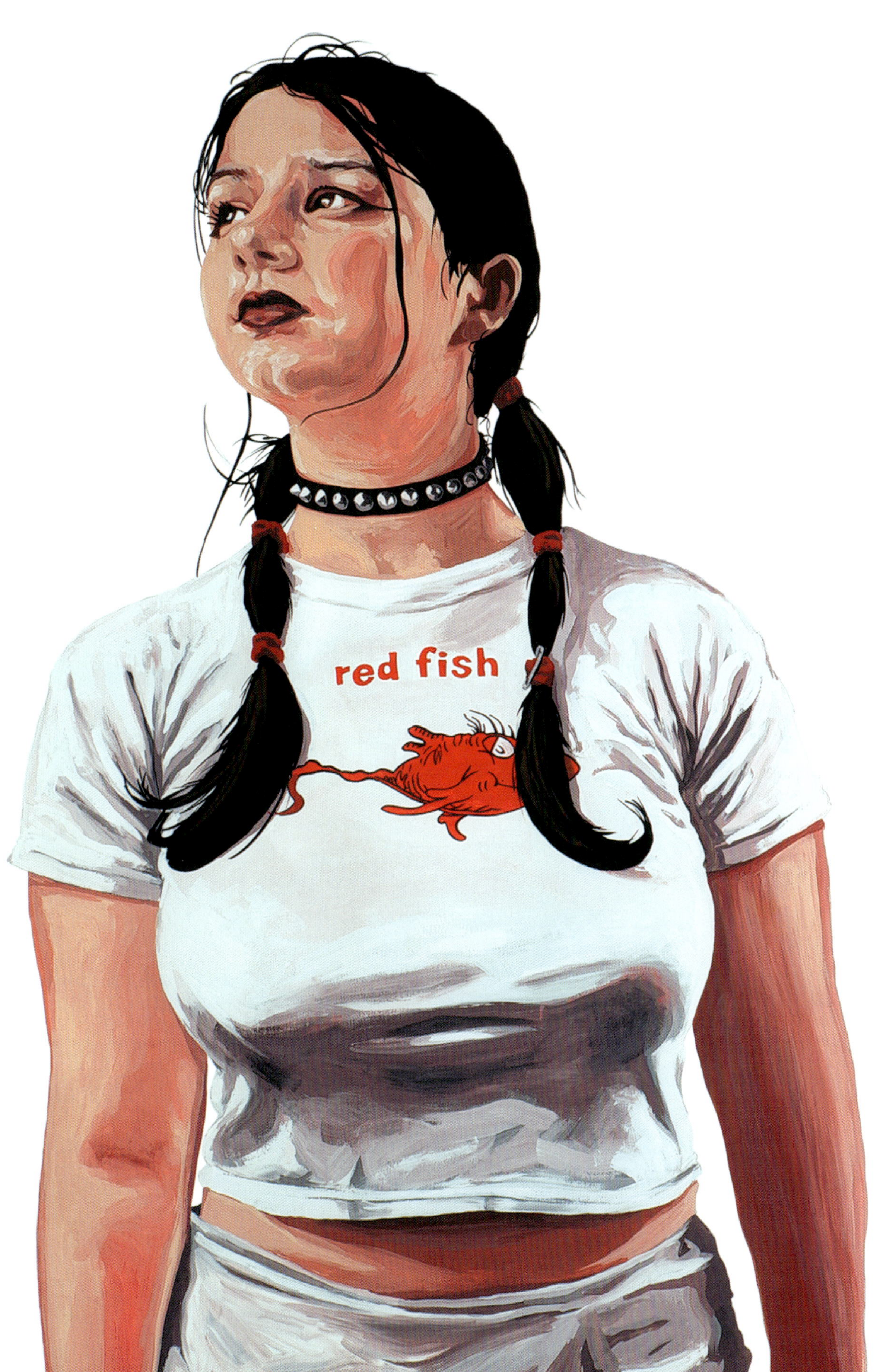
red fish

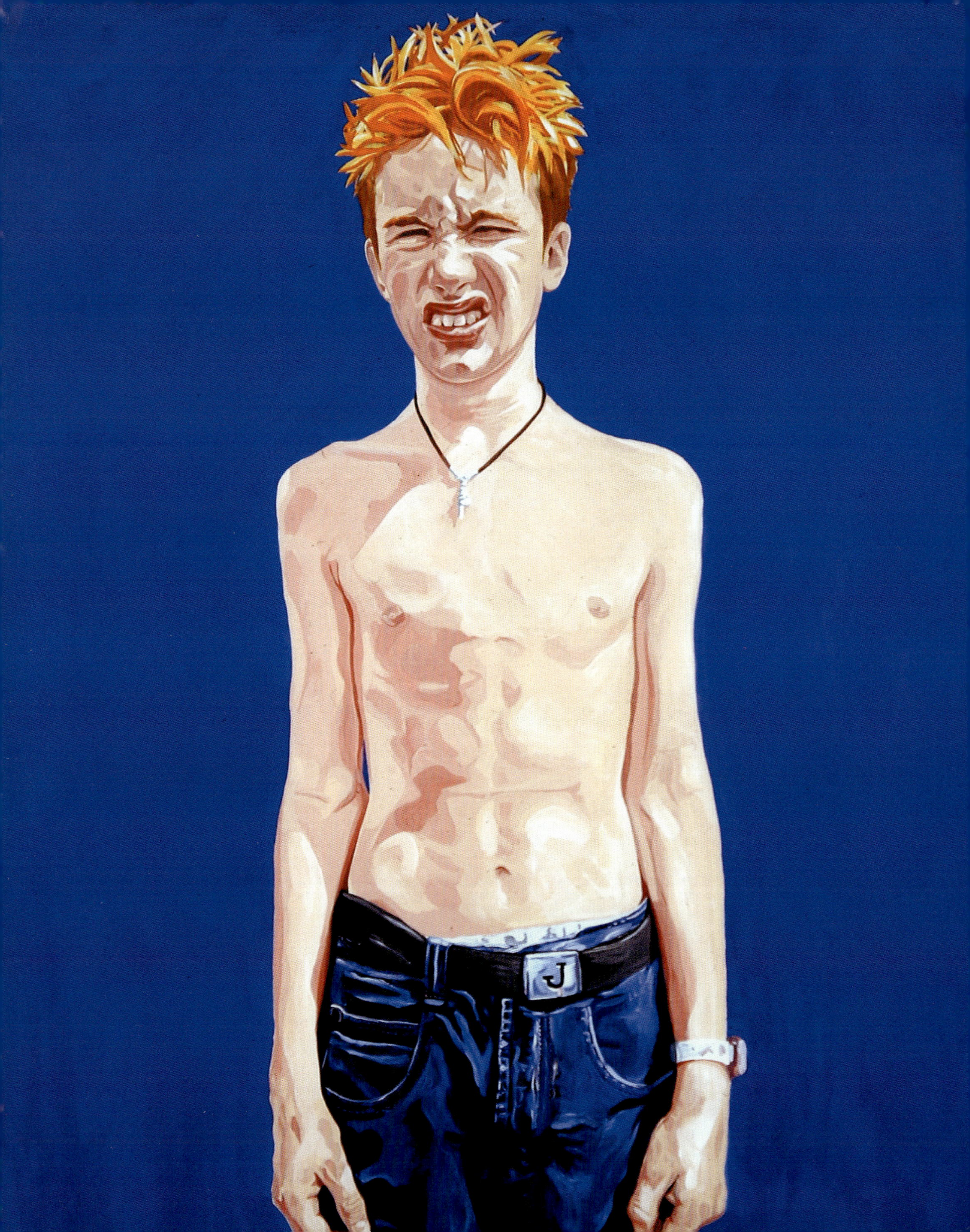

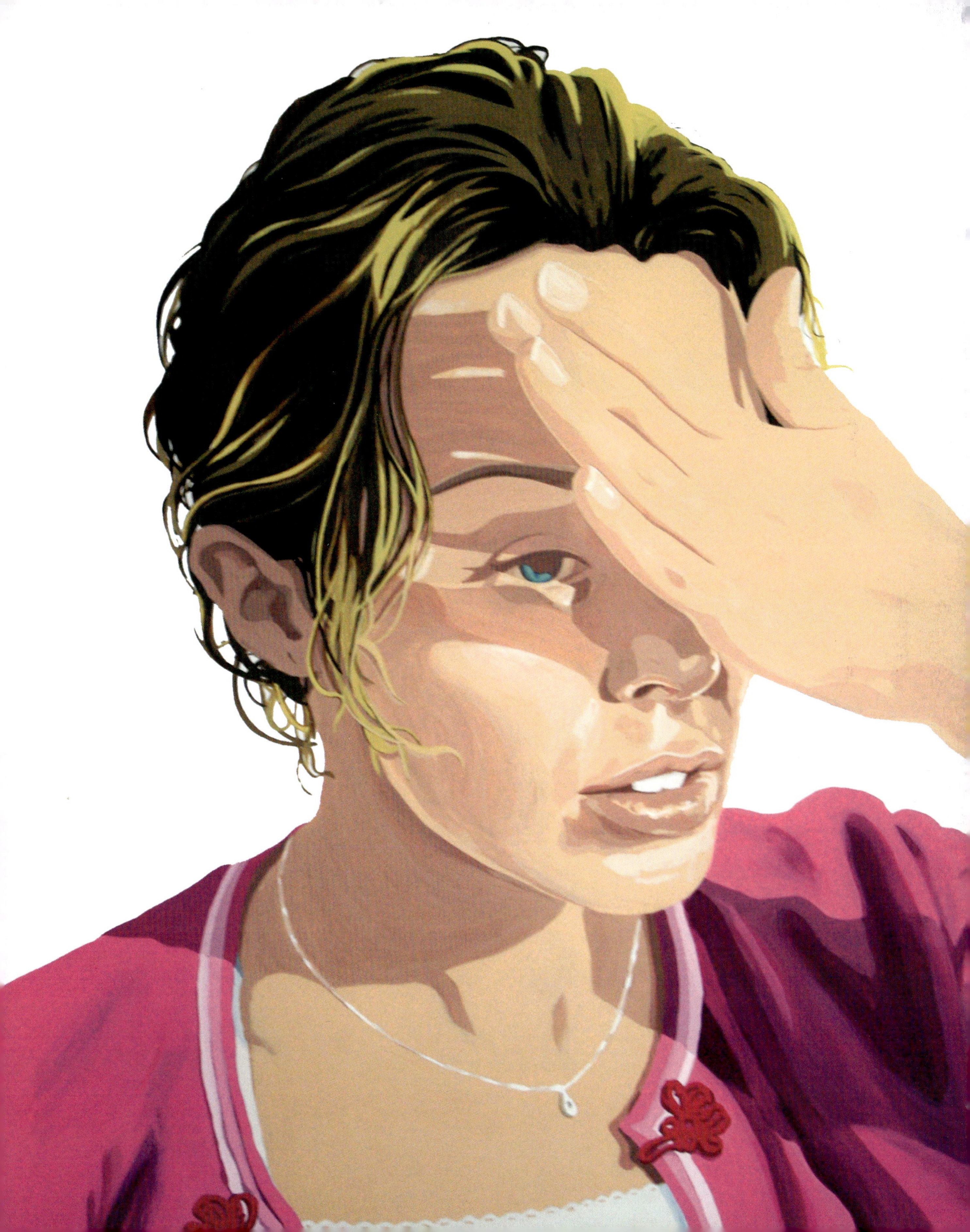

Helen age 18, London 2000
100 x 139cm Gouache on paper
Private collection Chicago.

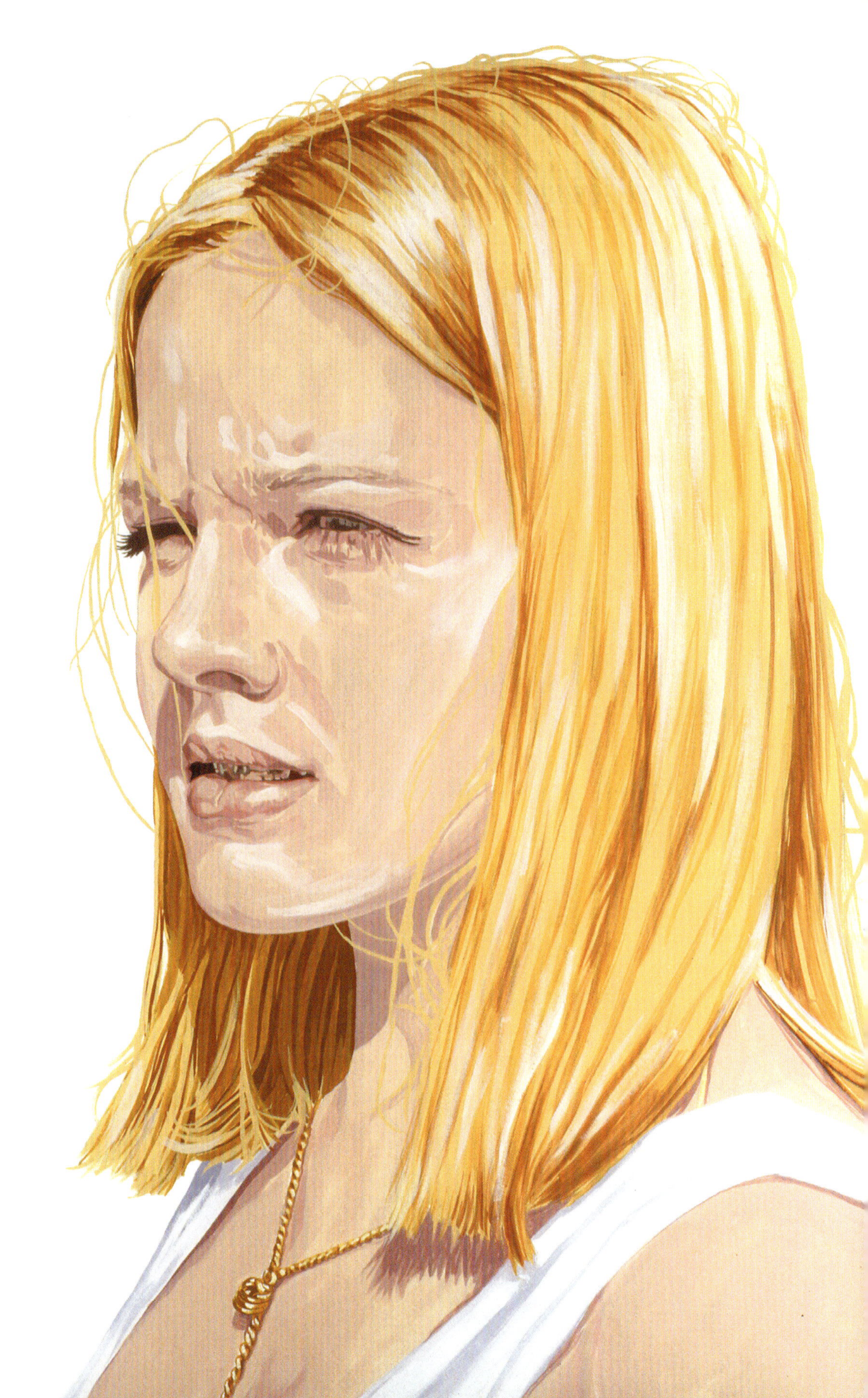

Sophie age 17, London 2003
100 x 139cm Gouache on paper
Private collection London.

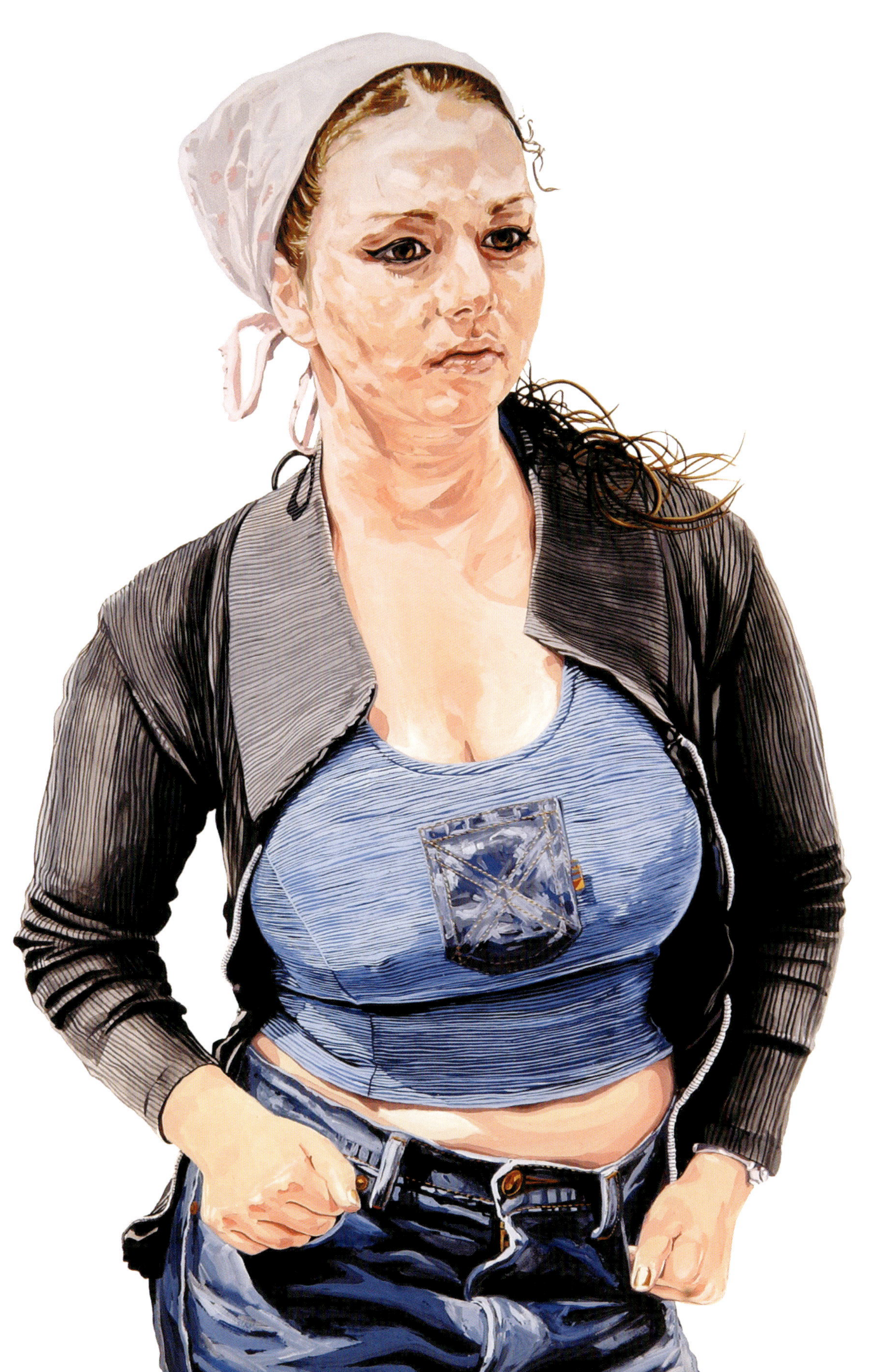

Joey age 14, Las Vegas 2000
100 x 139cm Gouache on paper.

Following Page

Toya age 12, London 2001
100 x 139cm Gouache on paper
Collection of Johan Renck, Sweden.

Jemma age 14, London 2000
100 x 139cm Gouache on paper
Collection of Johan Renck, Sweden.

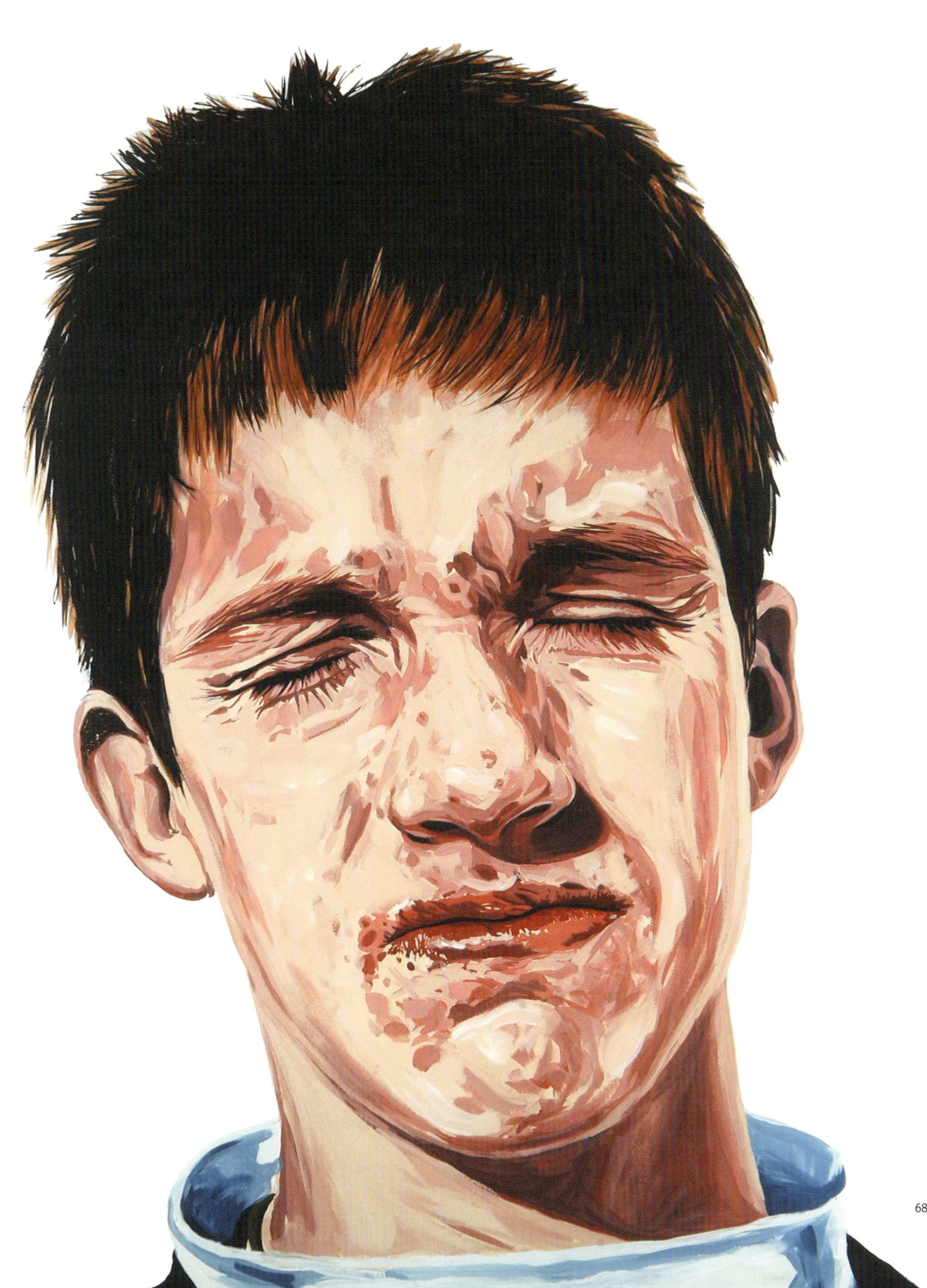

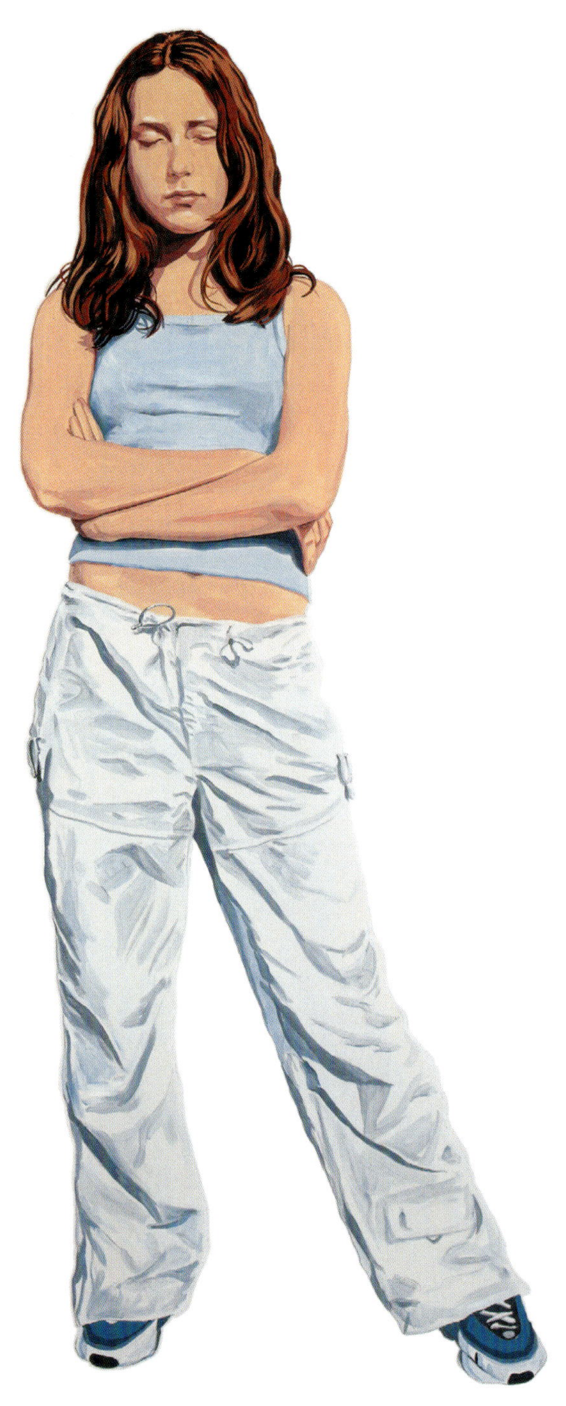

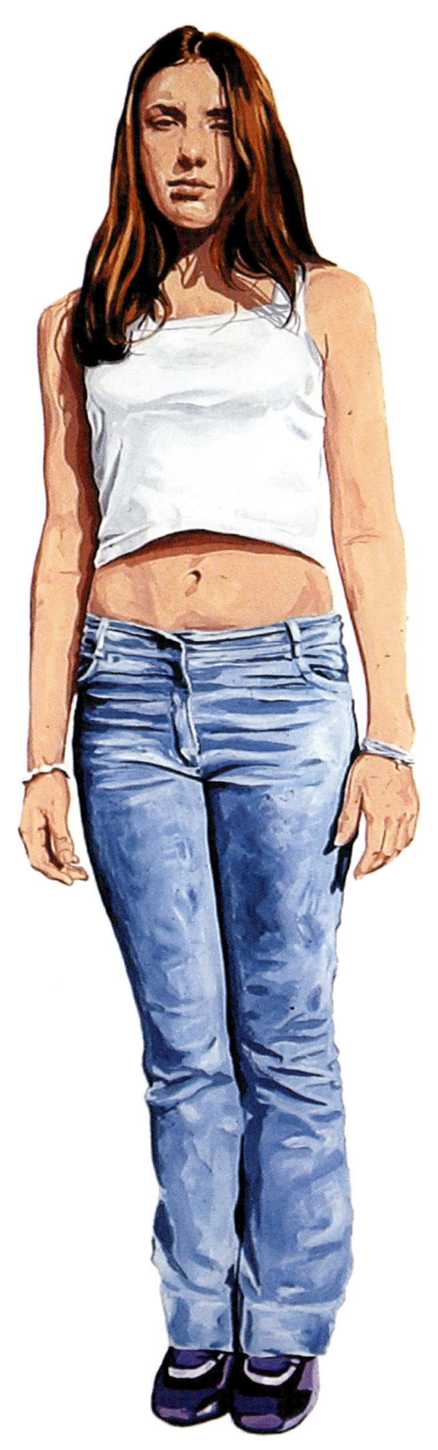

Miwa, London 1999
100 x 139 cm Gouache on paper
The West Collection, Philadelphia.

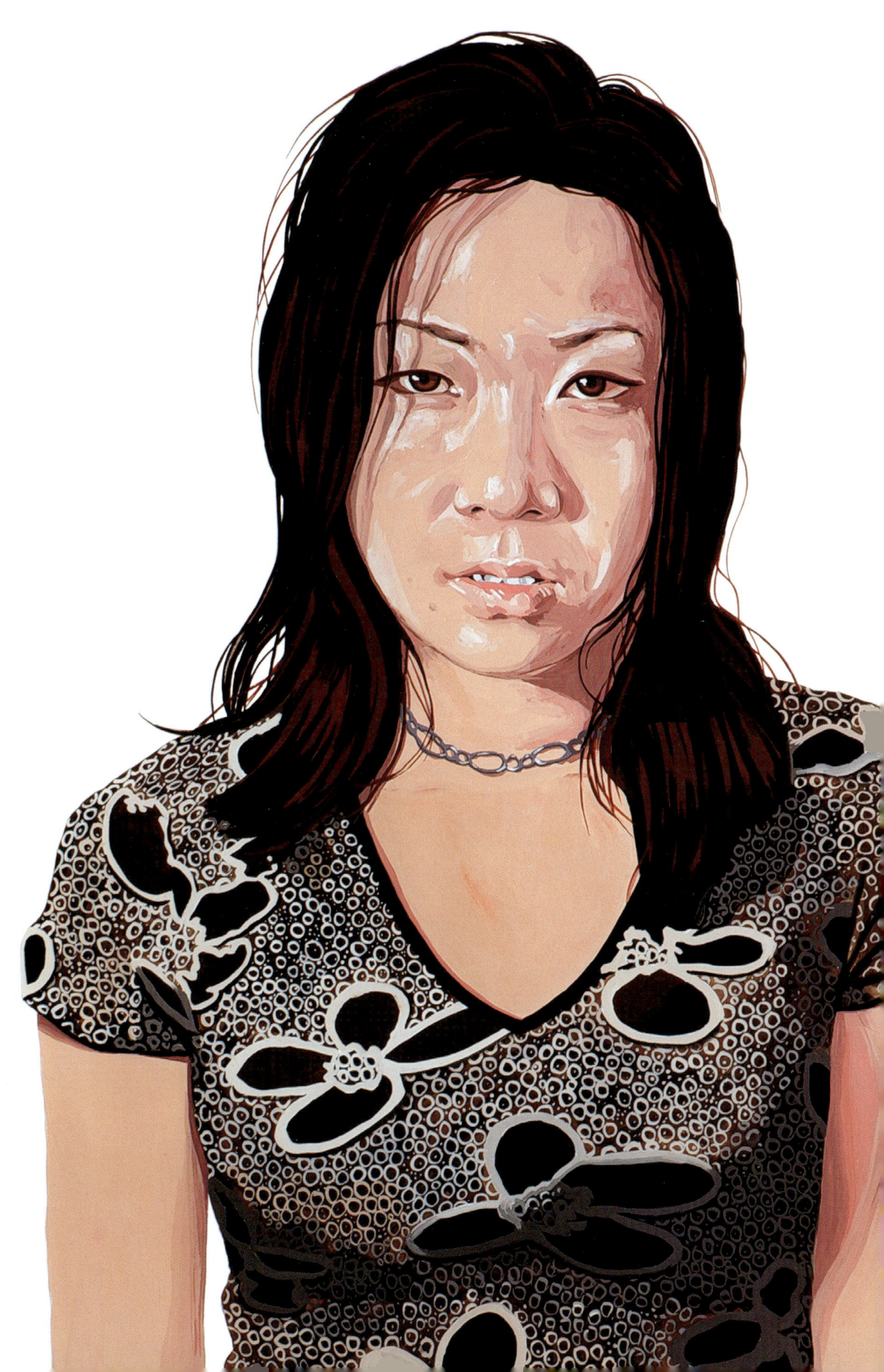

Riho, London 1999
100 x 139 cm Gouache on paper
The West Collection, Philadelphia.

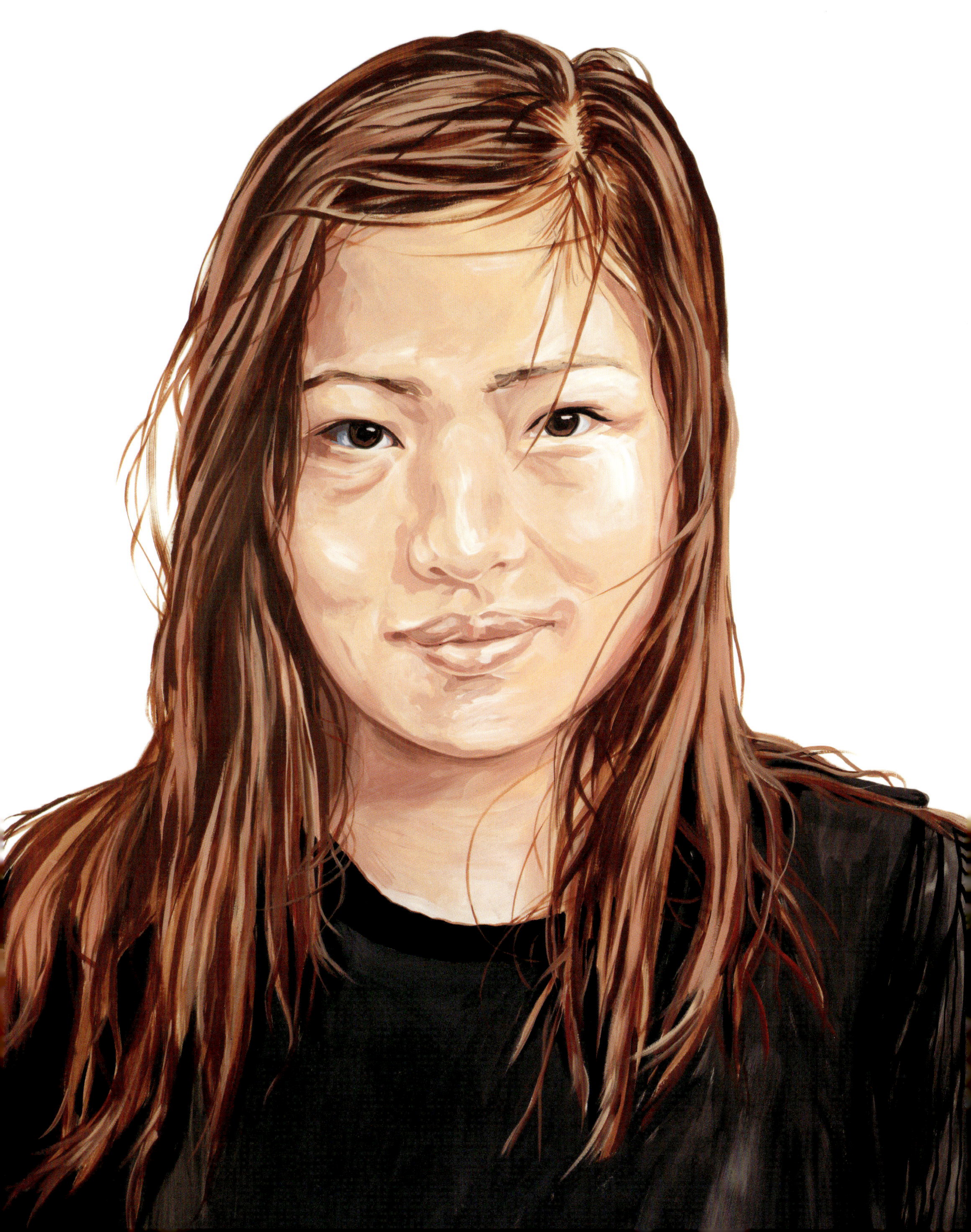

Natsuki, London 1999
100 x 139cm Gouache on paper
The West Collection, Philadelphia.

Following Page

Helen age 18, London 2000
100 x 139cm Gouache on paper.

Johnny age 10, Las Vegas 2000
100 x 139cm Gouache on paper.

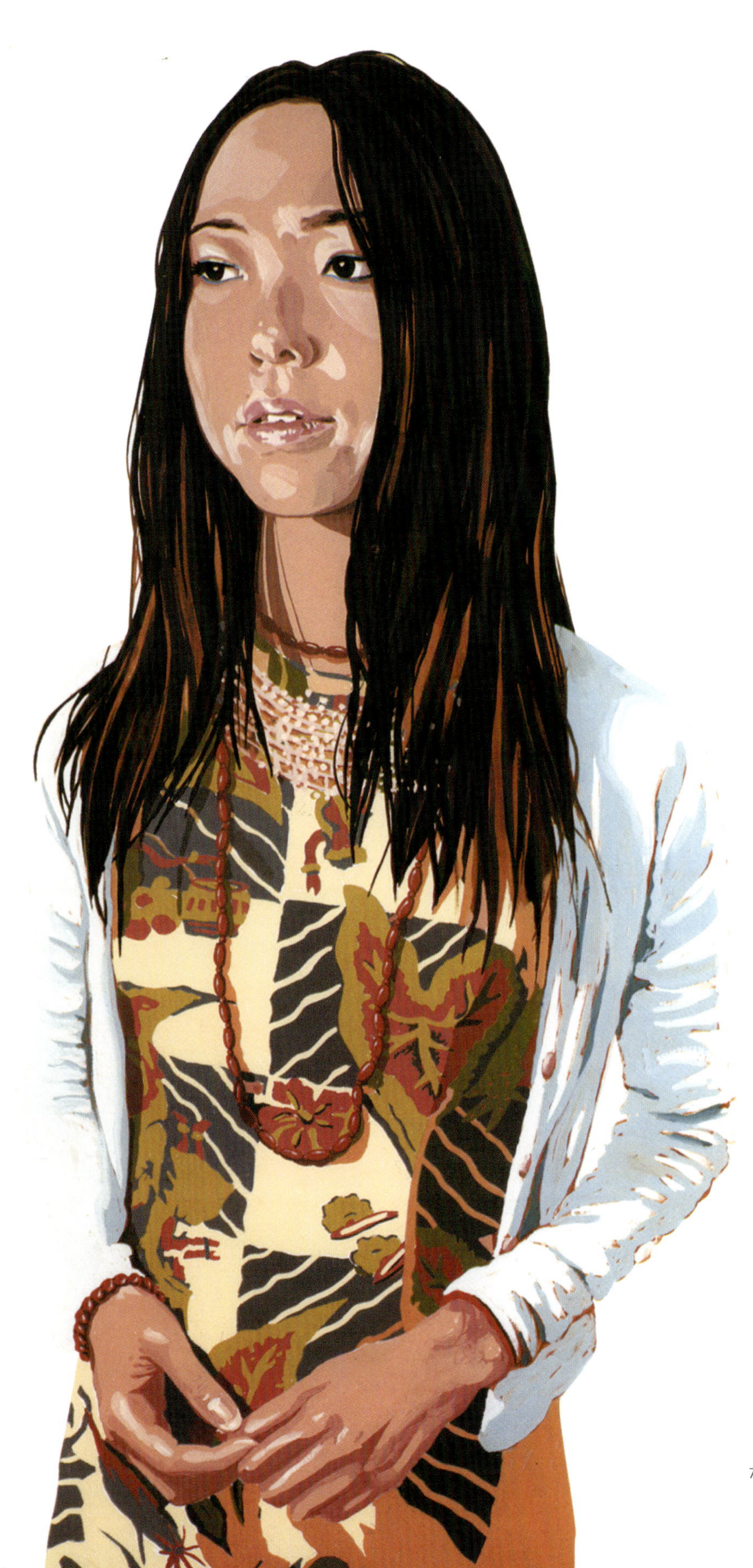

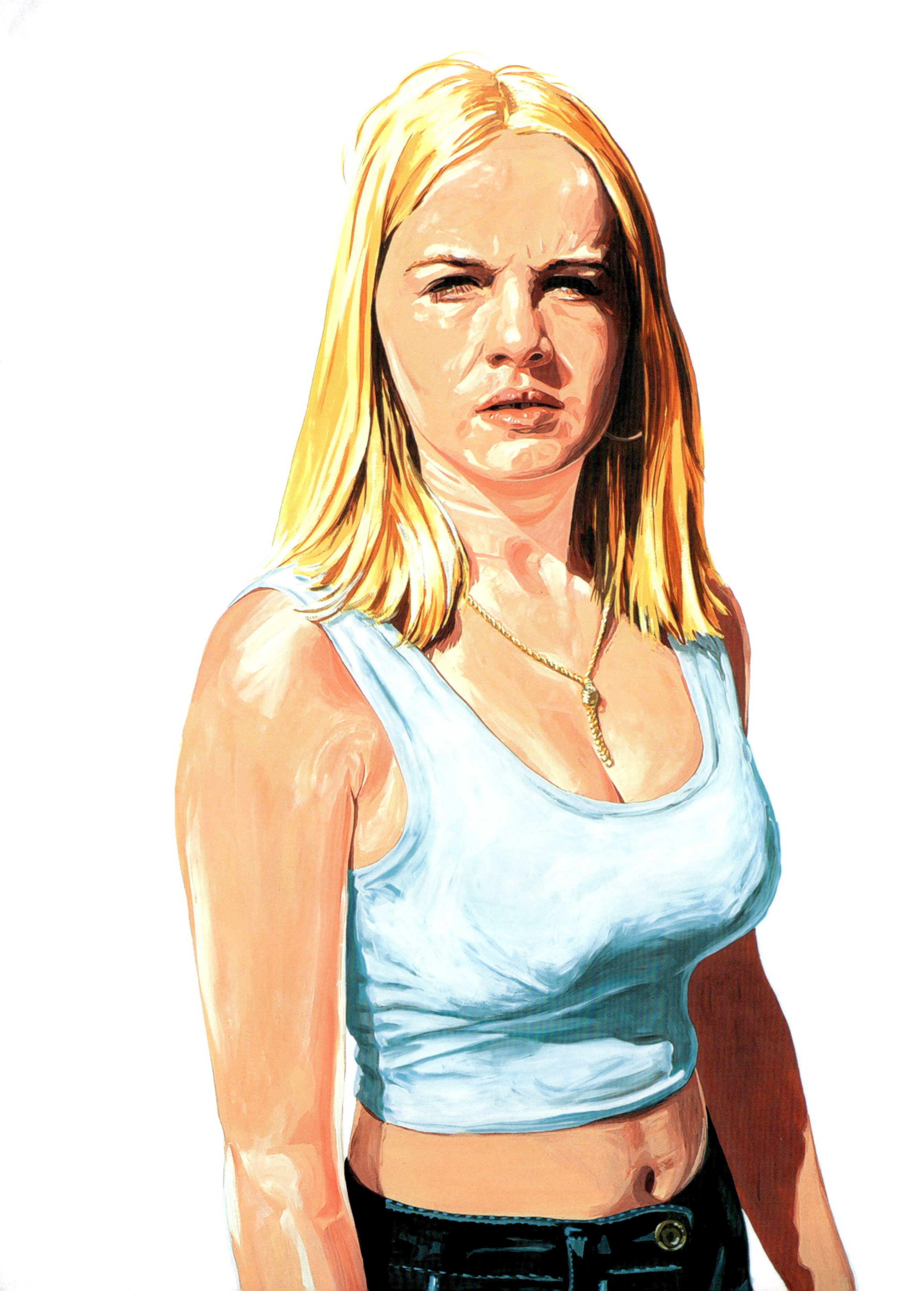

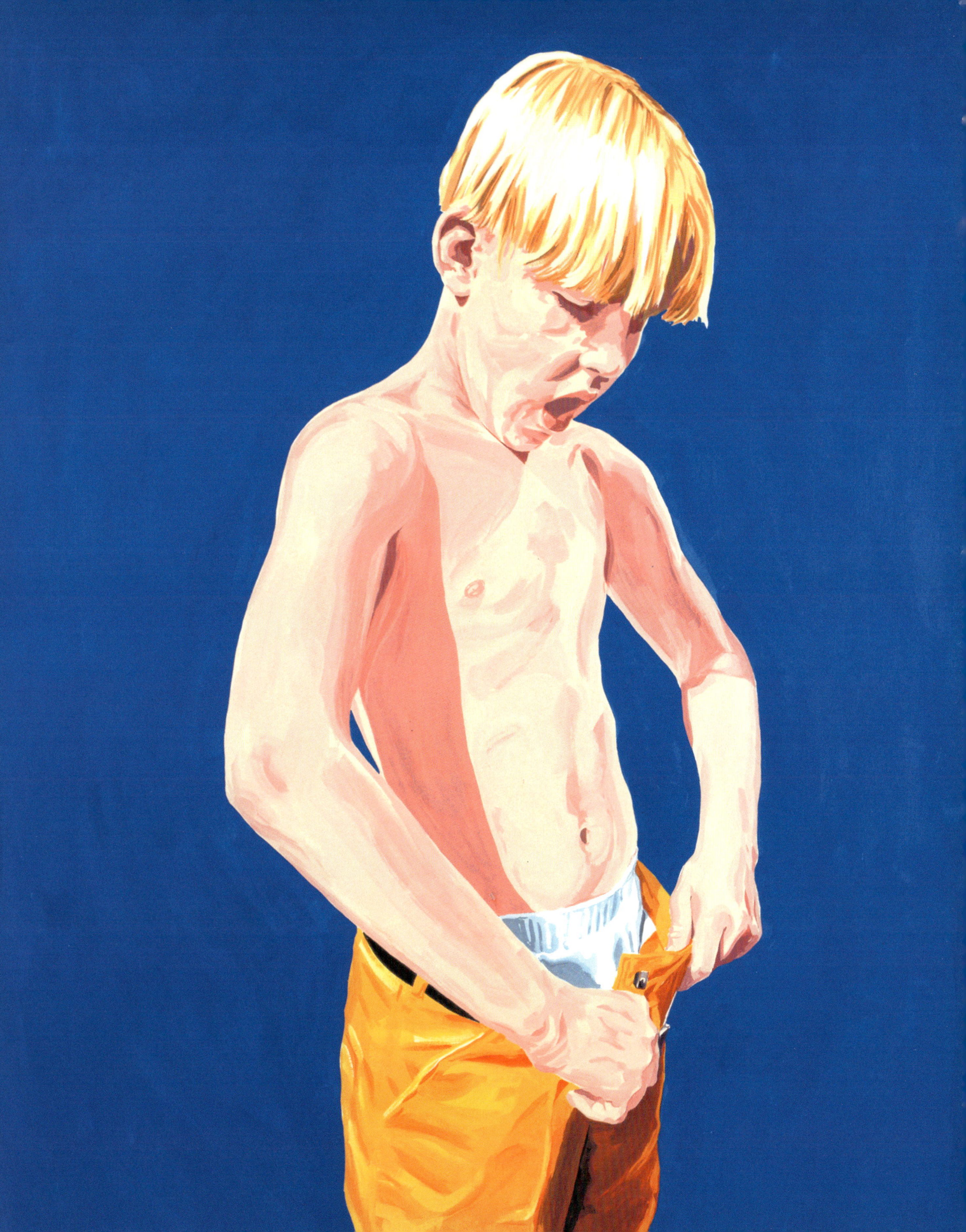

Henry Age 20, London 2002
100 x 139 cm Gouache on paper
Collection of Mario Testino, London.

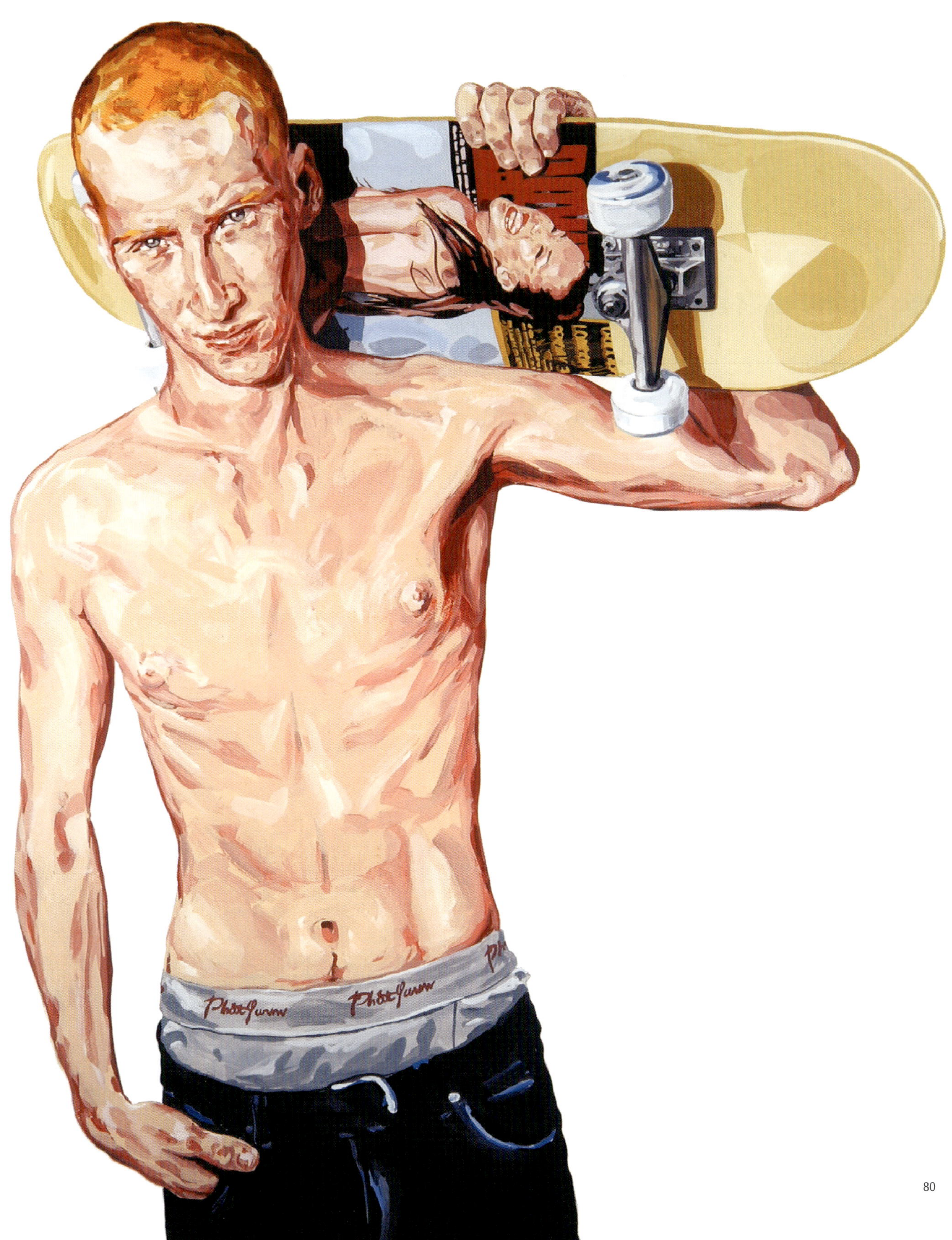

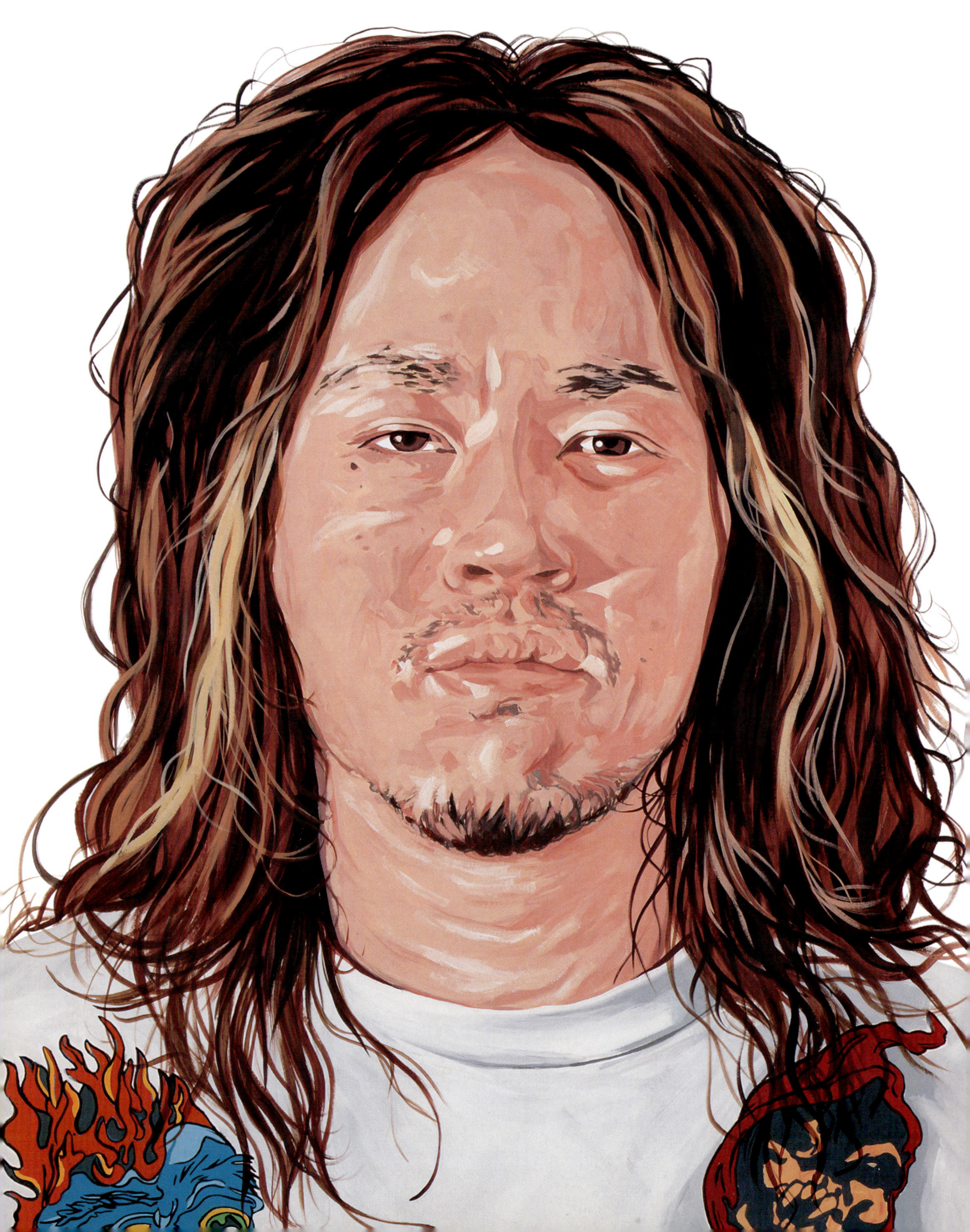

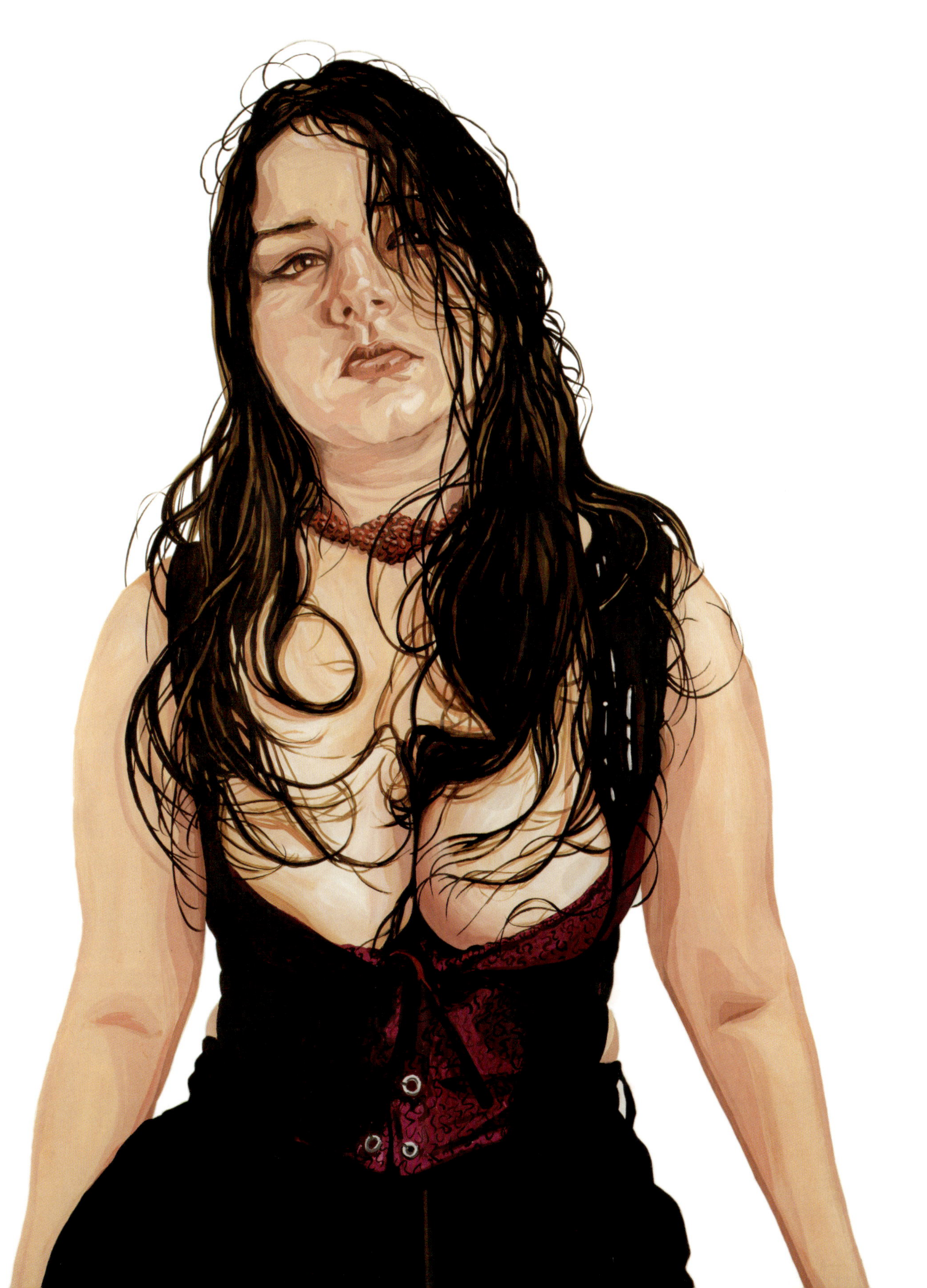

Devendra age 22, New York 2004
100 x 139cm gouache on paper
Private collection Paris.

Previous Page

Ozzy fan, London 2000
100 x 139cm Gouache on paper.

Sophie age 18, London 2000
100 x 139cm Gouache on paper.

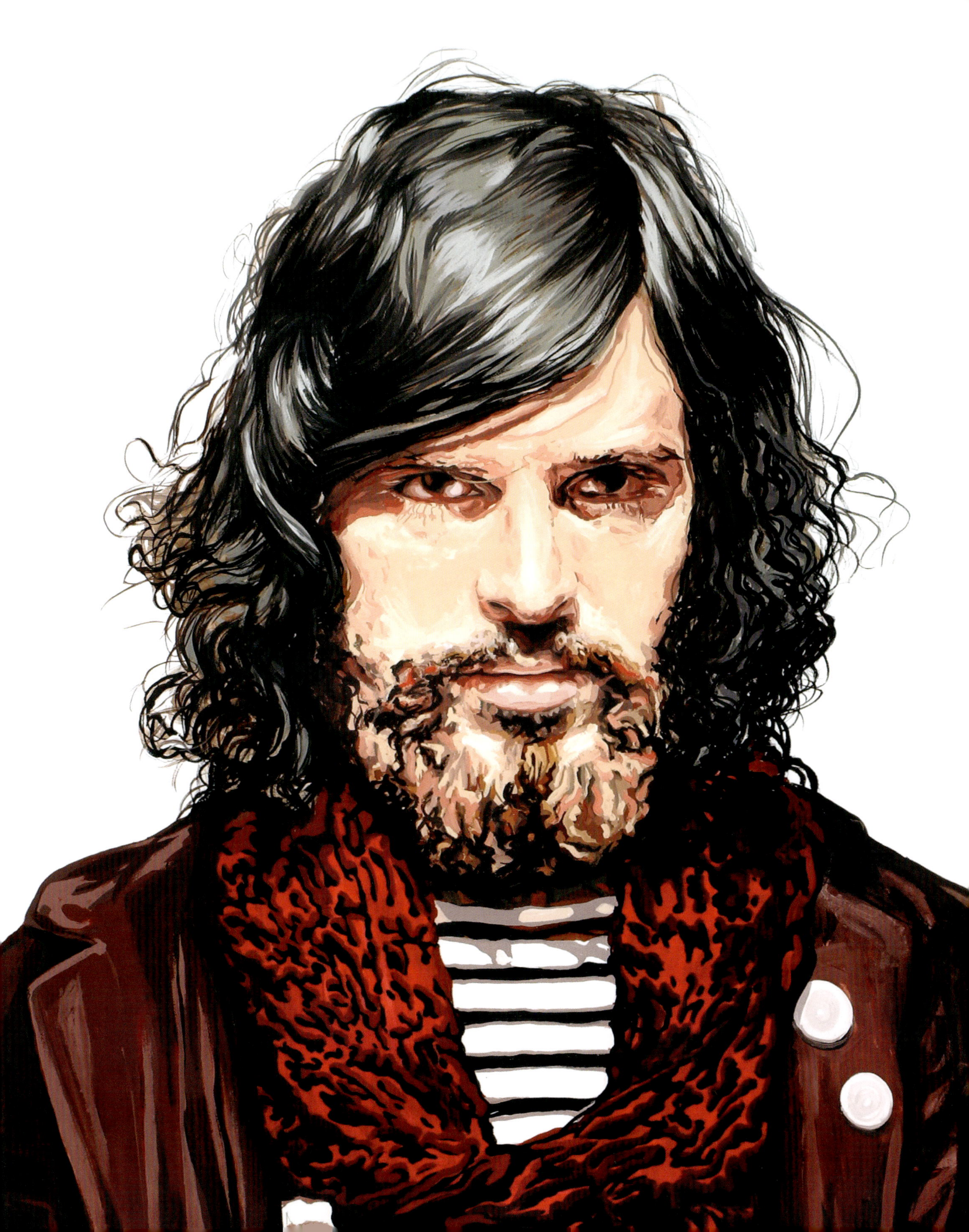

Liesl age 14, Chicago 2003
100 x 139cm Gouache on paper
Collection of Christophe O'Reilly and Charlotte Bavasso, London.

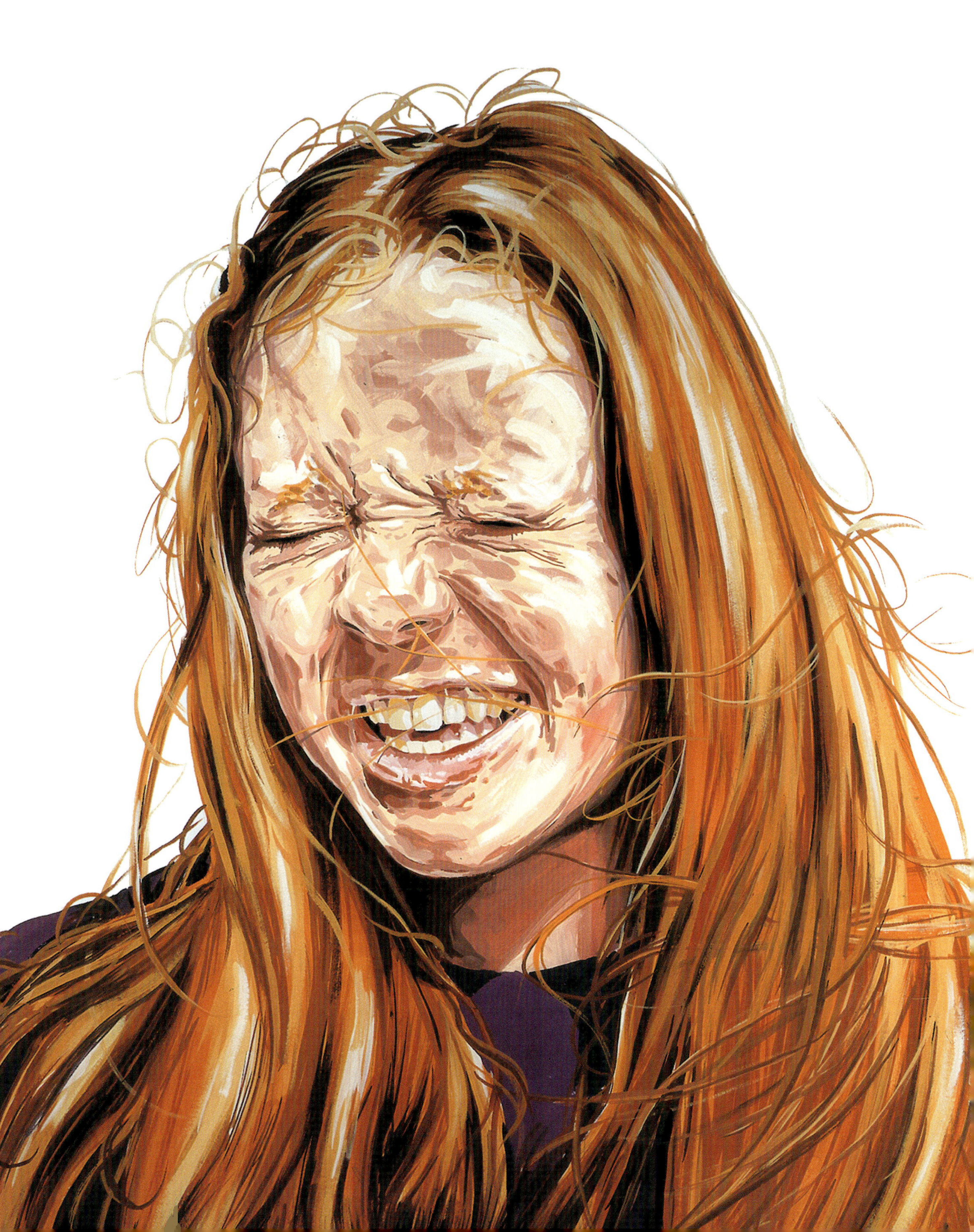

Charlotte, London, 1999
100 x 139 cm Gouache on paper.

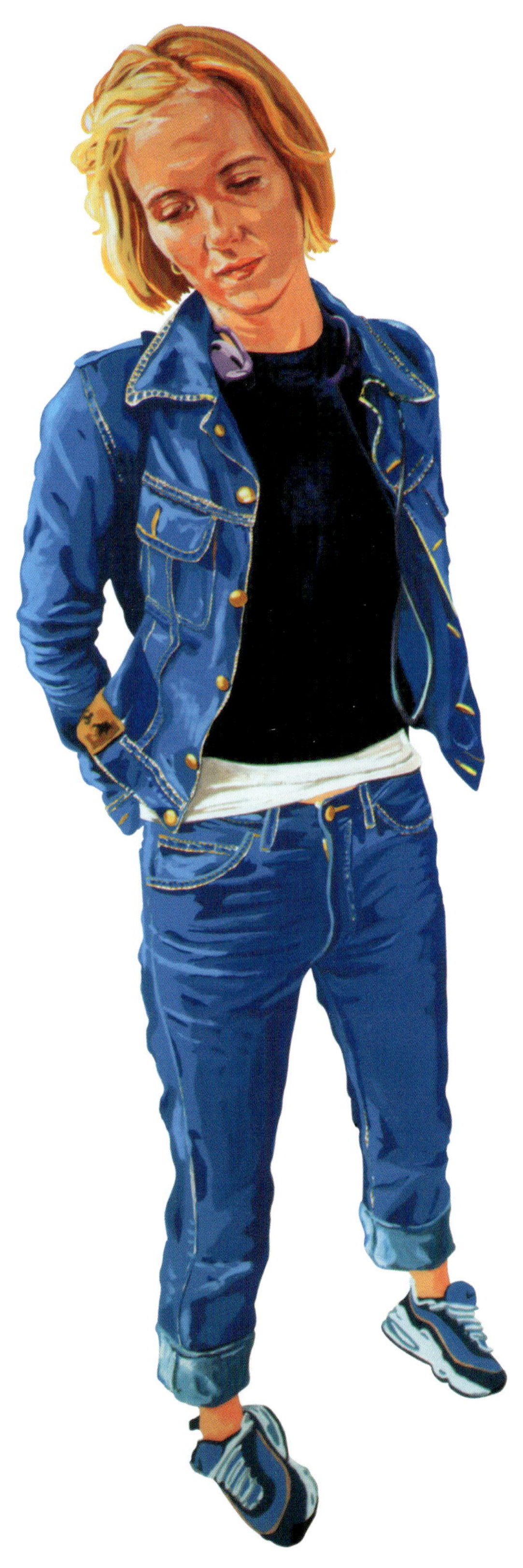

Jemma age 17, London 2003
100 x 139 cm Gouache on paper
Collection of Eric Decelle, Brussels.

Following page

Chicago Landscape - 2003
130 x 225 cm Gouache on paper.

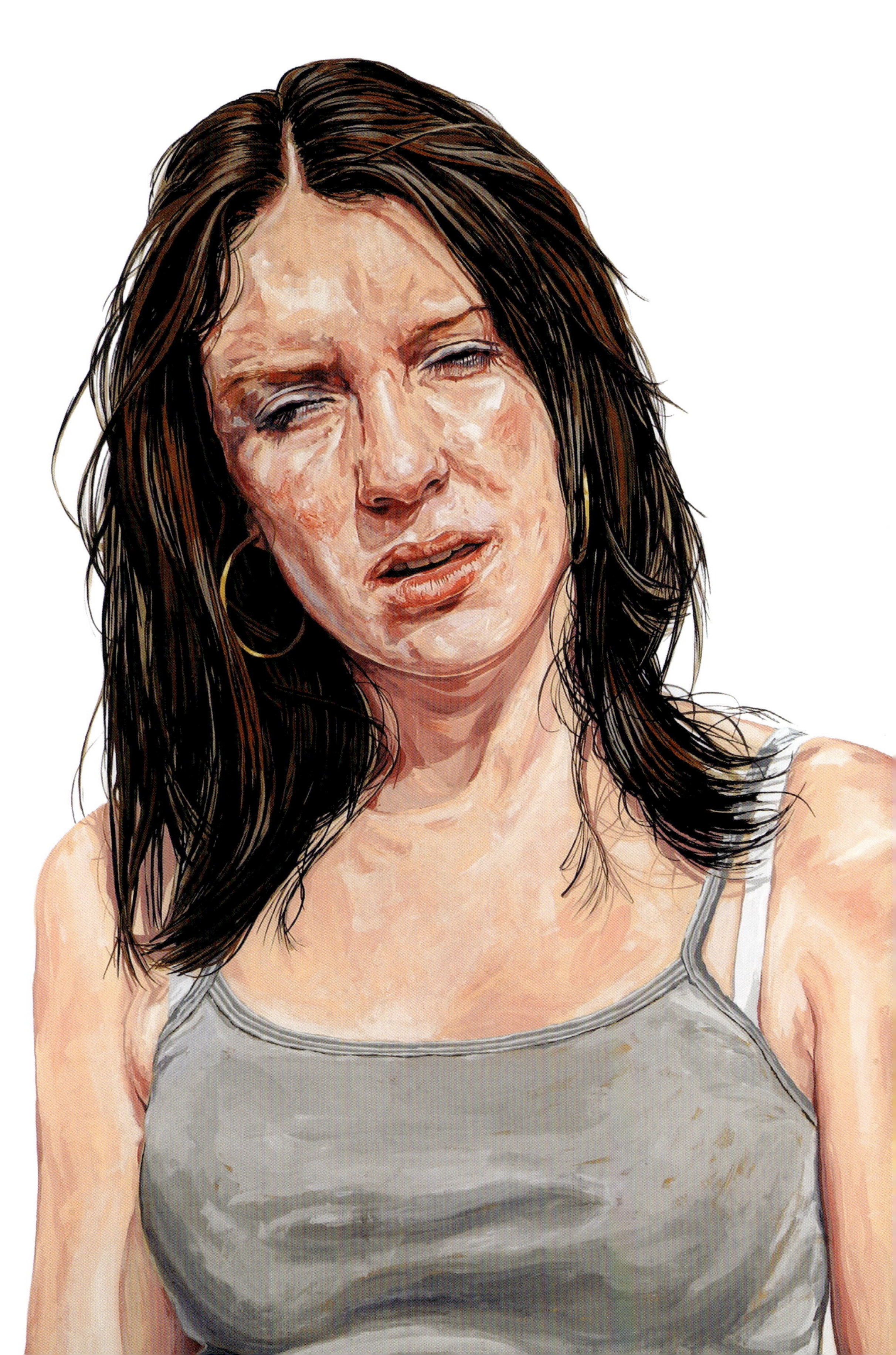

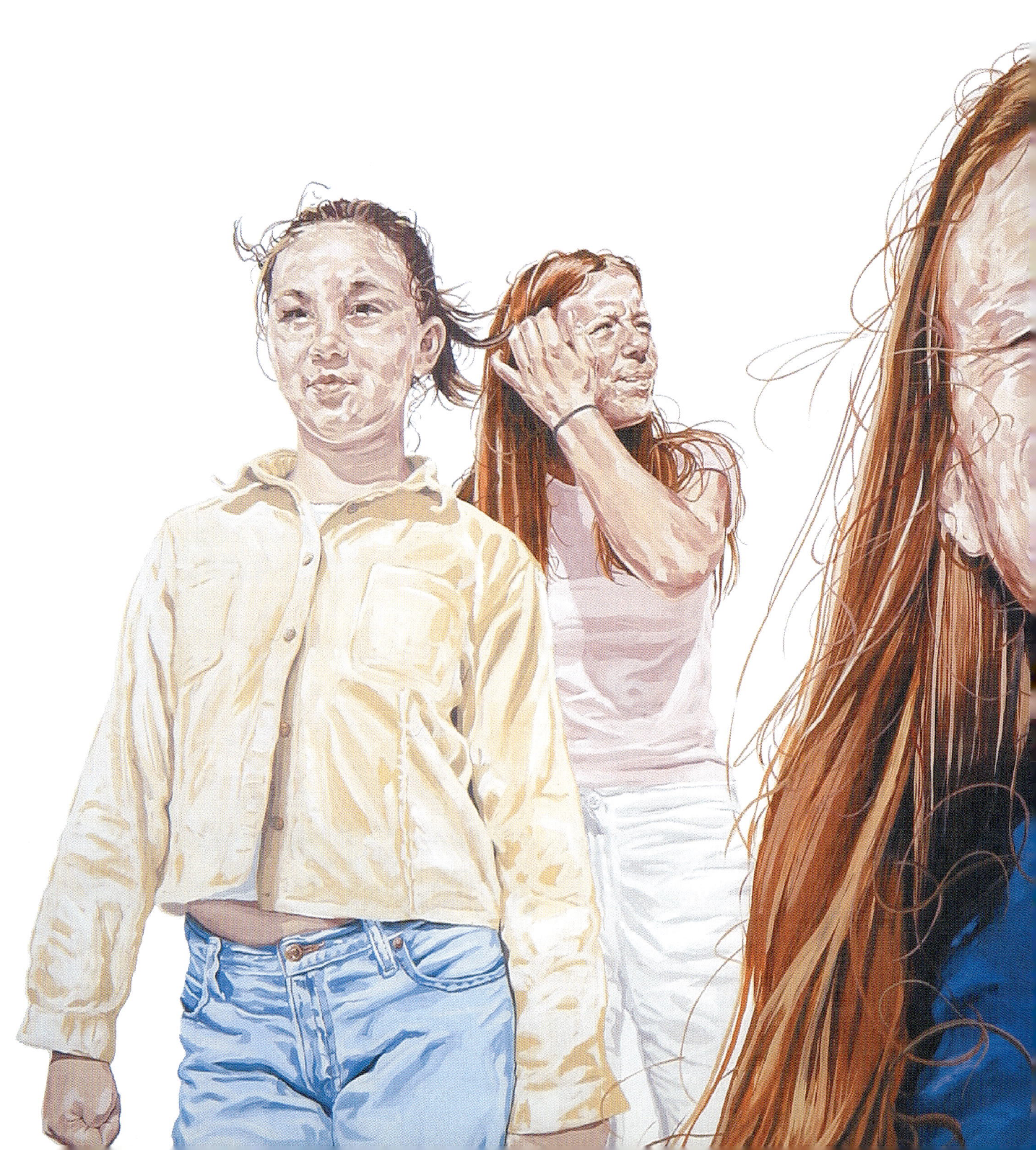

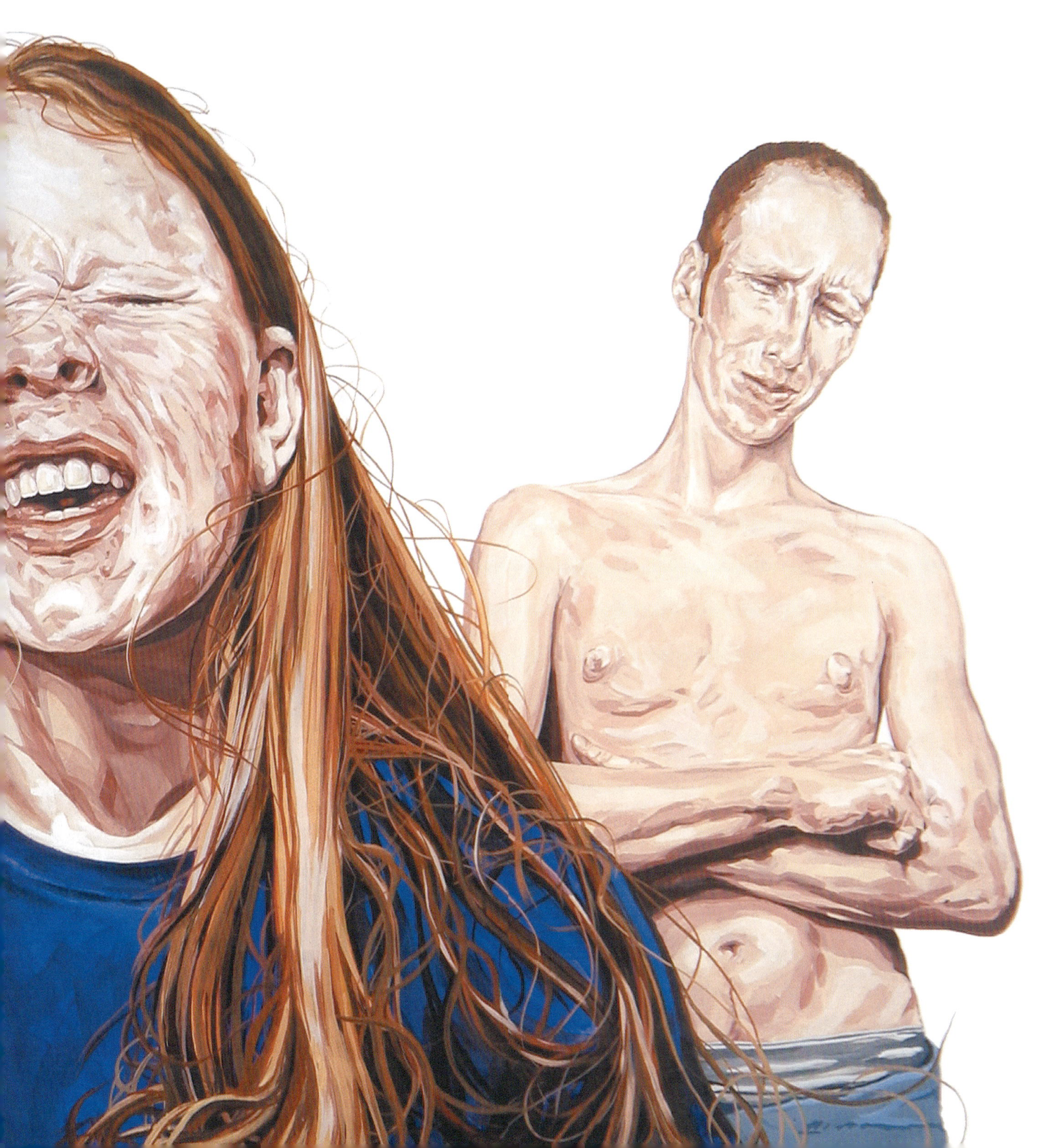

Charlotte age 23, London 2003
100 x 139cm Gouache on paper
Private Collection, London.

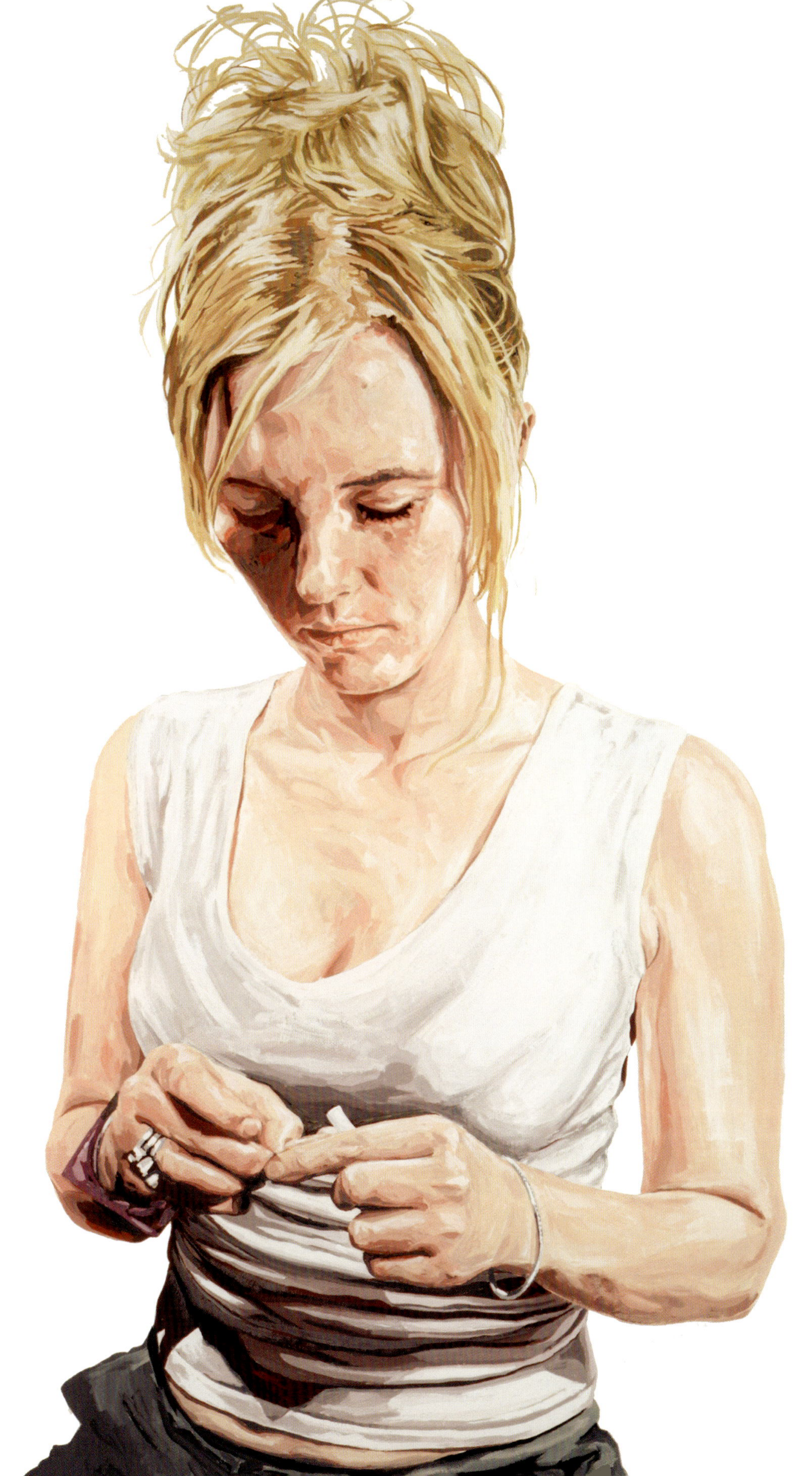

94

Sequins

Roisin Murphy

Not only the subject but the artist
contained there within the frame

The first time I encountered Simon's paintings they left a big impression on me. It was in his studio and some of the "Kido" pictures were propped up against the walls. What struck me most was facing the tangible presence of not only the subject but the artist contained there within the frame. Having worked only with graphic artists, photographers, and video directors in the past in the mass production of images, those paintings standing finished and complete in one single object of intense work had an energy that could not be replicated in a million commercial images, It was only an honour to be asked to sit for my portrait. I almost fell to the floor.

Roisin Murphy London 2005

(Detail) Sequins number 3 , 2005
100 x 139cm Gouache on paper.

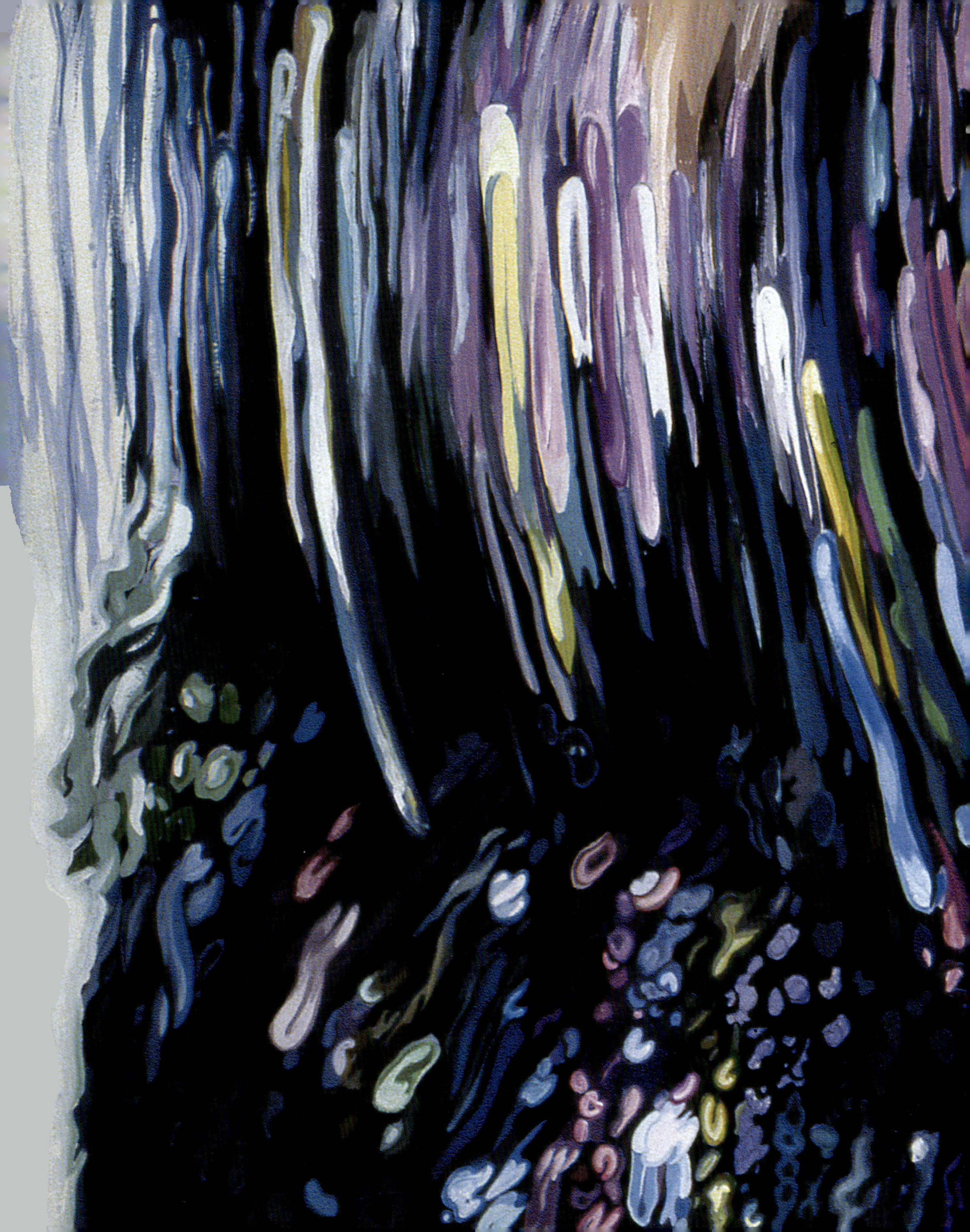

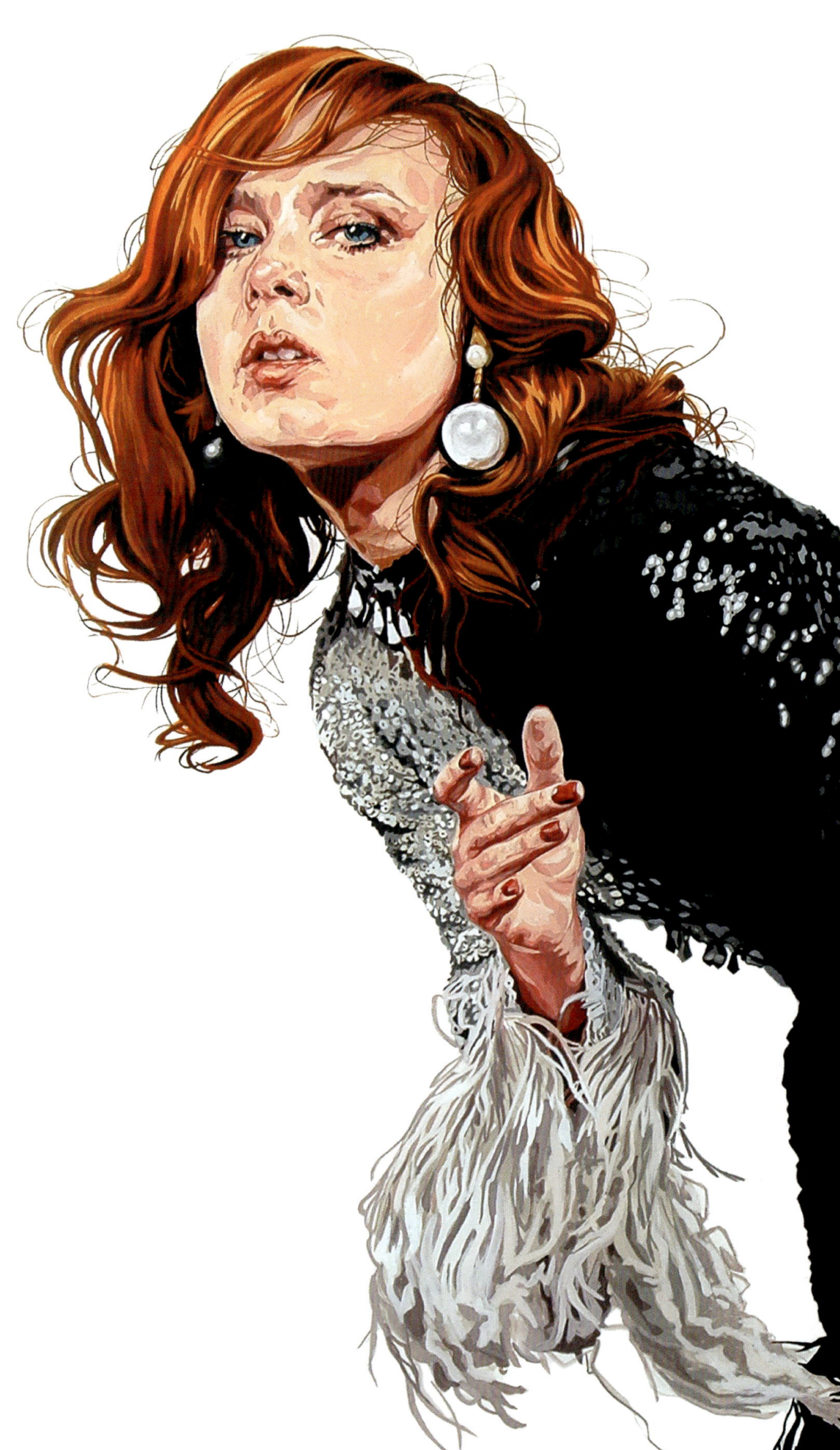

Ruby Blue - 2005
139x 100cm Gouache on paper
Private collection London.

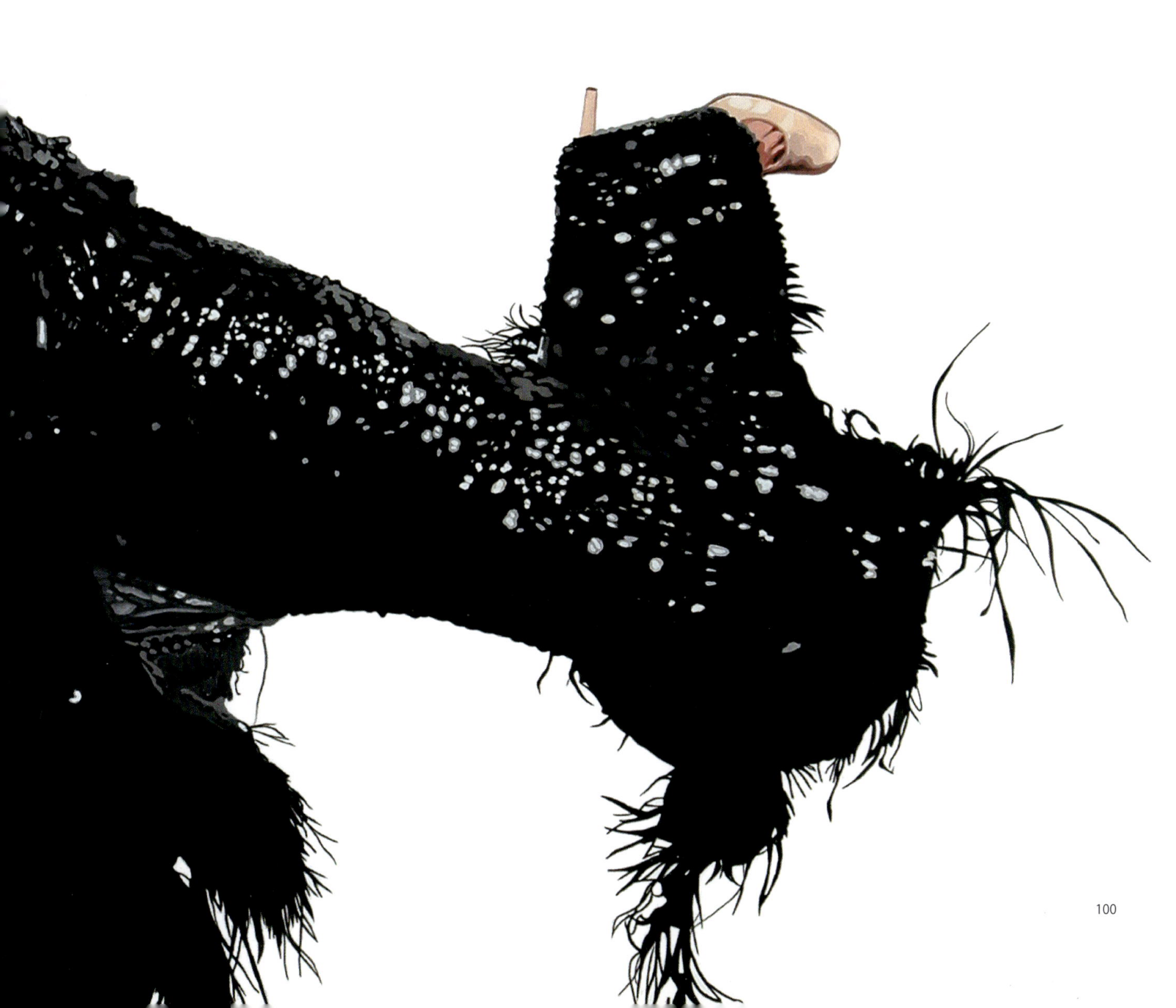

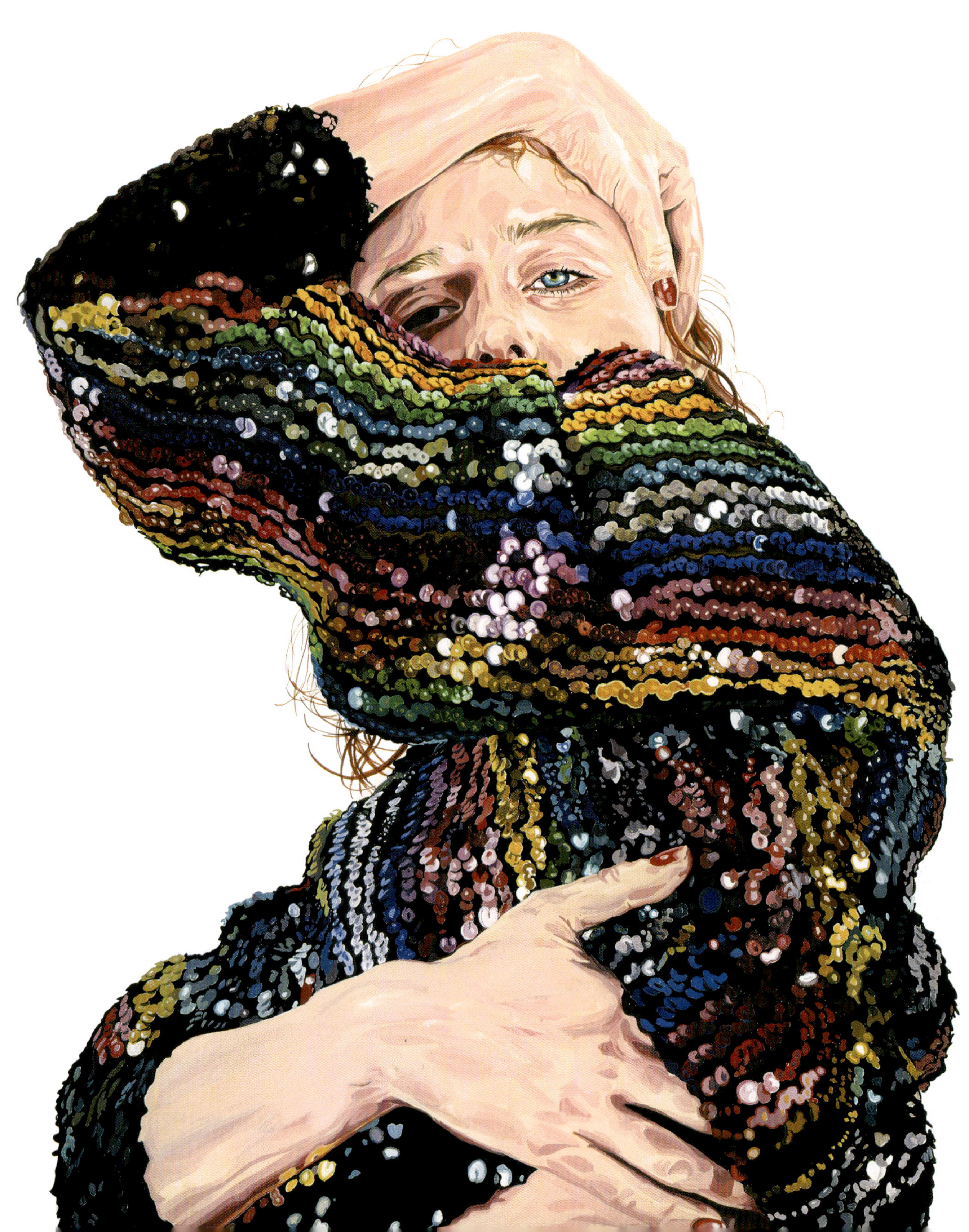

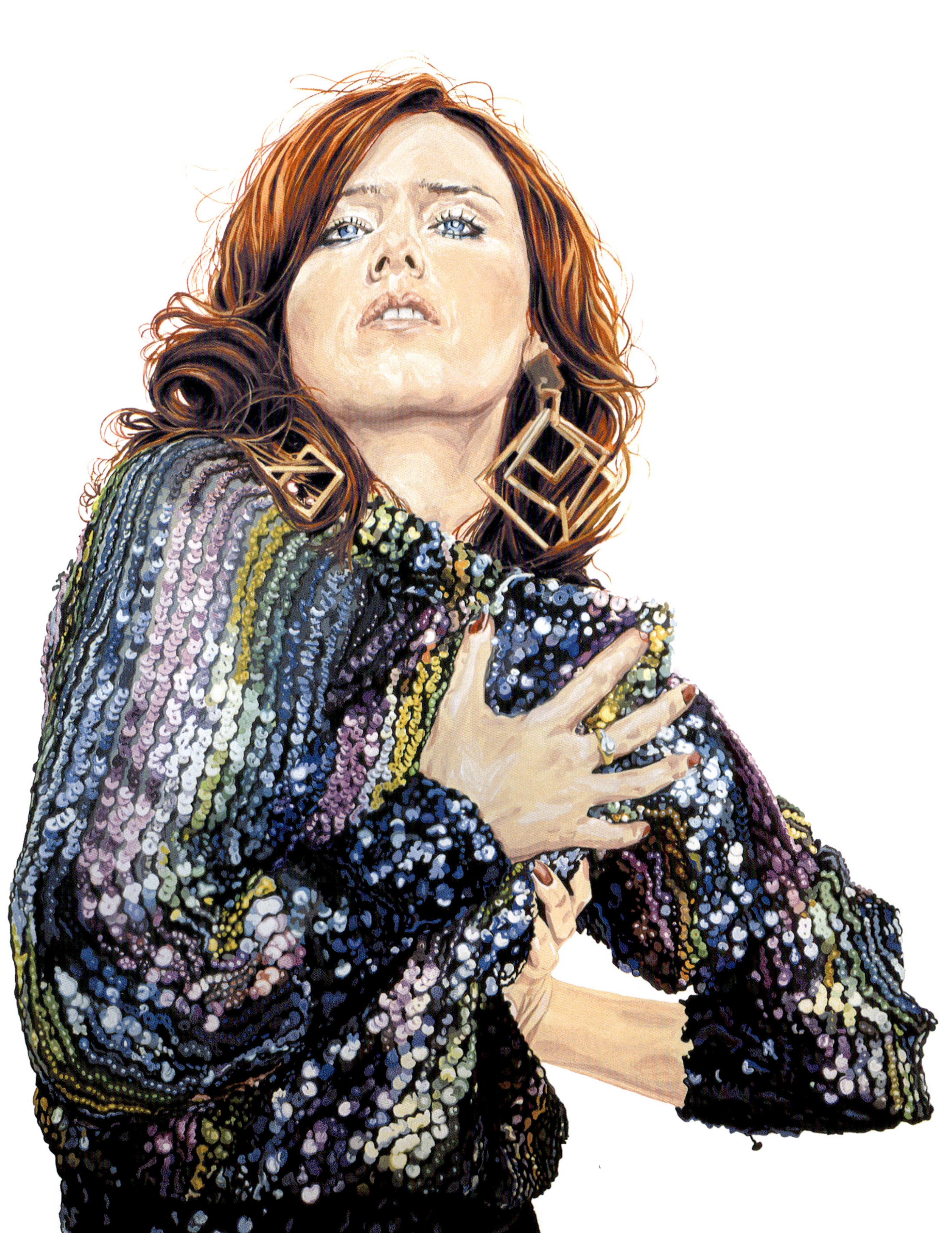

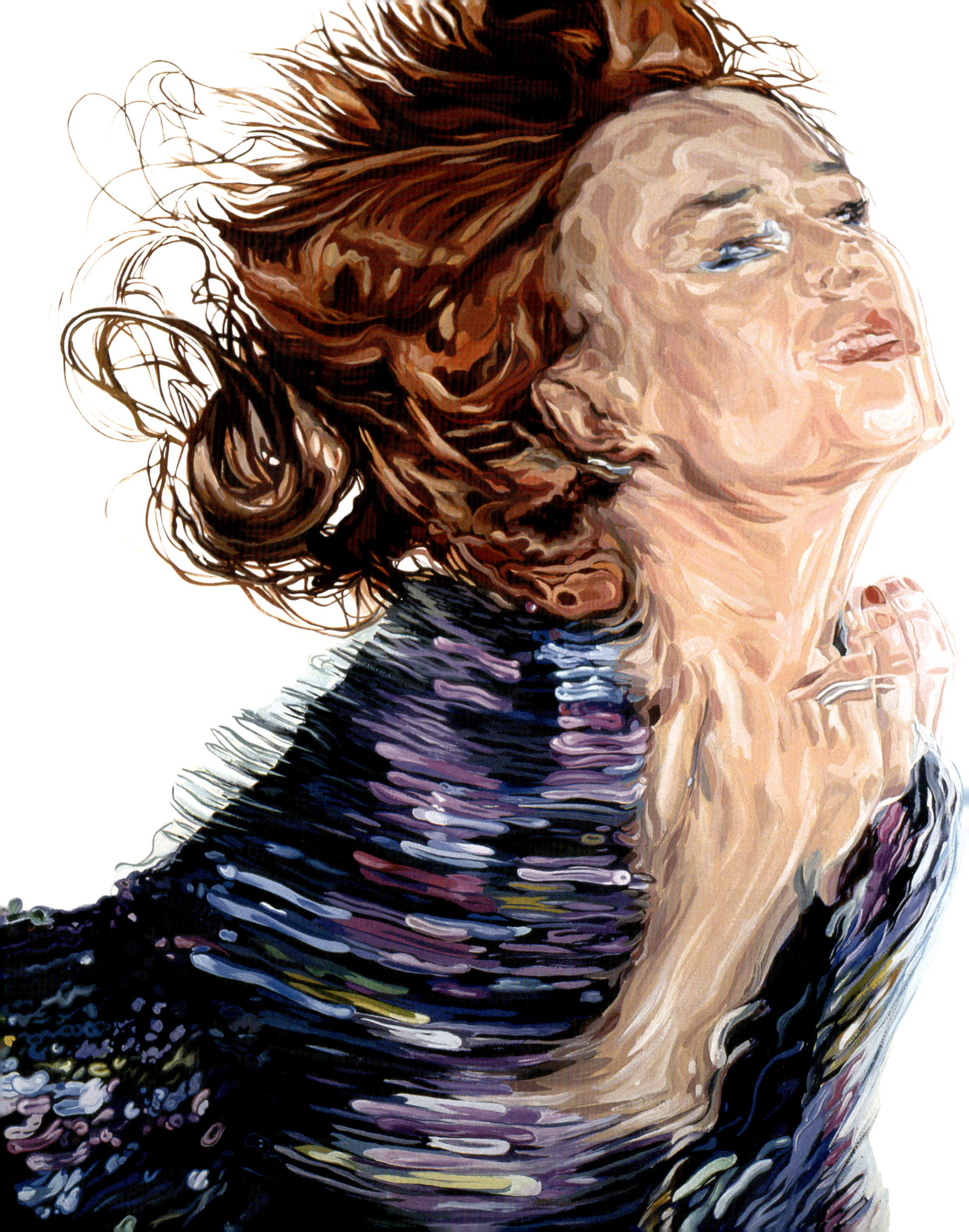

Previous Page

Cricklewood Paintings 2005 - 2008

Girl With Orange, London 2006
100 x 139 cm Gouache on paper.

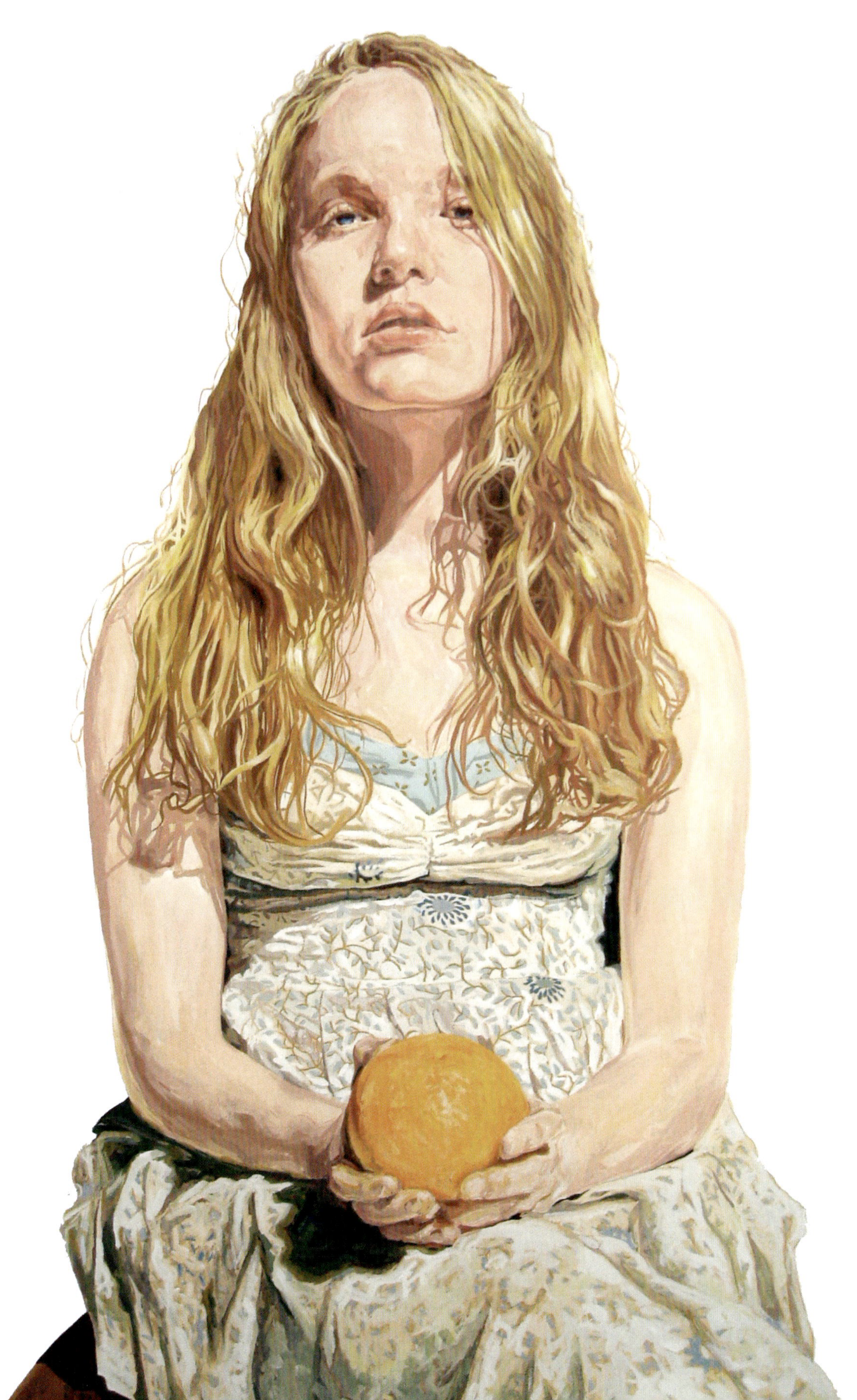

Tamzin Merchant, London 2006
90 x 70 cm Oil on canvas.

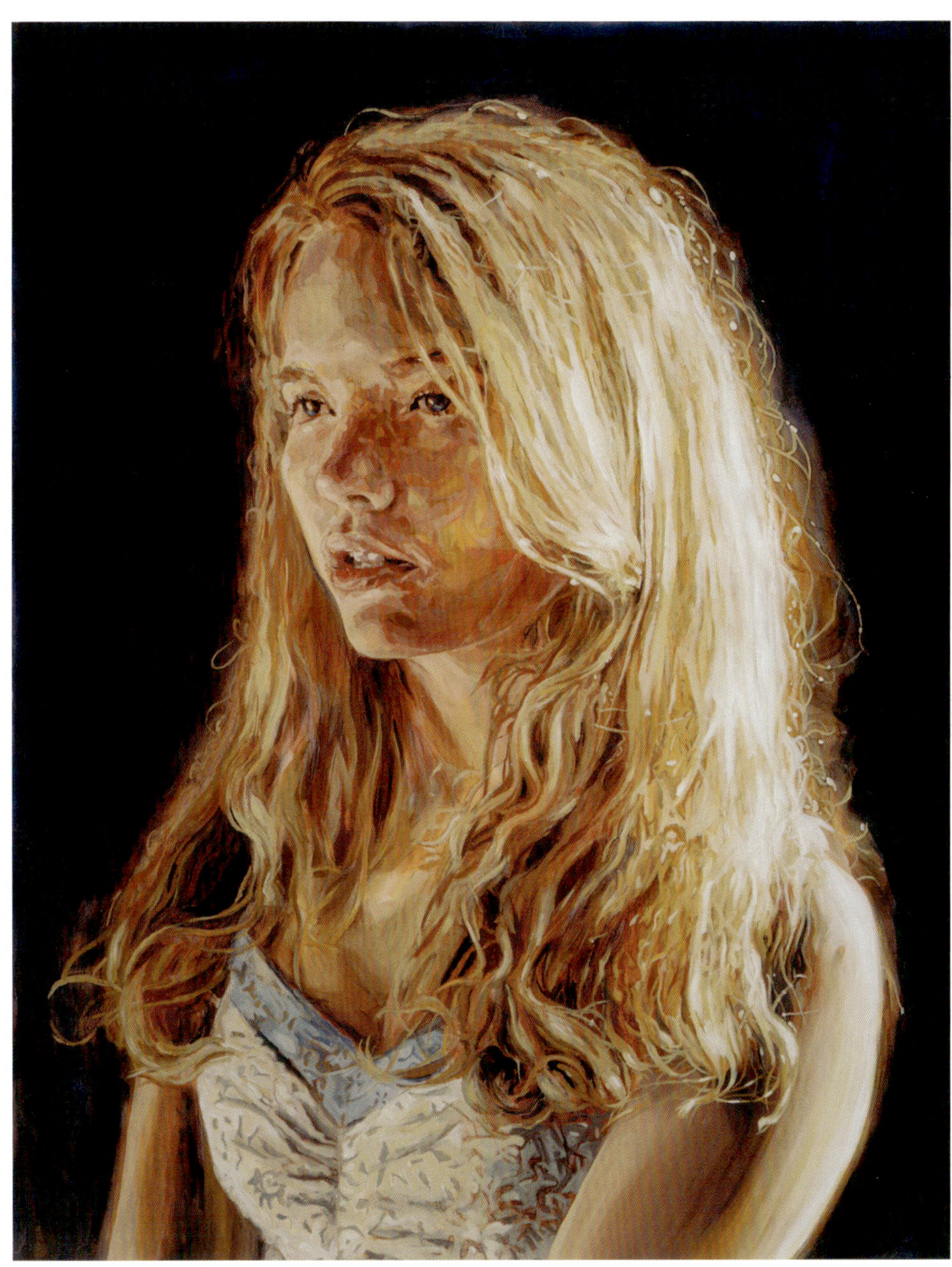

Blind Marquis, 2005
30 x 20 cm Oil on board
Private collection London.

Following Page
Installation view

Sophie, 2008
35 x 50cm Oil on canvas
Private collection Paris.

Untitled, 2008
35 x 50cm Oil on canvas
Private collection Paris.

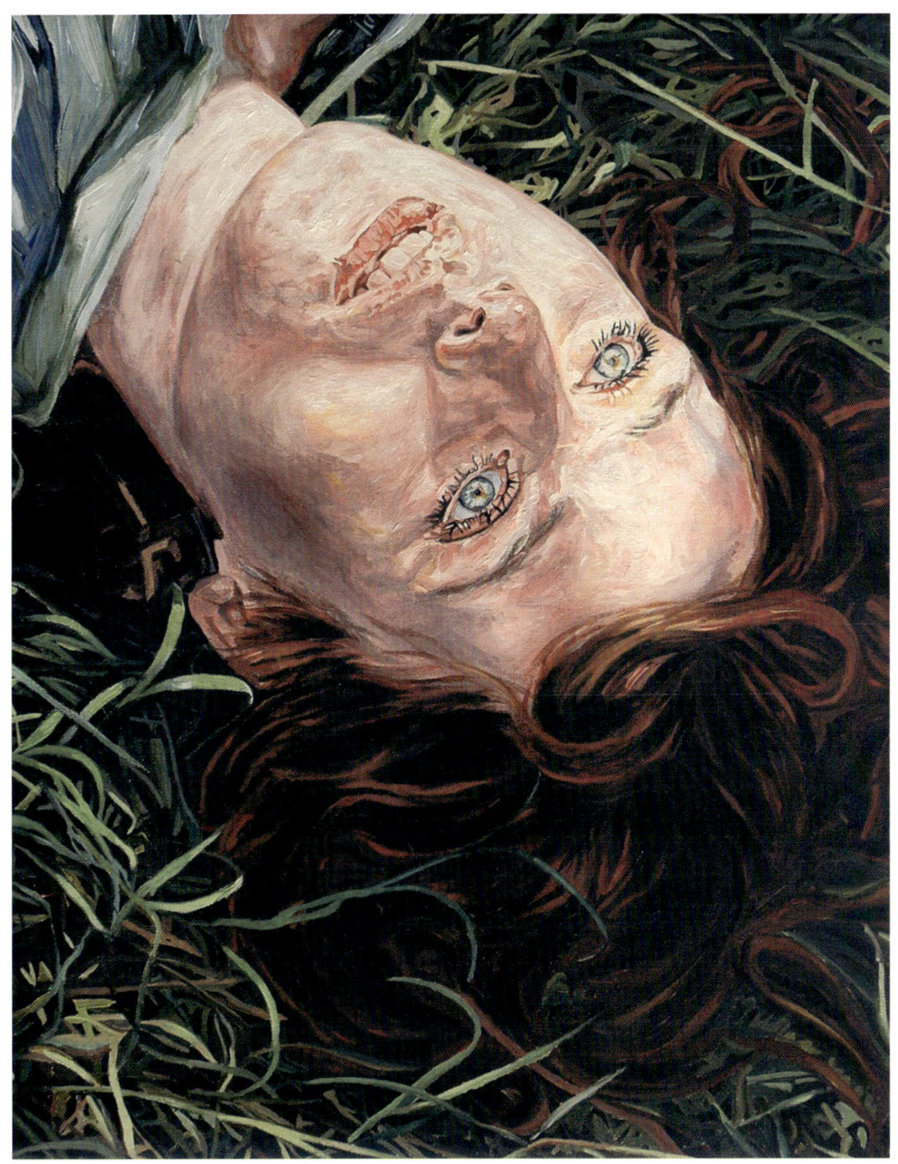

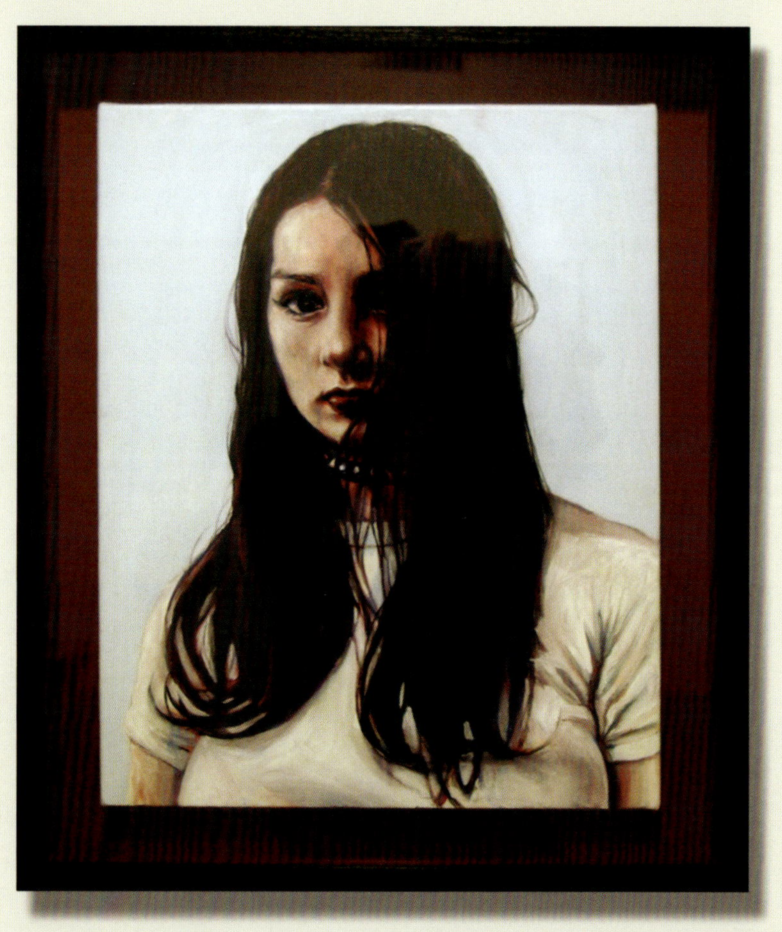

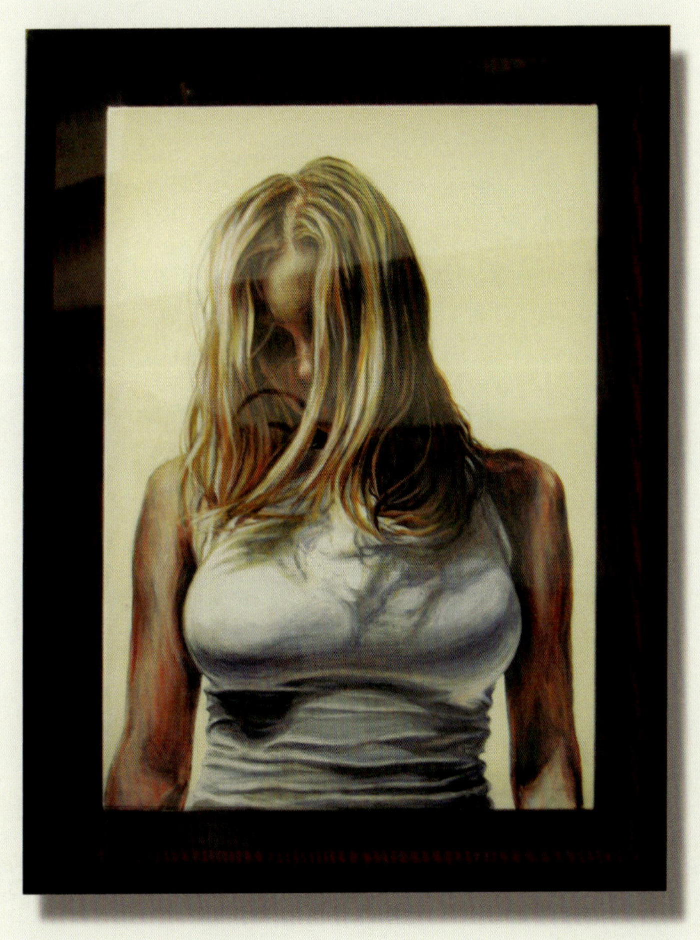

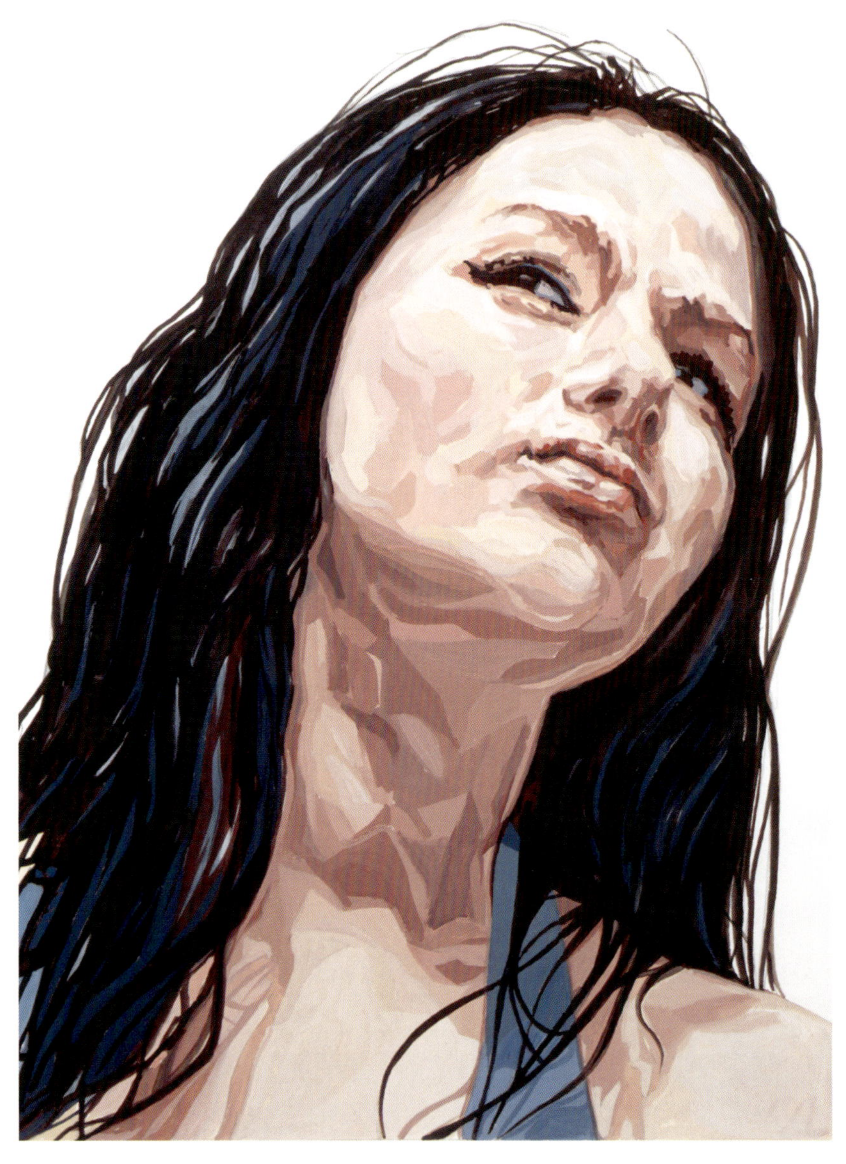

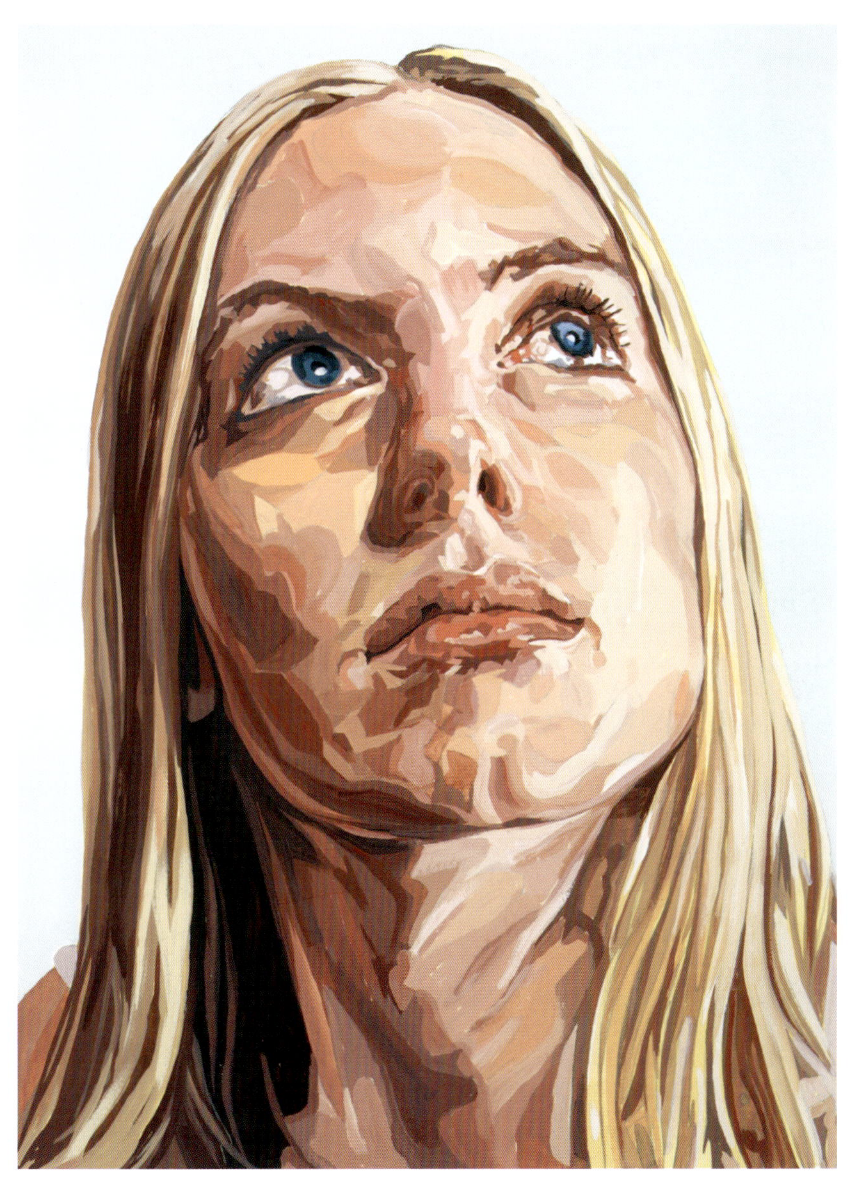

Sam, 2006
10 x10 inch Gouache on paper.

Previous page

Sophie, 2006
14 x 10 inch Gouache on paper
Private collection, Brussels, Belgium.

Samantha, 2006
14 x10 inch Gouache on paper
Private collection, Brussels, Belgium.

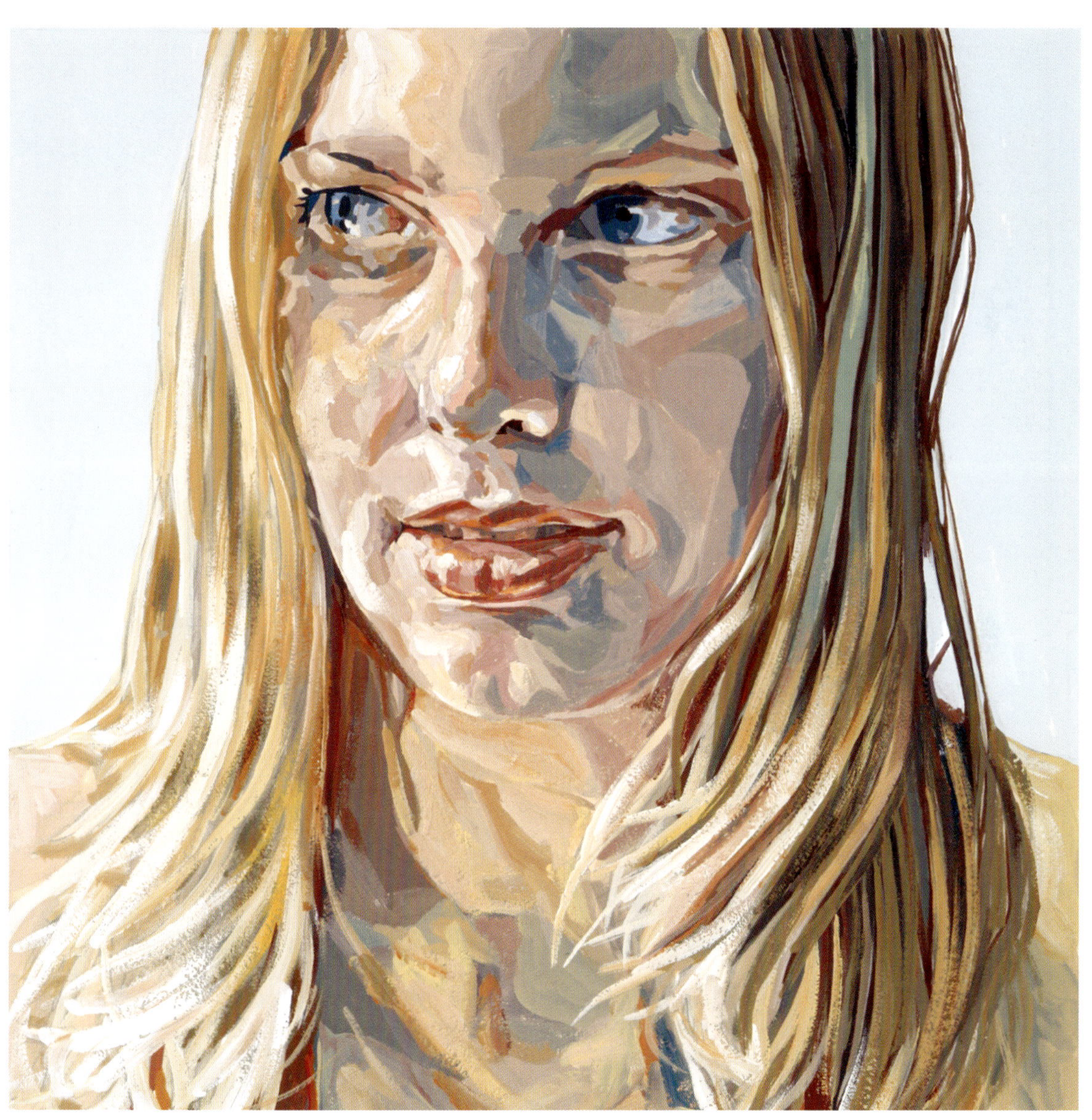

Melanie, London 2006
Installation view
100 x 139 cm Gouache on paper.

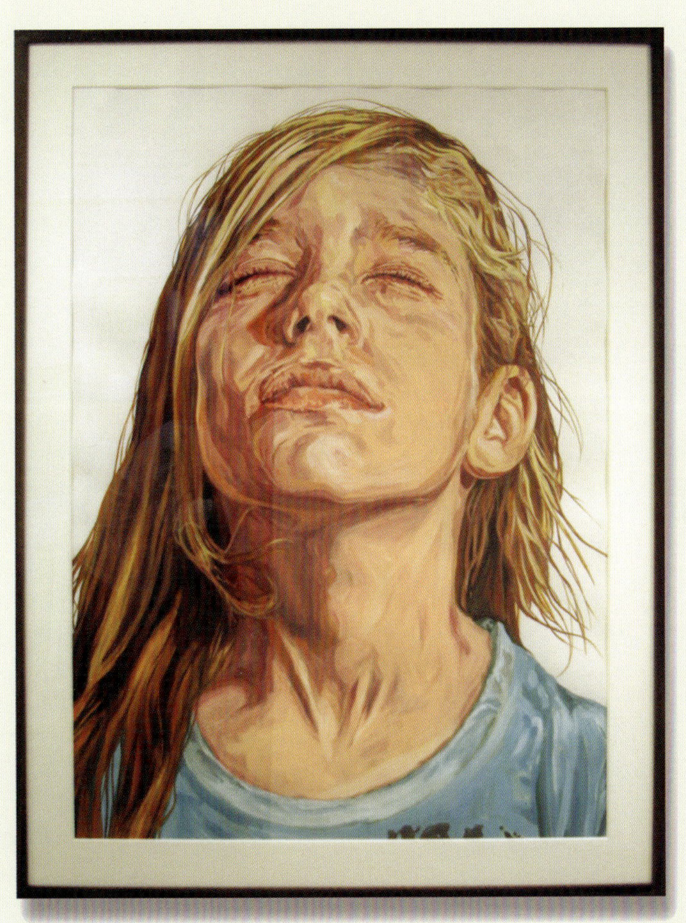

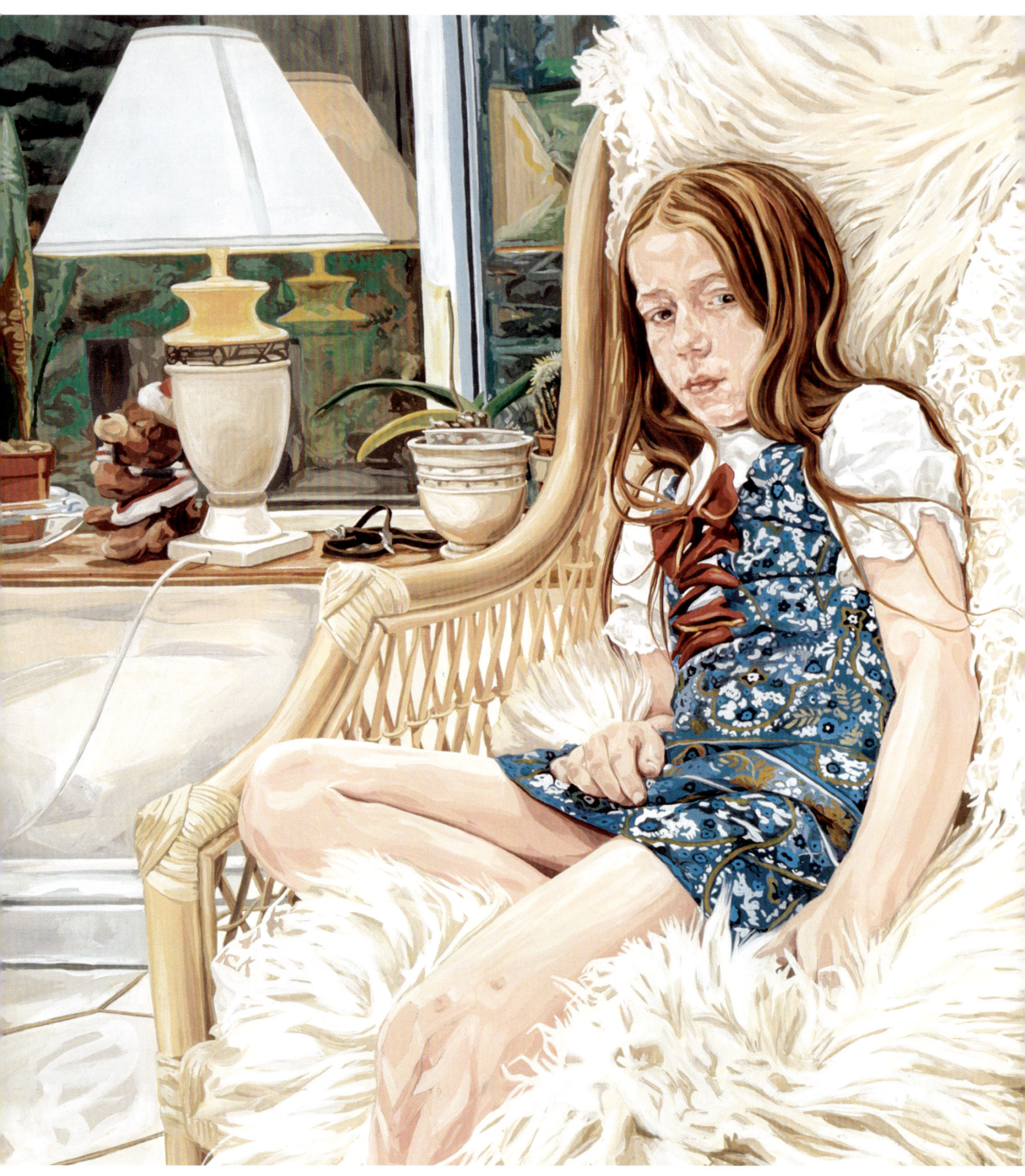

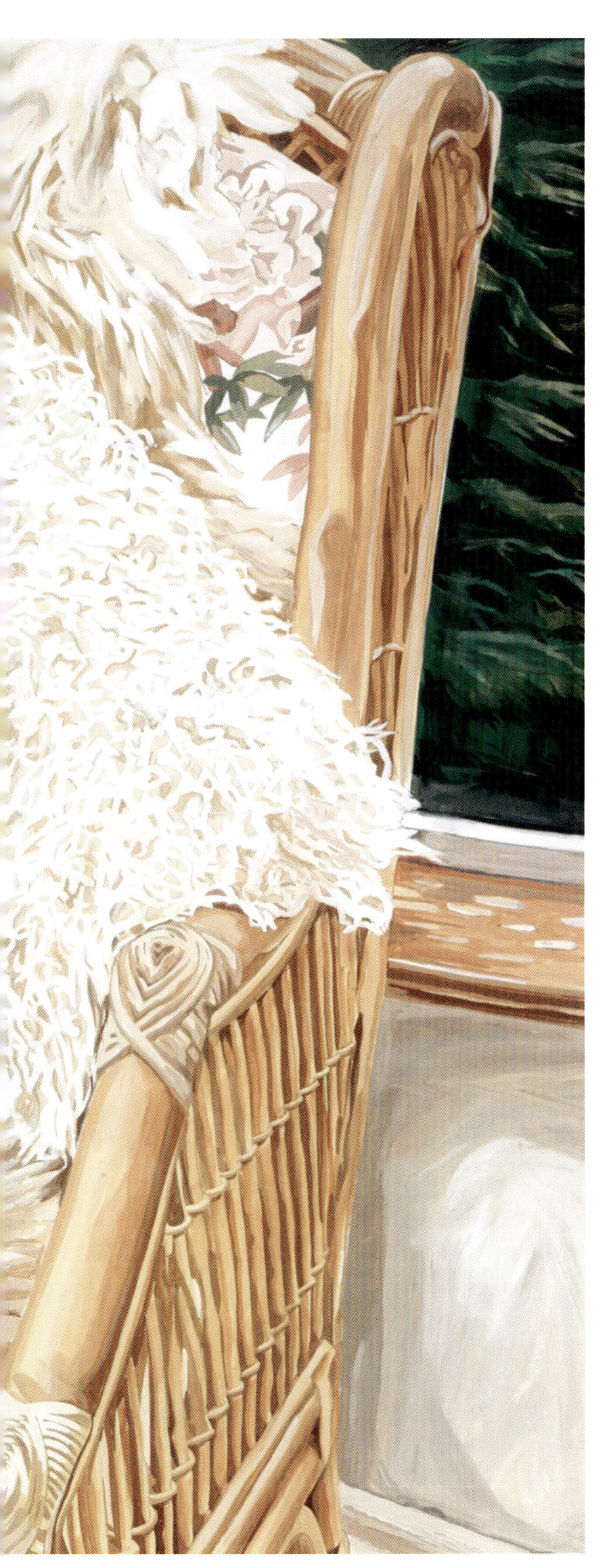

The Vale of Avoca, 2006
139 x 100cm Gouache on paper.

Previous page

Little girl number one, 2006
(14 cm) paper size A2 Gouache on paper.

Little girl number two, 2006
(14cm) paper size A2 Gouache on paper.

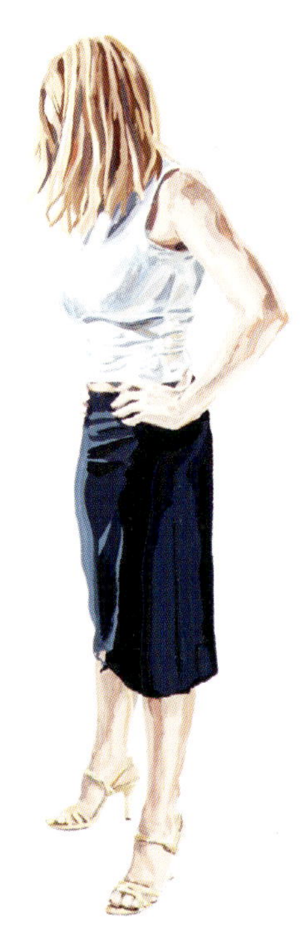

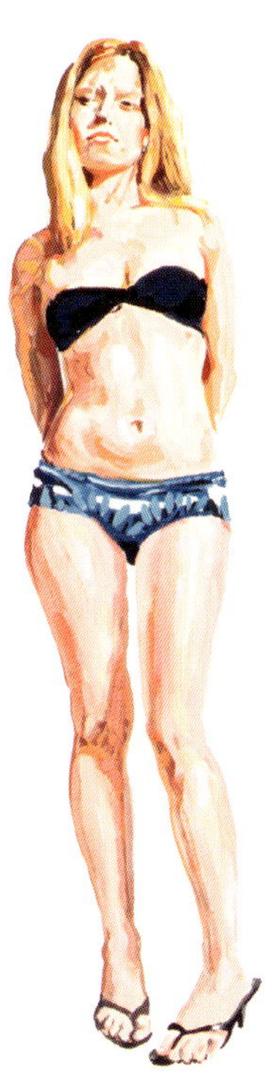

A last chance of recognition in a failed career

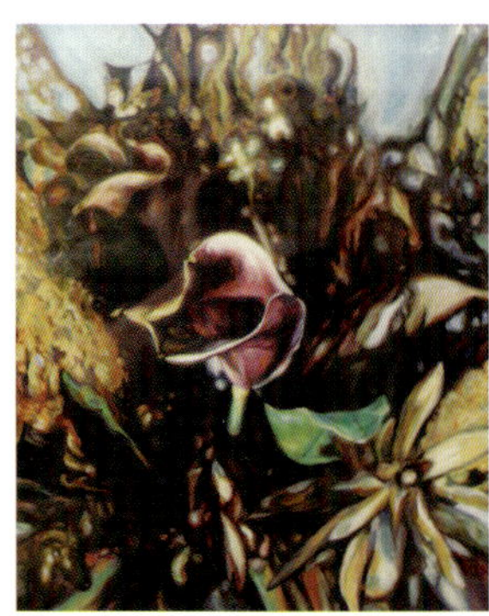

Failing Flowers, 2006
14 x 20 inch Oil on canvas.

This recent body of work is titled "There for the grace of God" and feature portraits of strangely familiar, but failed and unknown actors . The first pieces were shown in Paris and then a larger set followed in New York last year (2007). They are taken from found photographs. In some cases job lots of negatives, which I have made my own prints from. The paintings are in oil and built up using multiple layers of primary colour. The final monochrome glazes allow these colours to bleed through. I call this technique of working "Mono-Prismic". For the actors they give a last chance of recognition in a failed career - that could so easily be there waiting for any of us.

Actress No.1
2008 Oil on canvas (90 x 70 cm)

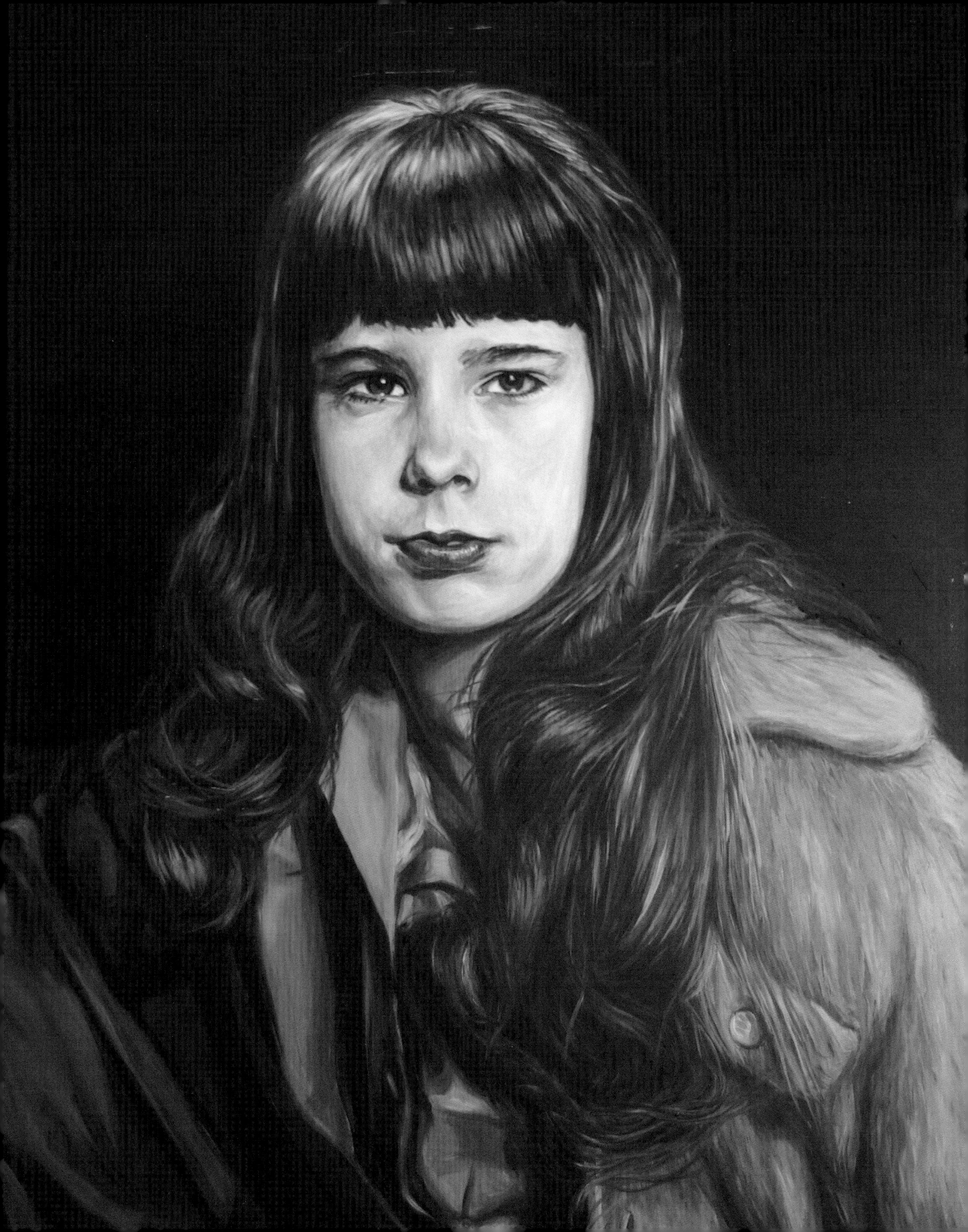

There For The Grace Of God
2007 oil on canvas (140 x 170 cm)
Private collection, New Jersey.

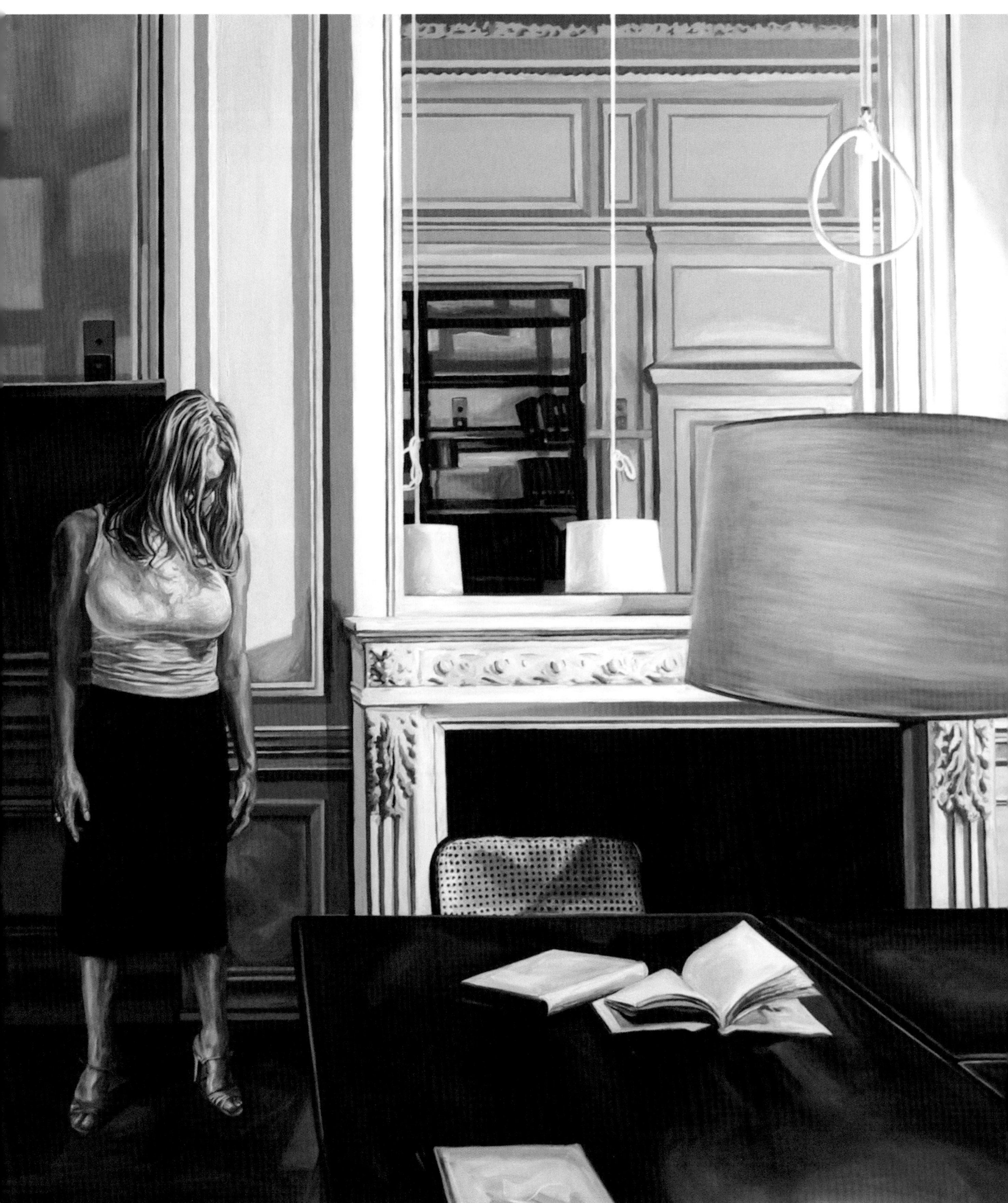

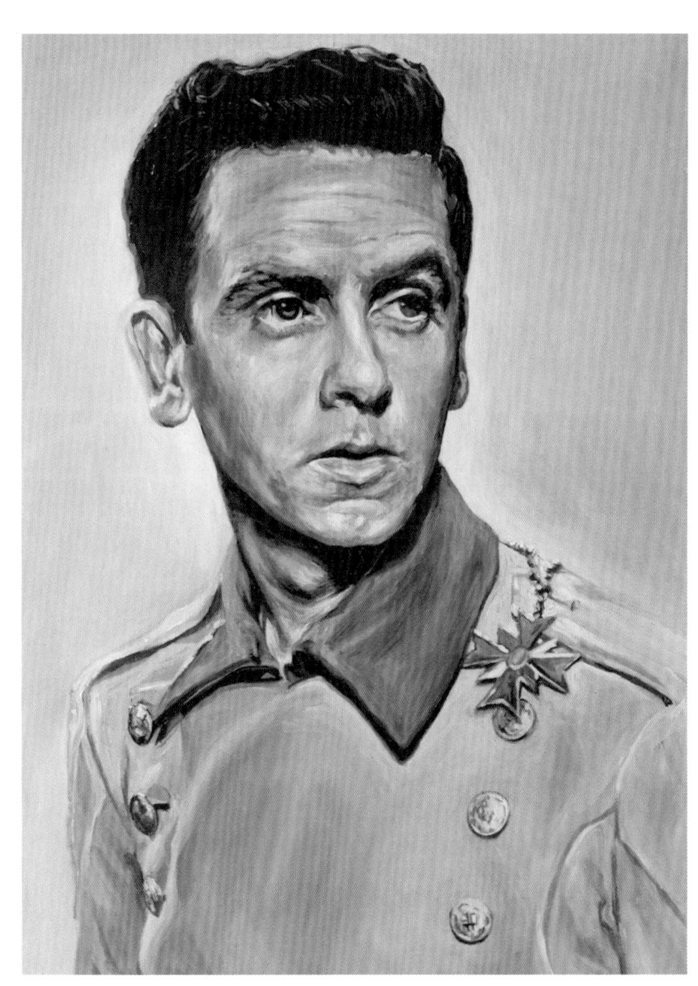

Actor No. 2
2007 Oil on canvas (35 x 50 cm)

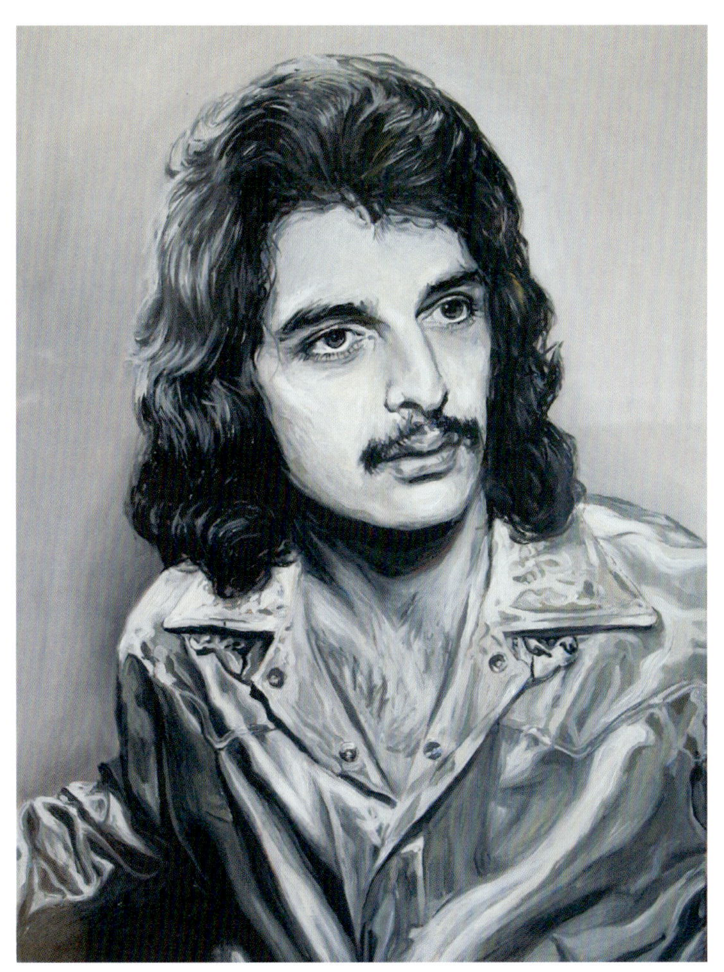

Actor No. 3
2007 Oil on canvas (35 x 50 cm)

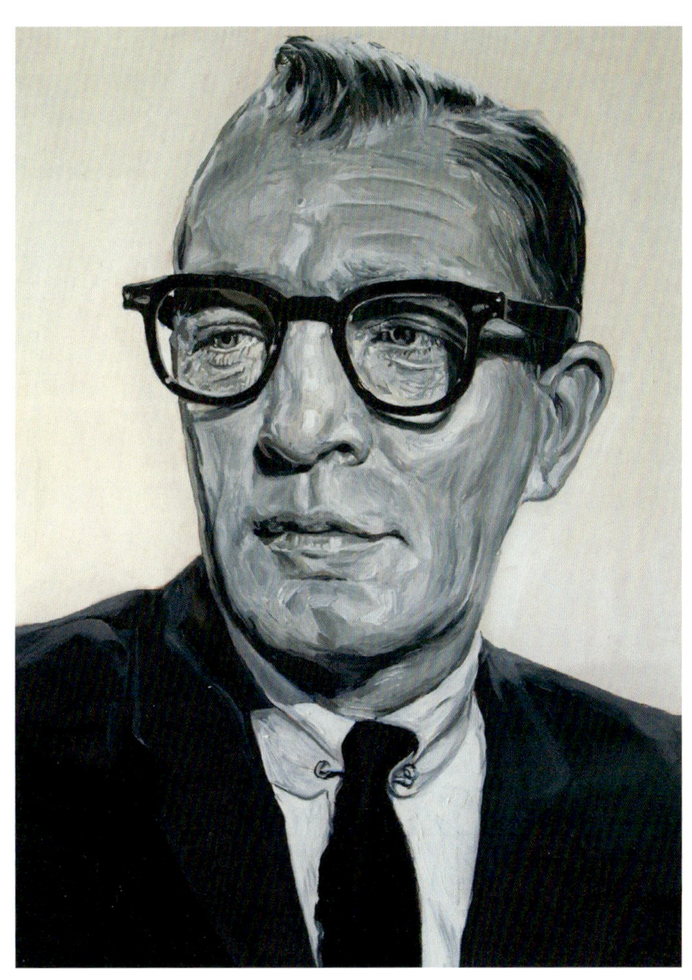

Actor No. 4
2007 Oil on canvas (35 x 50 cm)

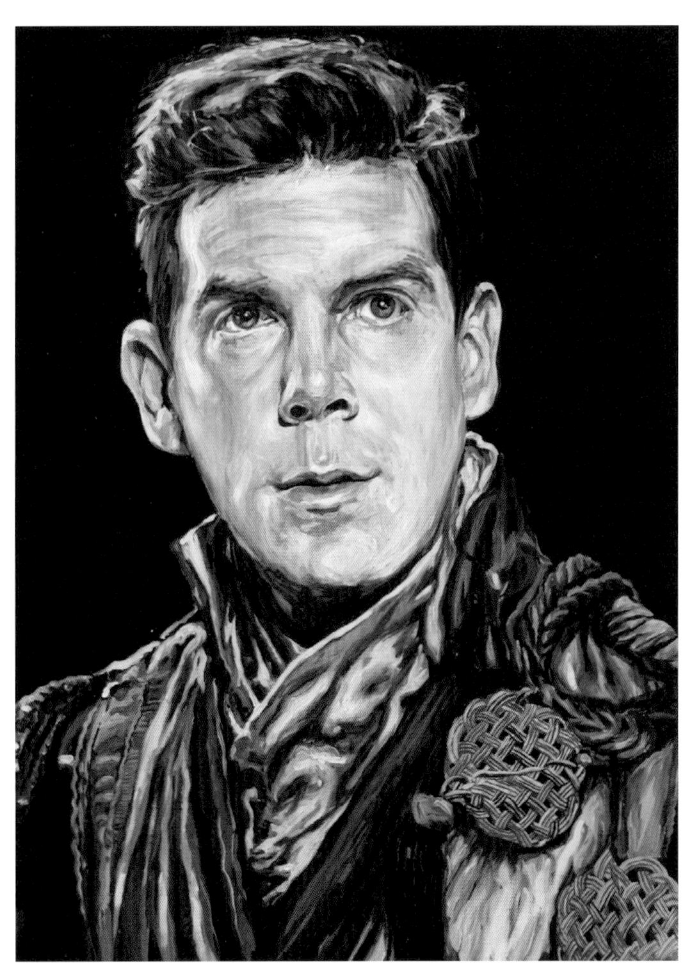

Actor No. 5
2007 Oil on canvas (35 x 50 cm)
Collection of Anthony Goicolca, New York.

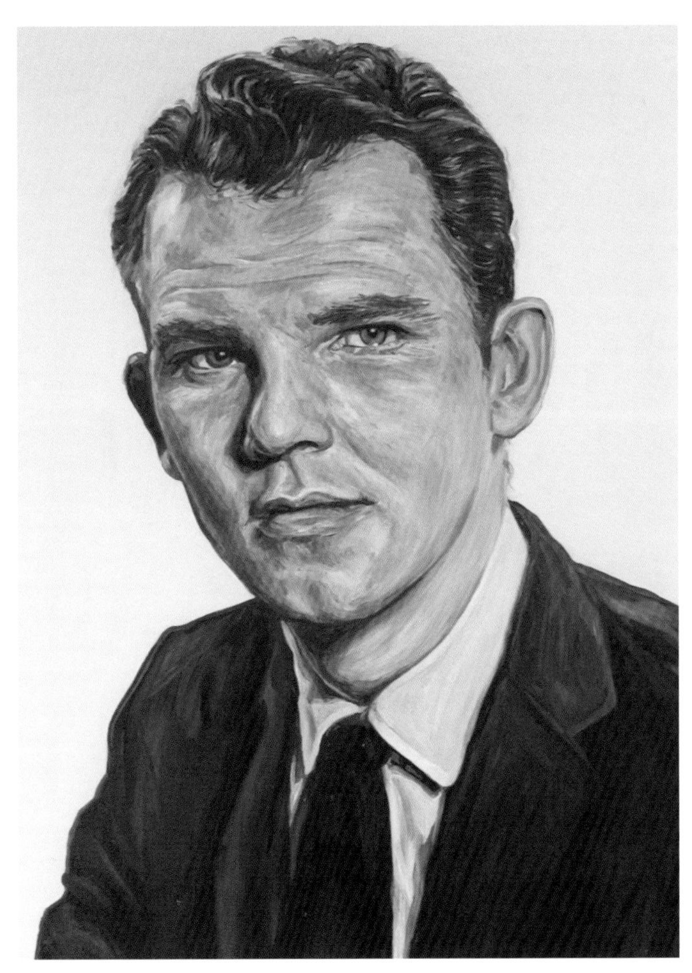

Actor No. 6
2007 Oil on canvas (35 x 50 cm)

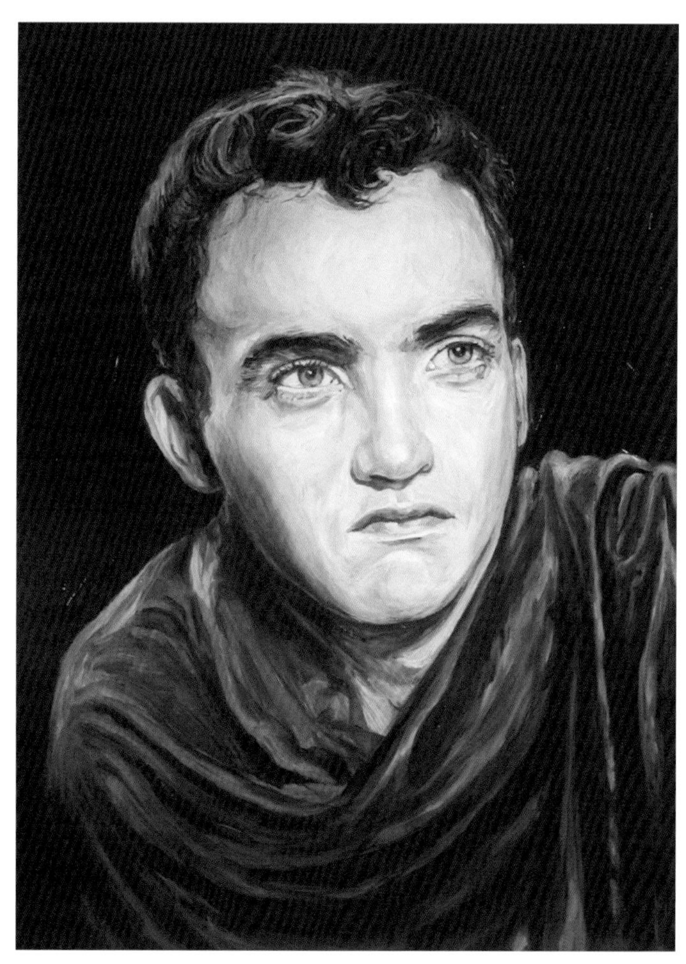

Actor No. 7
2007 Oil on canvas (35 x 50 cm)

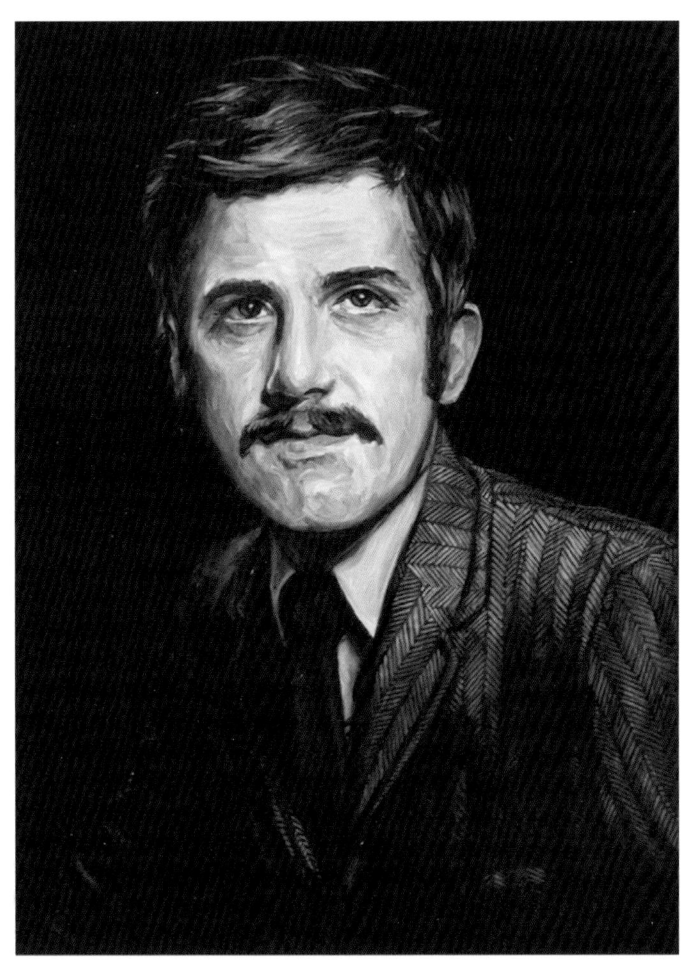

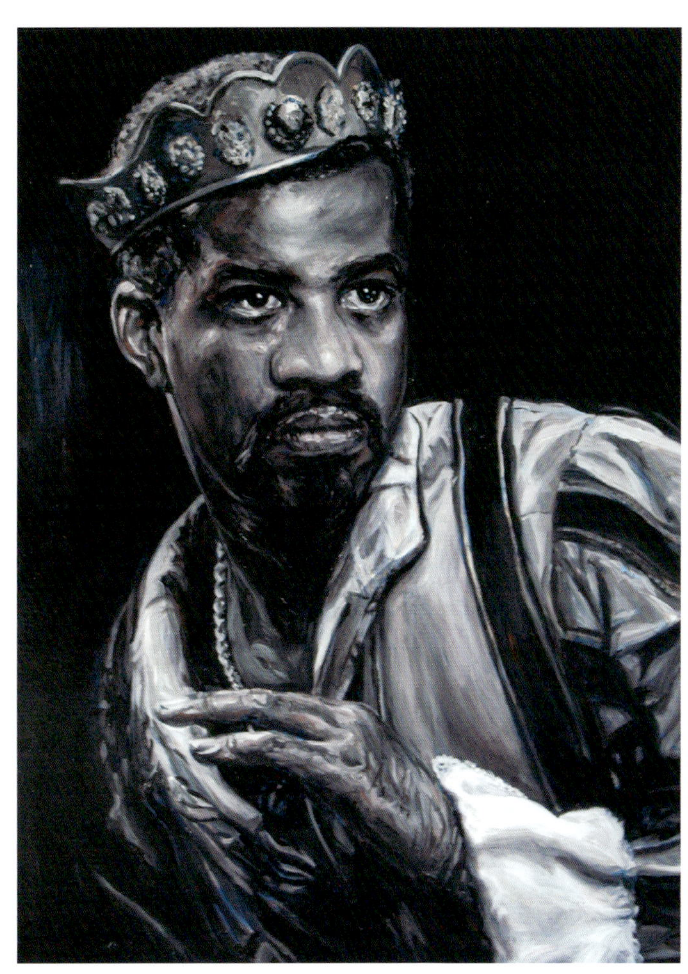

Actor No. 9
2007 Oil on canvas (35 x 50 cm)

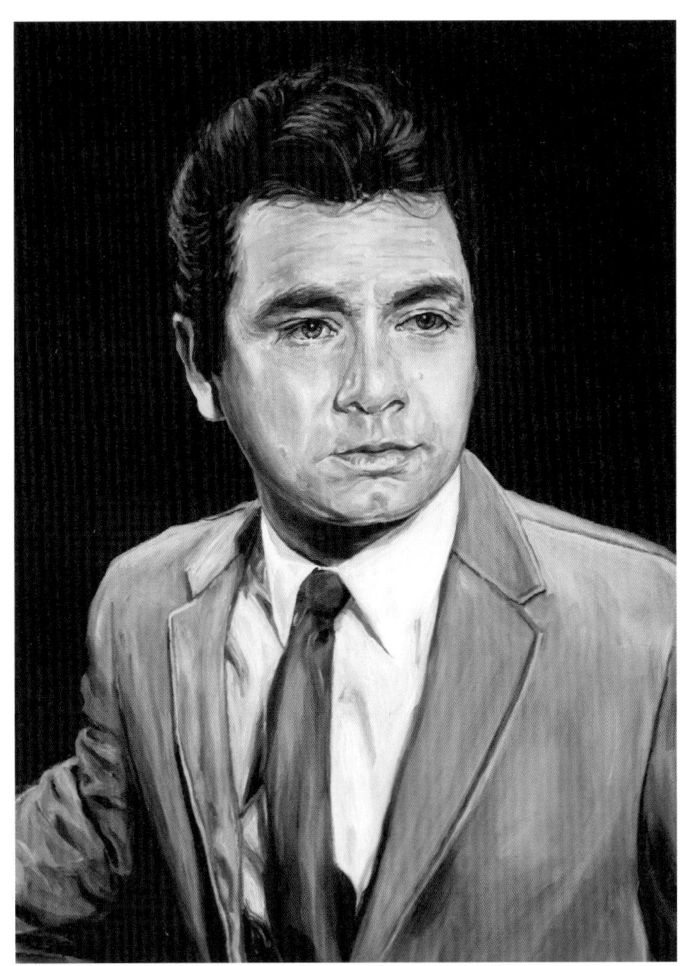

Actor No. 10
2008 Oil on canvas (35 x 45 cm)

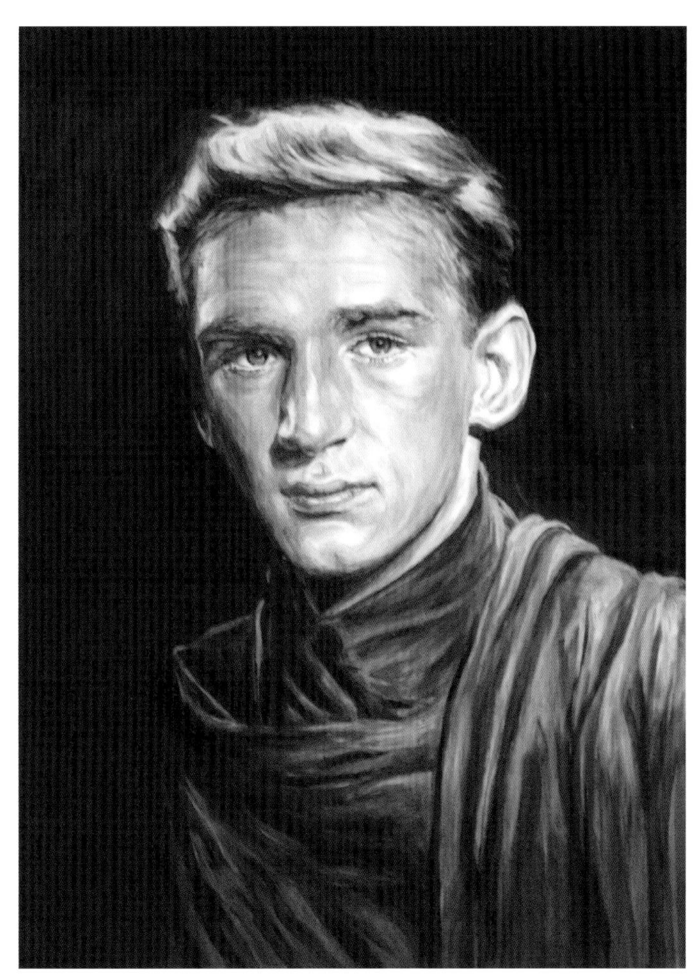

Actor No. 11
2008 Oil on canvas (35 x 45 cm)

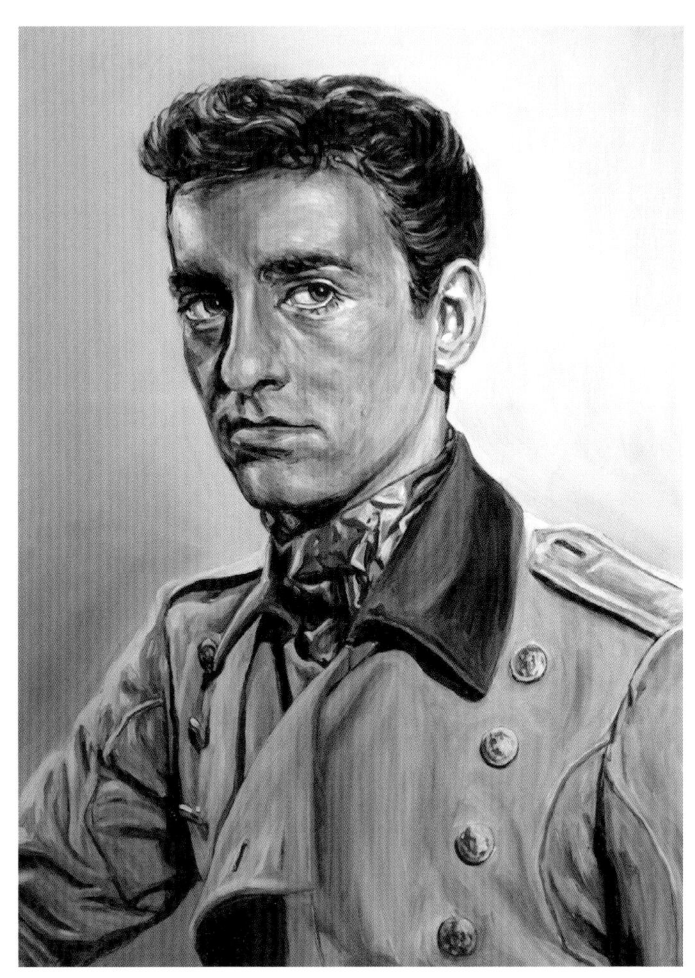

Actor No. 12
2008 Oil on canvas (35 x 45 cm)
Collection of Eric Decelle, Brussels.

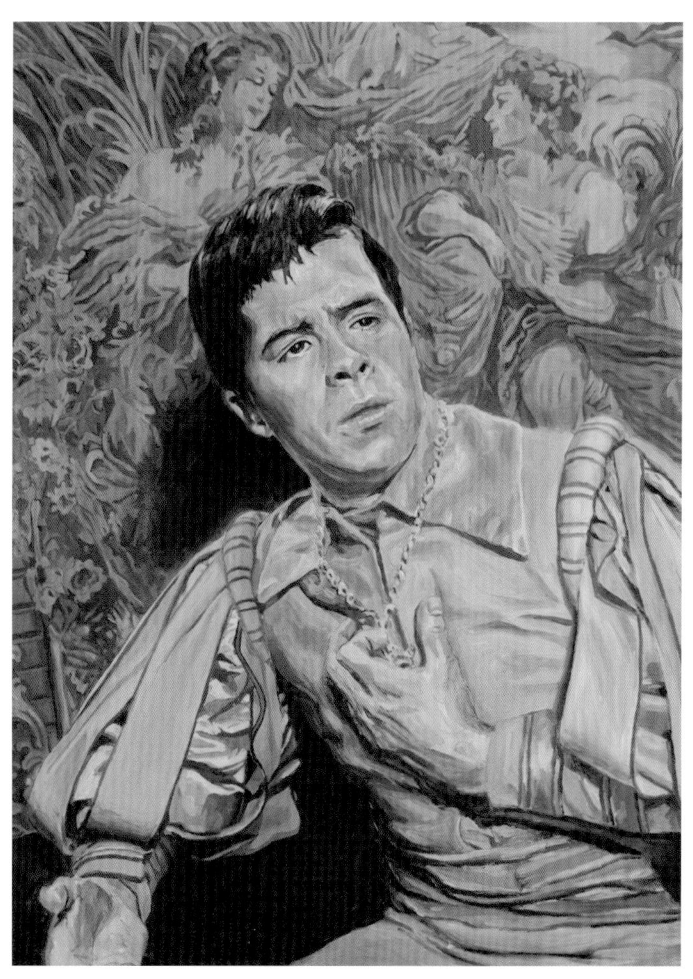

Actor No. 13
2008 Oil on canvas (35 x 45 cm)

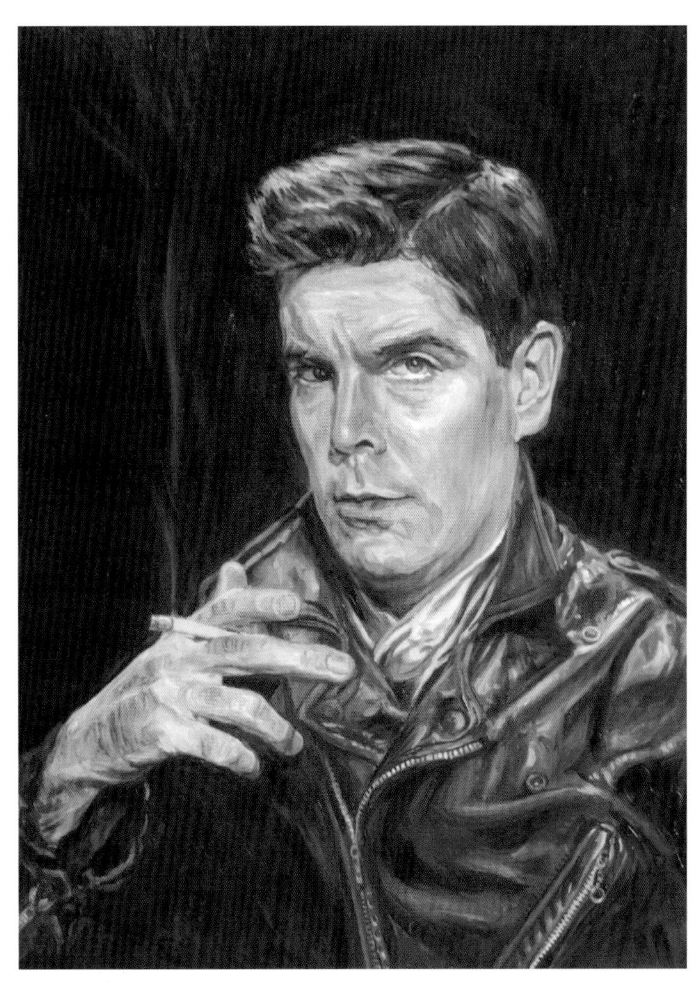

Actor No. 14
2008 Oil on canvas (35 x 45 cm)

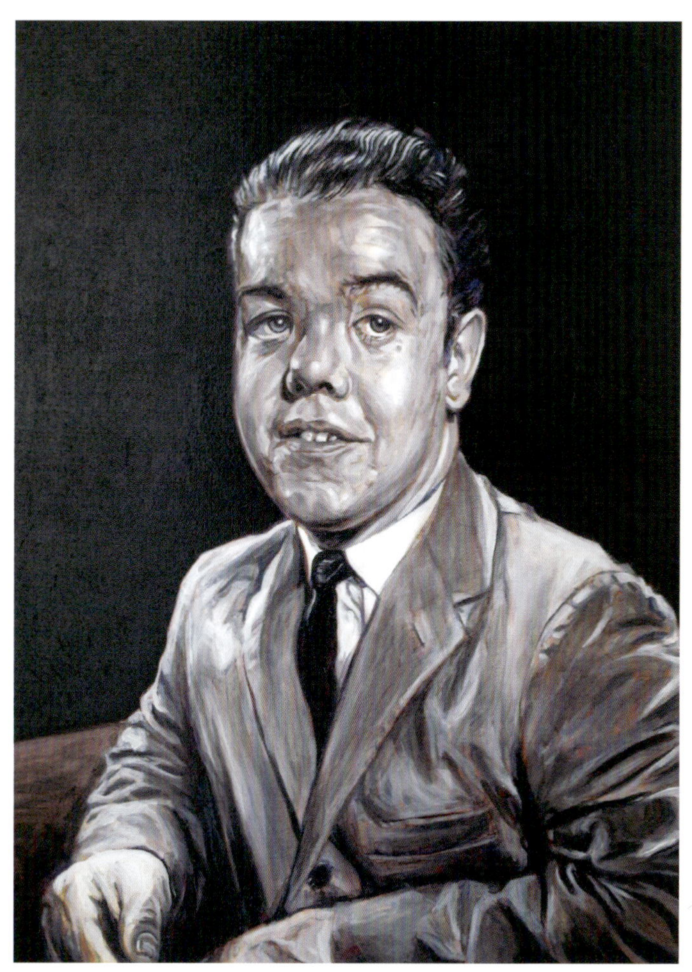

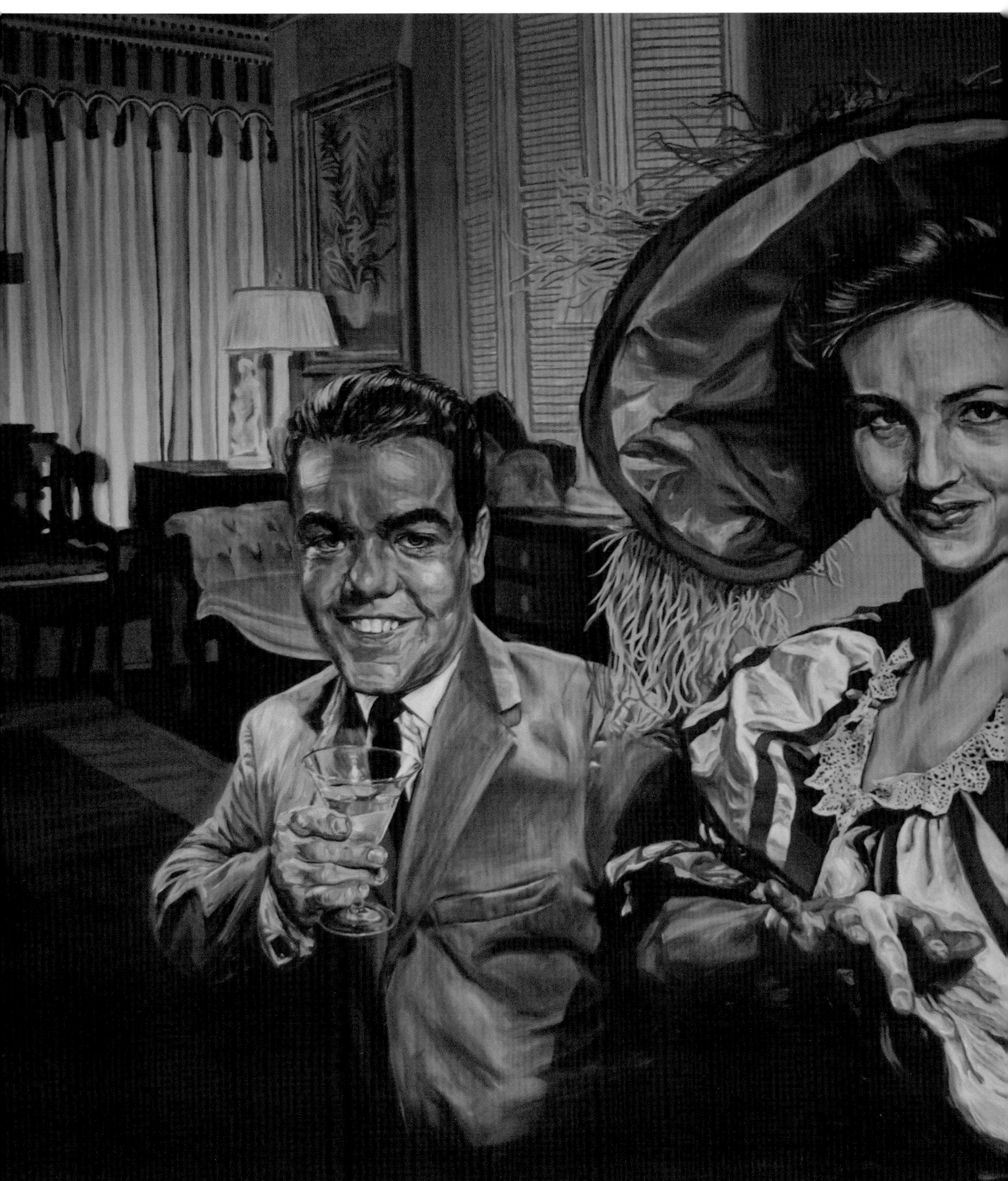

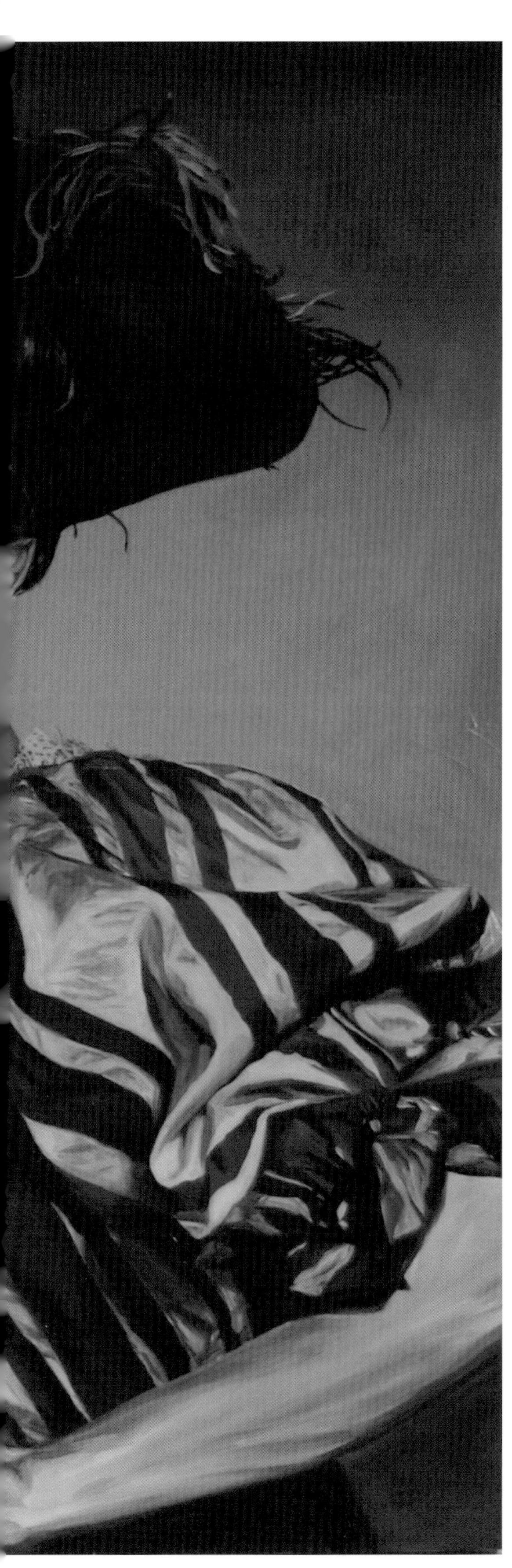

Gallant Company
2008 oil on canvas (140 x 170 cm)

Actress No. 2
2008 Oil on canvas (35 x 45 cm)

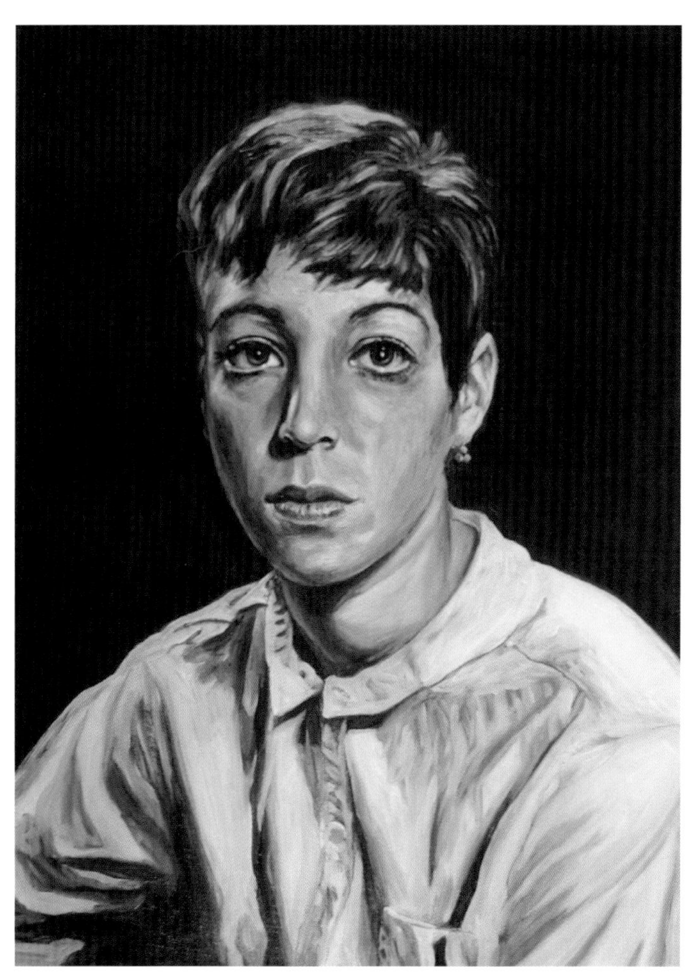

Actor No. 15
2008 Oil on canvas (35 x 45 cm)

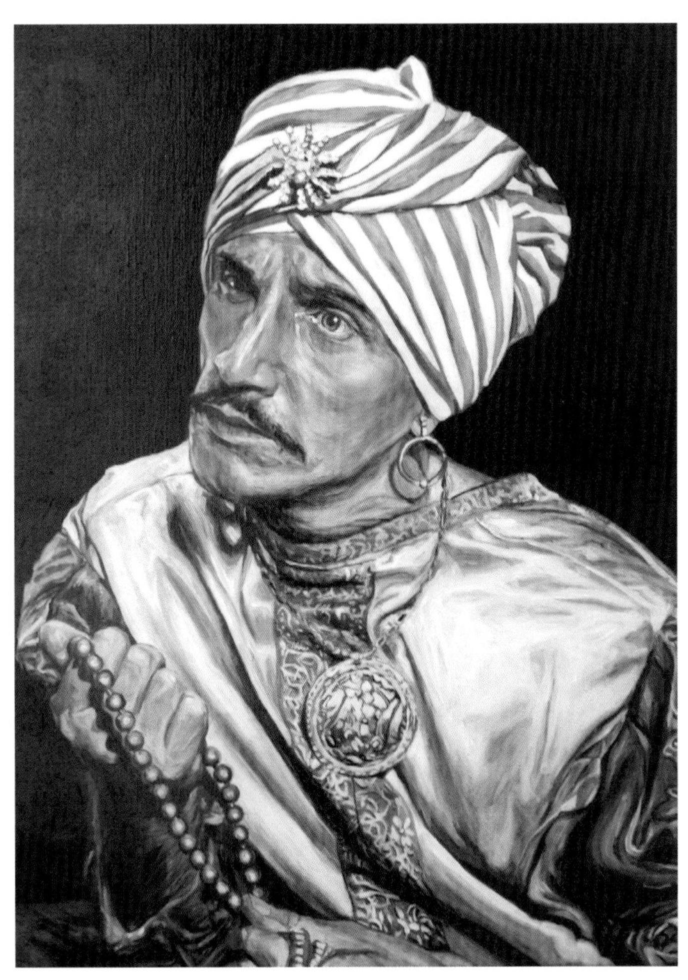

Animation and Early Graphic Works
Christian Haye

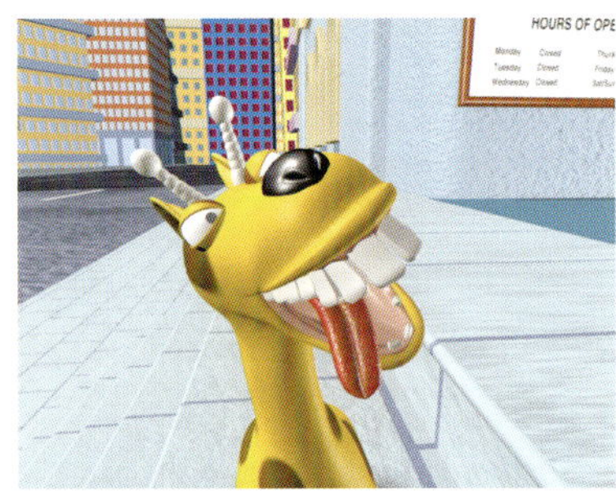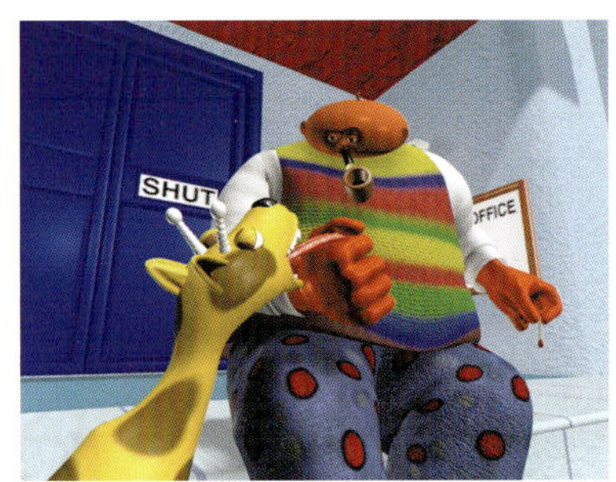
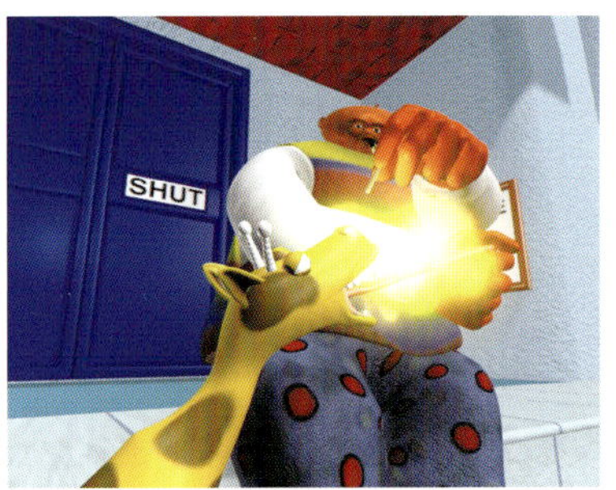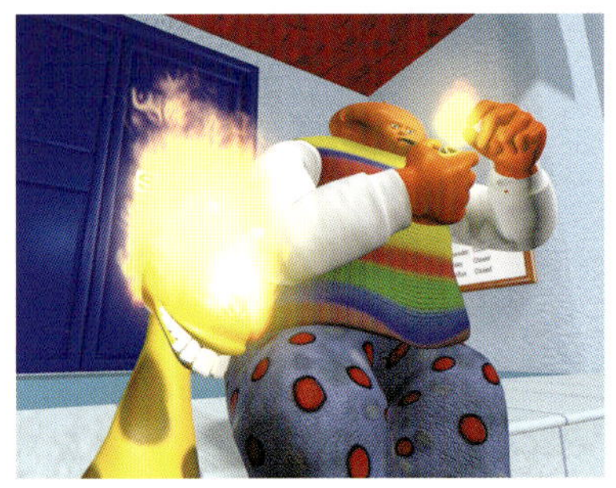

Film still sequence from Johnny
Pumpkin, 1999
Mr Pumpkin lights his pipe.

Opposite The tin plated toddler
Rendered still for Vogue, 1999.

Simon Henwood's slickly-made computer series Johnny Pumpkin is an over-the-top parody of big studio animation – specifically the personality driven narratives, overly detailed designs, and family-audience merchandise tie-ins of the Walt Disney studio and it's computer arm Pixar.

Like John Tenniel on acid or a techno-Bosch, Mr. Henwood throws so much plot and so many bizarre characters at us, we drown in his toxic, saturated colors and convoluted, ultimately nonsensical narrative.

John Canemaker

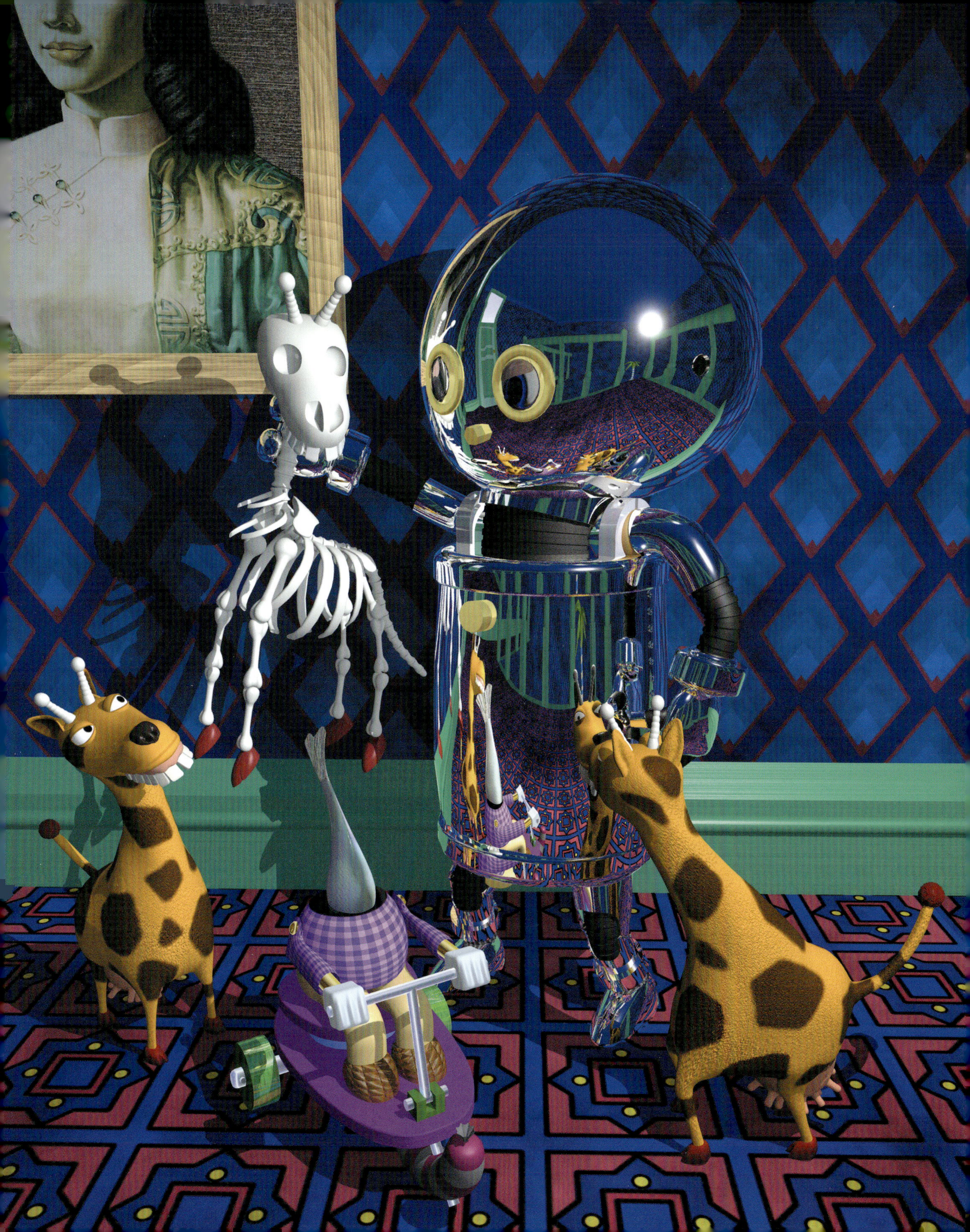

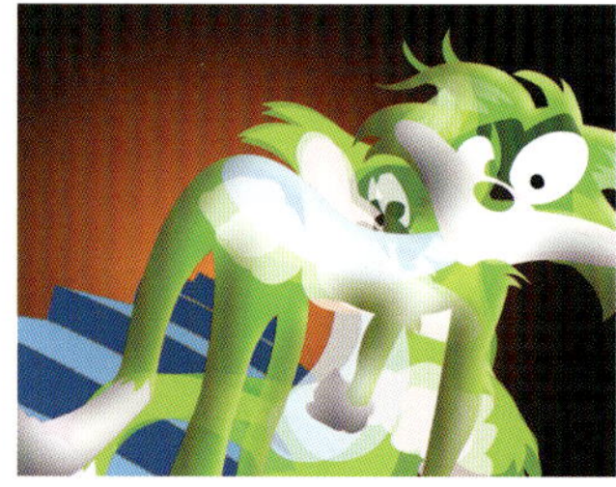

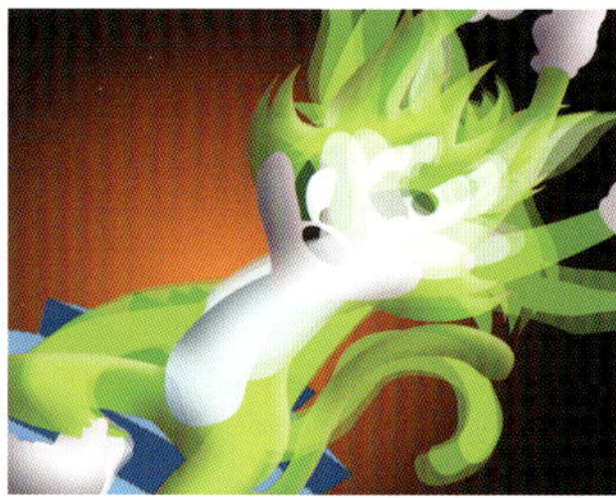

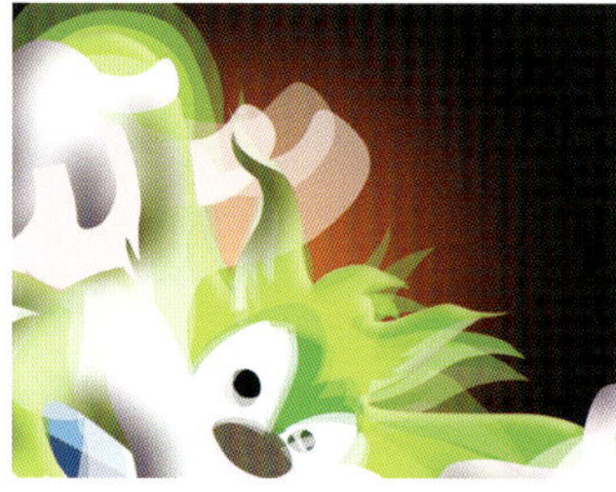

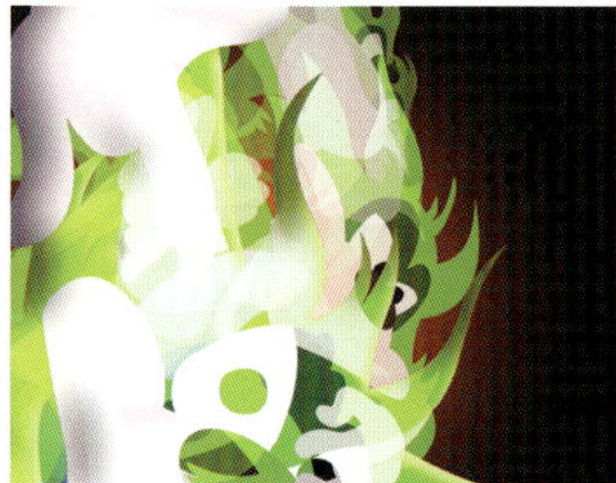

Film still sequence from Dude decending a staircase -Apollo 440, 2003.

Suburbia used to be the best place for resistance. The myth of conformity was the space where we were nonconformist. The creation, dissection and our attempted destruction of that space could be accepted as the industrial strength narrative of the twentieth century. The battle of normalcy has itself become mainstream. Later for suburbia that took too long. The same war happens instantaneously in cyberspace and it is won and lost in the blink of an eye. This is an age so dependent on recycling that yesterday's rebellion becomes tomorrows fashion at an astonishing speed. In the western world a new millennium has brought with it a tragic question. With no opposition to seemingly anything, what is there left to rebel against? Simon Henwood is not the answer (unless you're that bored) but Henwood ecstatically reanimates the question. A painter of spoiled adolescents and humanoid blobs, an illustrator of sanguine gothics tales for children, an animator of fantastical visions of worlds eerily like this one but not close, a publishers of indie magazines that bring together the cacophony of voices that hover between the marginal and the traditional, a collector of high and low cultural artefacts and an ever growing media presence who neither bites nor strokes the hands that are feeding the uber producer: Simon Henwood.

To begin to unravel Henwood's cultural production would probably induce the schizophrenia that might appear to be at the roof of that production. But Henwood is actually very simply stated a saviour of the root of that production. Melancholy mixed with spurts of joy and exaltation attempting to break out the coffin of boredom in that oft related tale of pubescent angst. What Henwood does brilliantly is locate that angst to the point that an 80 year old will feel it as if it were acne, and the endless quest for something new to do was a disease of the elderly and not the young. In the paintings we discover mellifluous snapshots of all the moments that define this stage paired with anthropomorphic realisations of those moments. They bring a delicate balance of horror and seduction that Henwood will then spin out into narrative. In Johnny Pumpkin for example, a creature seems to exist solely to tempt children with an orifice that once they enter they turn said creature inside out. What lurks in the mind of the madman is eerily similar to what is lurking in the mind of everyman. In Henwood's entire opus the evidence of everything is gingerly peppered about.

Accessing the pop culture database is a mammoth task and Henwood is a maestro. References collide like American trains throughout all the narrative work. Star Trek, Johnny Quest, Ed Gorey. Men in Black, the Betty Pages, Kirby (both Jack and the Nintendo icon), Manga and Steven Spielberg all sit comfortably in the tableau of Johnny Pumpkin for example. The encyclopaedic knowledge it would take to read all of the references would make Derrida happy but also serve to point out the populist sentiment at the heart of this body of work. Unlike some of his colleagues however Henwood isn't simply borrowing the culture but his conscious choice of diversifying his output to include comics and television, let's say, as well as paintings, separate him from the herd.

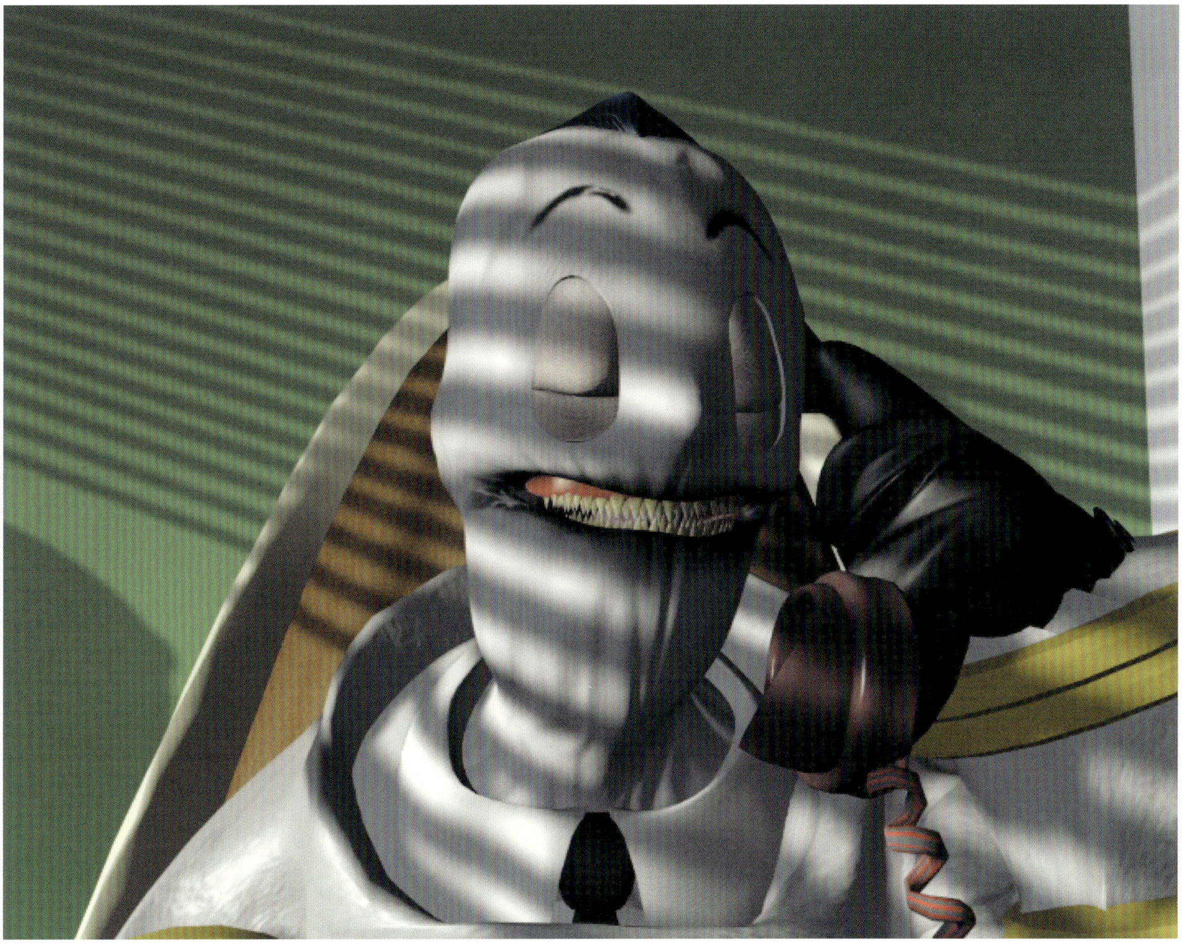

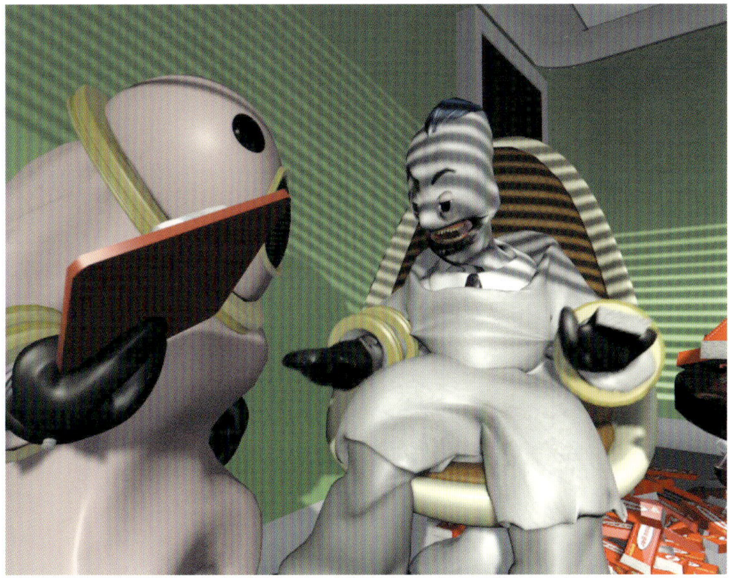

Film stills from Johnny Pumpkin, 1999
Dr. Godbreed in his office.

Following page
The cast of Johnny Pumpkin
Edition of one. Digital print 30 x 120 inch
UCLA Hammer museum projects, 2000.

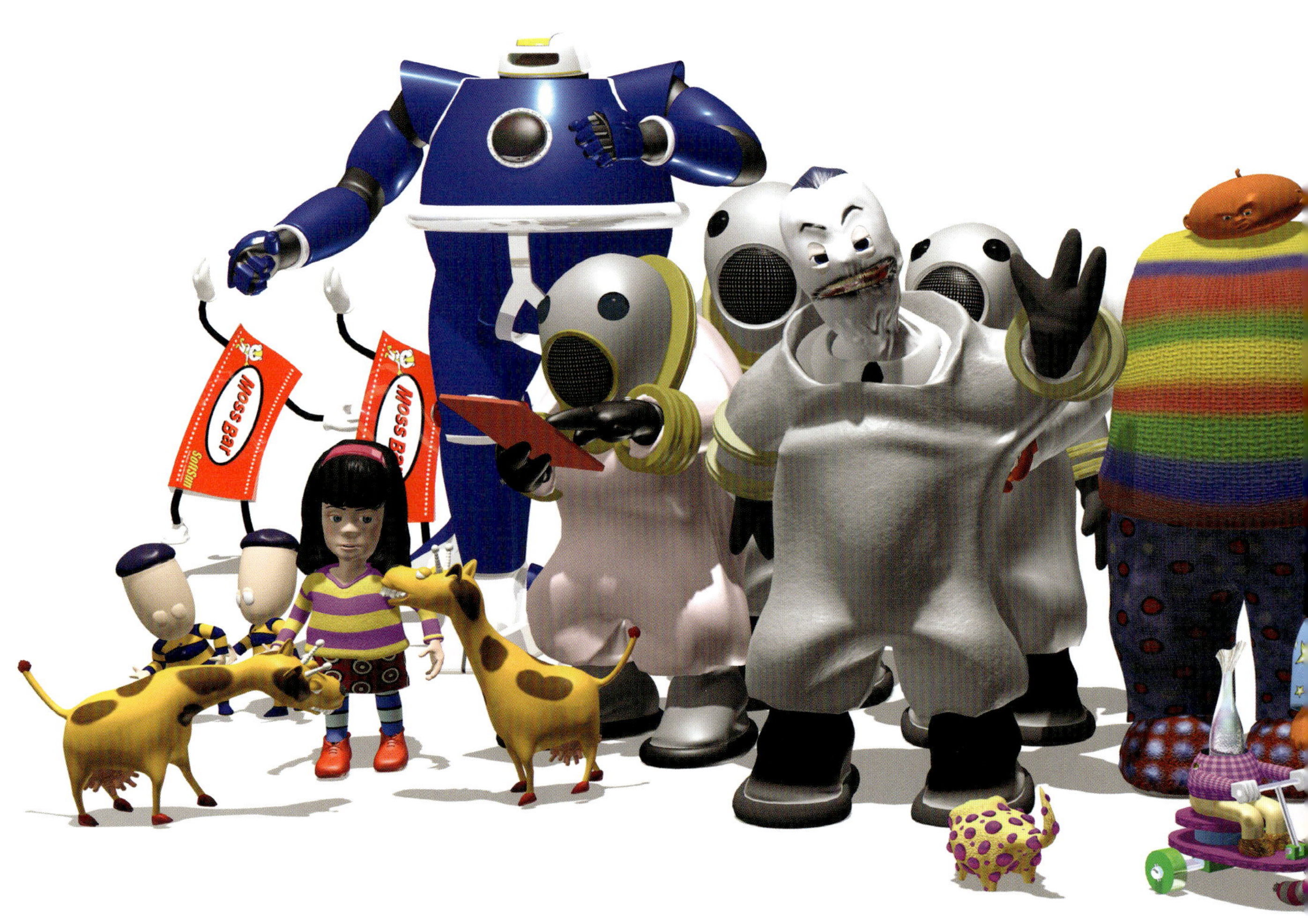
Moss Bar
SoftSim
Moss Bar
SoftSim

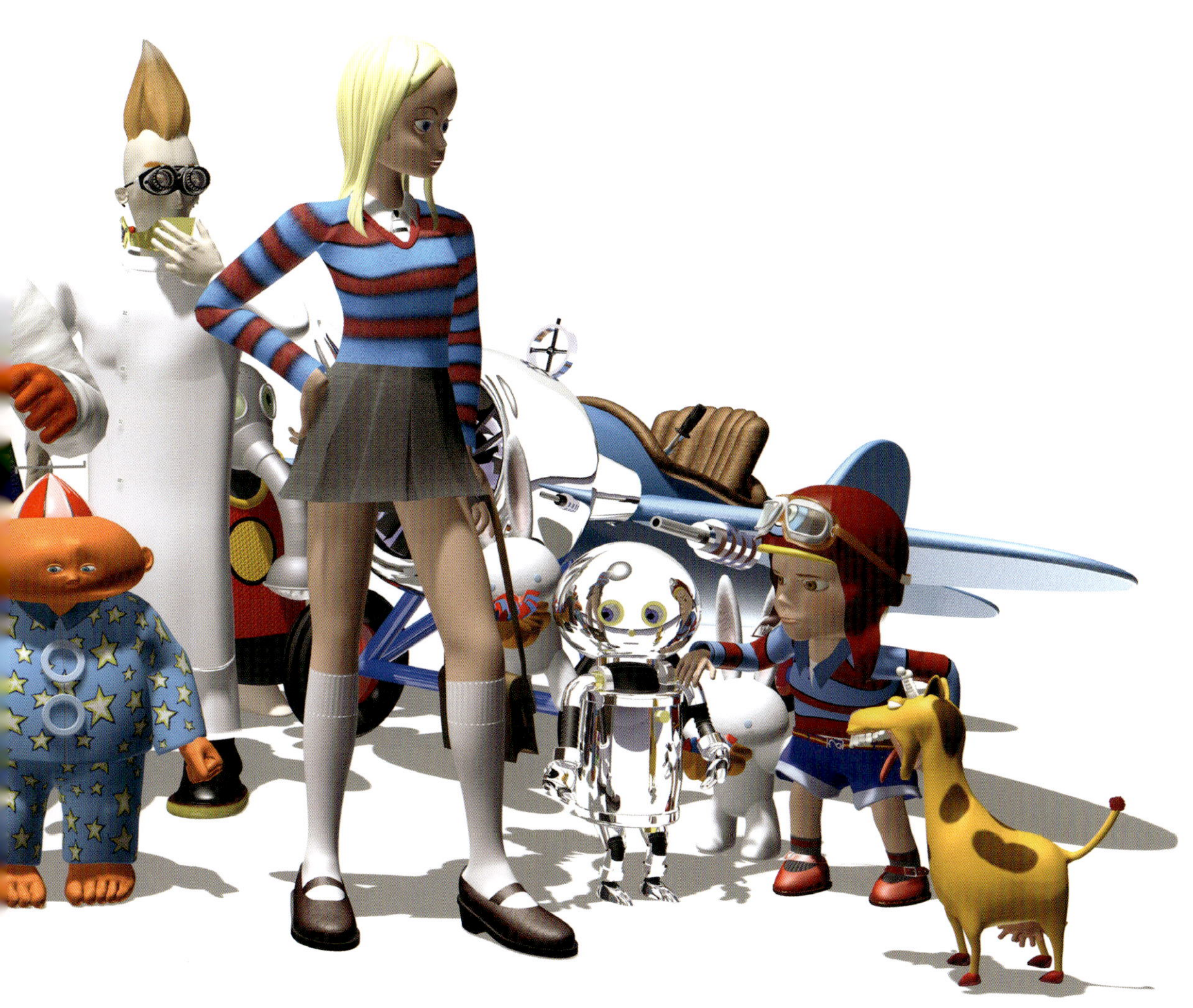

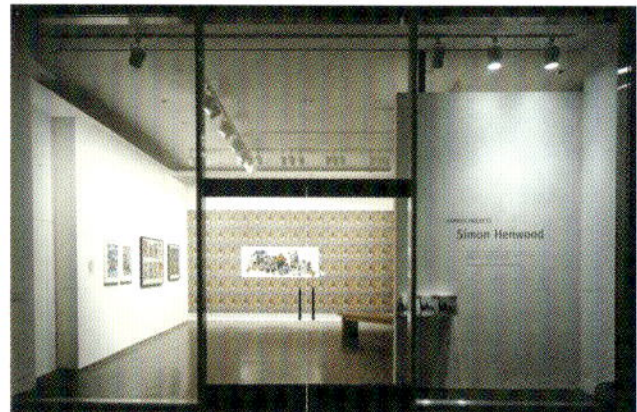

Installation views from UCLA Hammer museum, Projects - Simon Henwood, 2000 Featuring edition wallpaper, original production drawings and digital print

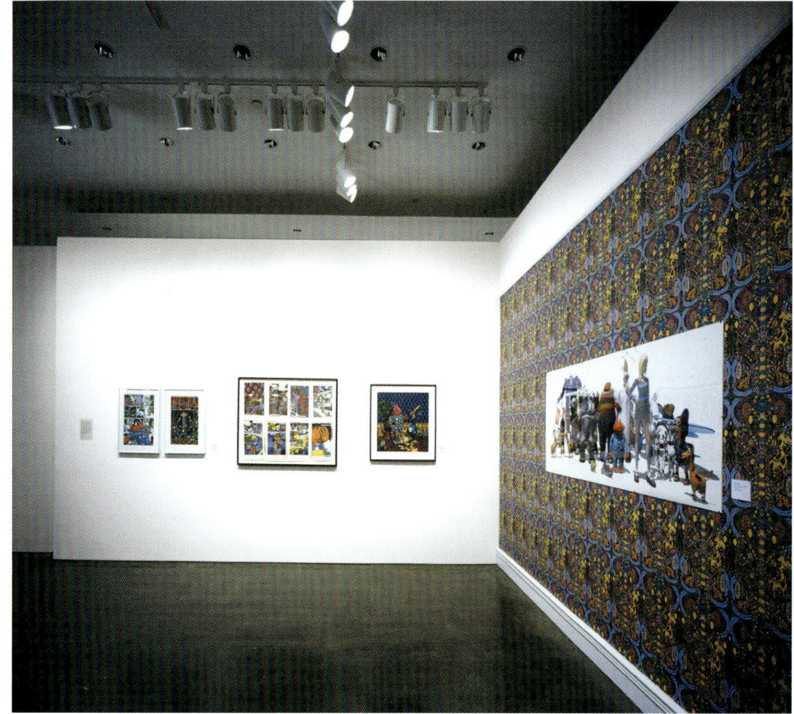

This is also why the books, especially the catalogue for Spoilt Children and White Kitten, prove so invaluable. They contextualize the work in a normally problematic format: reproduction. The interesting thing about Henwood is that the reproduction provides simply another opportunity to read the work instead of a shadow of the original.

Larry Clark and Takashi Murakami come to mind when musing the production of Simon Henwood. Clark's investigations of childhood sexuality have brought him to the edge of America's fascist moralism. In Europe, for the most part, kids are acknowledged as sexual beings. While the women in Henwood's labour and not solely relegated to babeland, it is not unusual to find a Betty Page type lurking around not so casually forever emasculating a pure excuse for masculinity. Murakami's cultural output comes from the same self-produced hyper-machine that Henwood must access. Murakami produces his own line of manga inspired sculptures crossed with an anime X-rated presence which finds women playing jump rope with their own breast milk or boys using their cum as lassoes. So innocent is the boy! Henwood has yet to go so hardcore preferring to maintain the bubble of fragility that softcore embodies. Although, I've seen the naughty bits lying around his flat and would not be surprised if a Henwood red light district pops up somewhere in his universe.

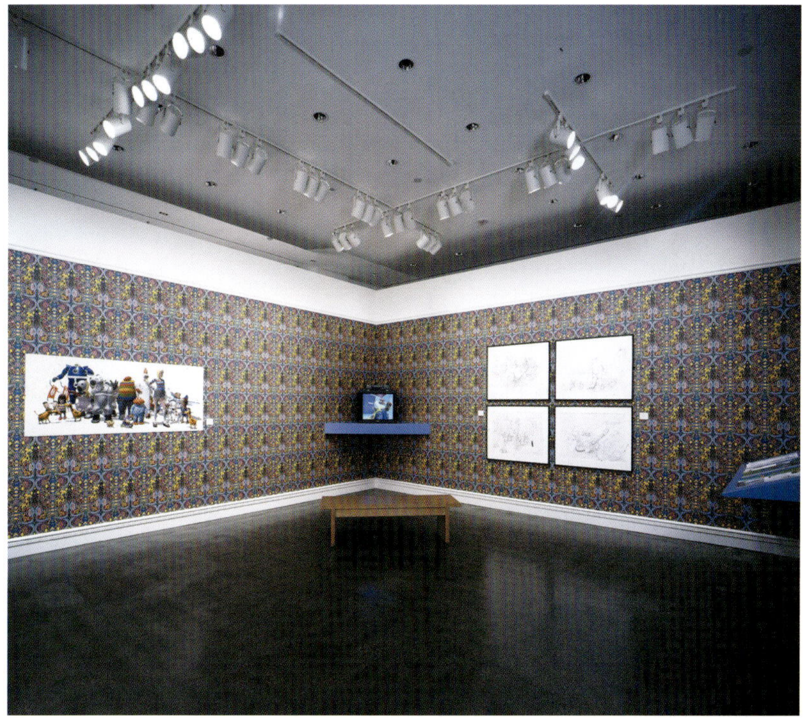

From Damien Hurst to Puff Daddy it has become evident that the best way to leave cultural production untainted by the big machine is to be ones own machine. The unrealised potential of the Internet as a place where anyone can be anything has already been diluted by the fact that very few people want to be everything. The next millennium is not about artists as cultural producers but cultural producers who make art. A breakdown of class structure is inherent in the elevation of mass entertainment and the devaluation of the temples of culture. This is the age of hypernation. One role is no longer enough if ever it was. The misnomer of Renaissance man applies to Henwood in only the capacity of someone who does many things. The reality of the situation is that Henwood is doing the same thing in all available formats. Visually narrating the moment just before that boring switch gets turned and we become adults (some of us, anyway). Sometimes this will call for a painting and sometimes an elaborate animation. Typographic interventions carry the same weight as bold brushstrokes fraught with the weight of philosophic dilemmas in a true democracy. We are quickly approaching that blissfully egalitarian moment when the mixture of culture and commerce isn't an indicator of compromise. The future is Henwood. Open up and swallow it.

Christian Haye

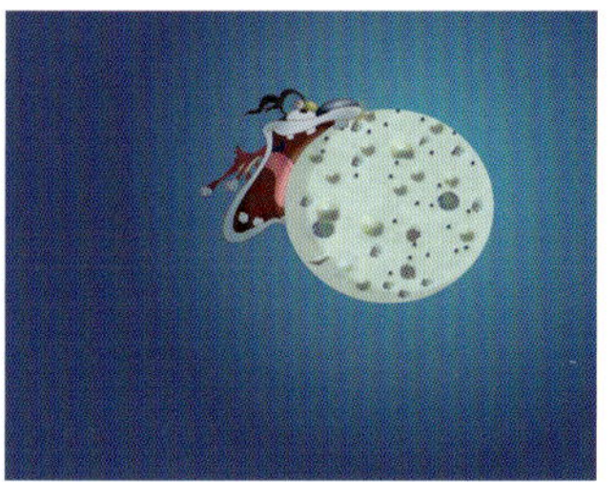

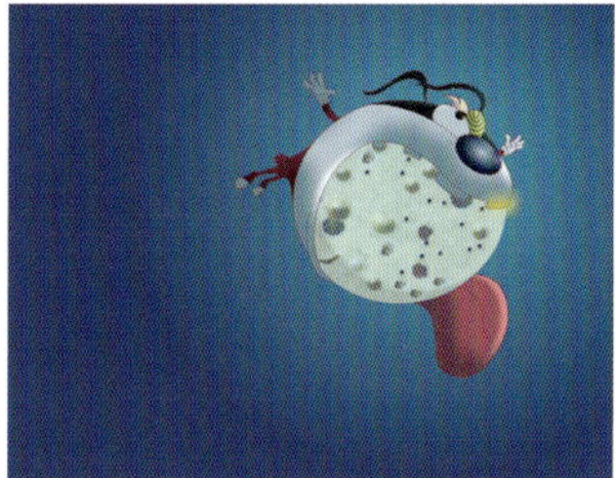

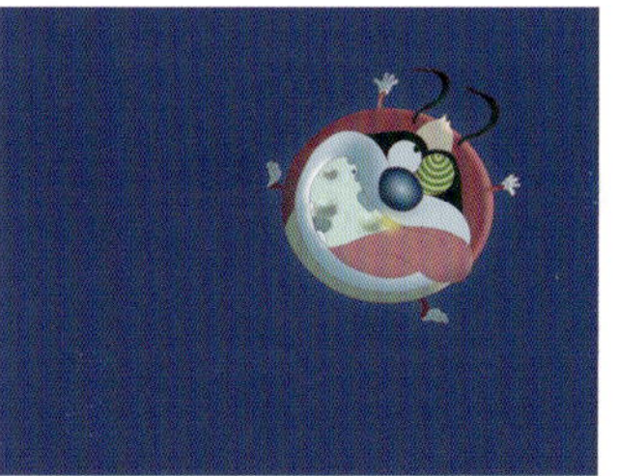

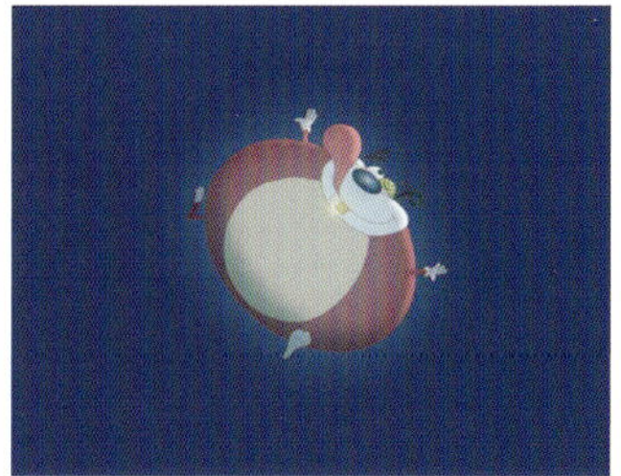

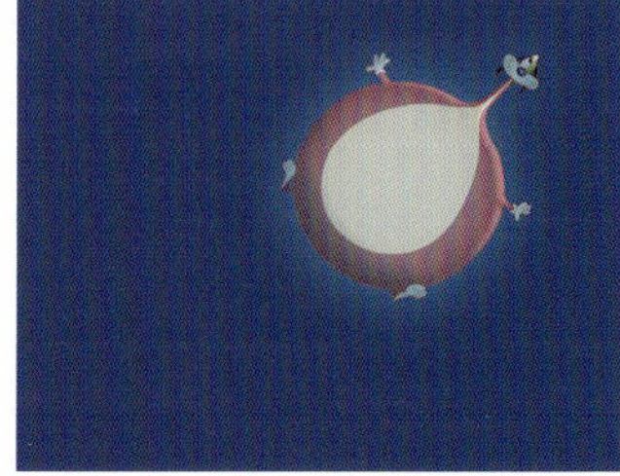

Film still sequence from Dude decending a staircase -Apollo 440, 2003.

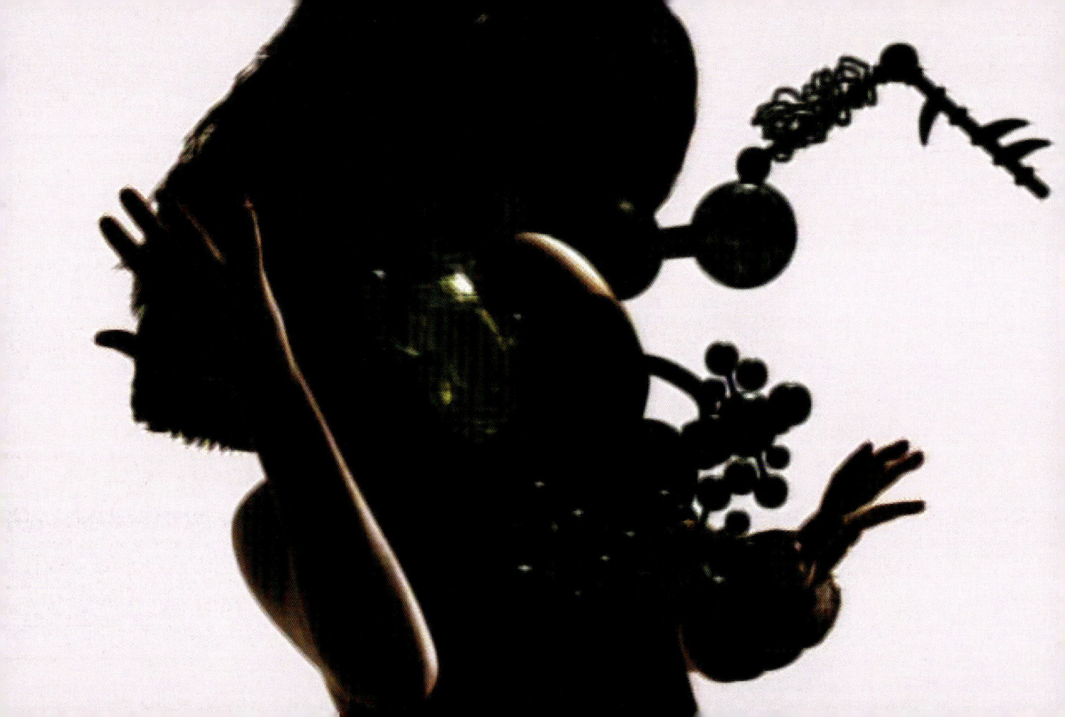

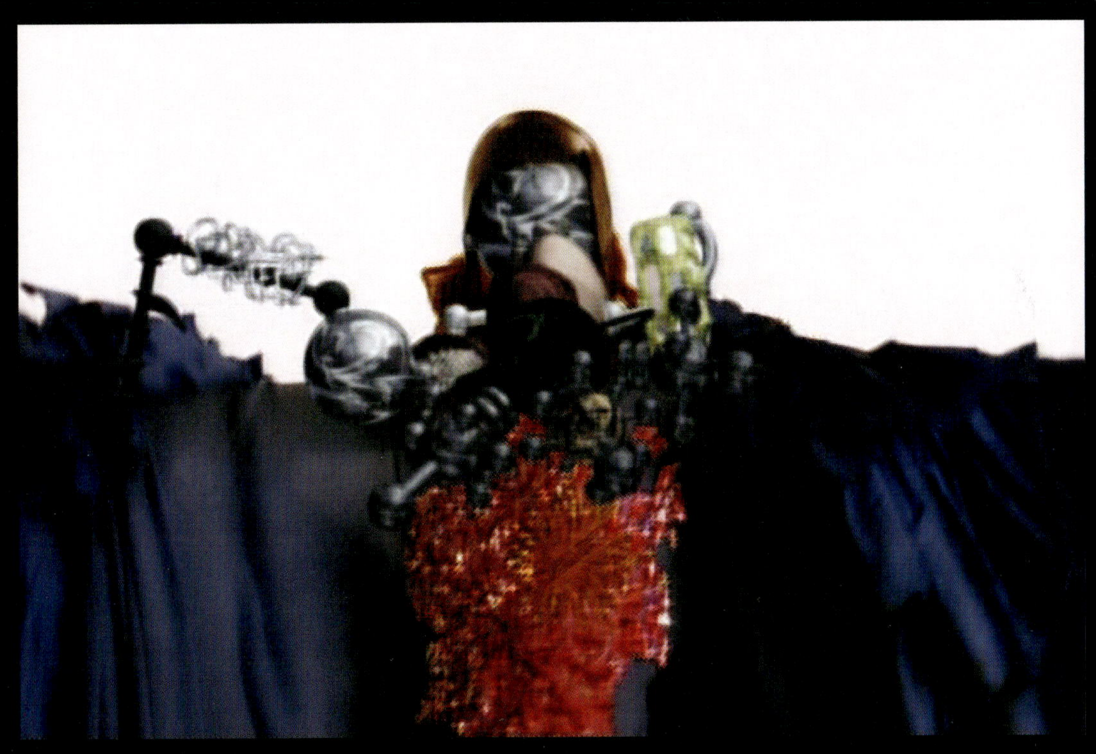

The following pages present a
selection of production paintings,
drawings and comic strips
produced between 1994 and 1999.
All pictures for Johnny Pumpkin
are gouache and pencil on paper,
and vary in size.

Previous Page

*Film stills from Sow into you -
Roisin Murphy. 16mm and
CGI Animation, 2005.*

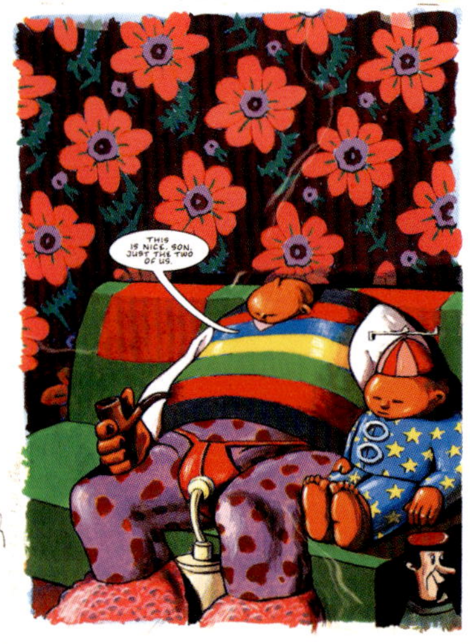

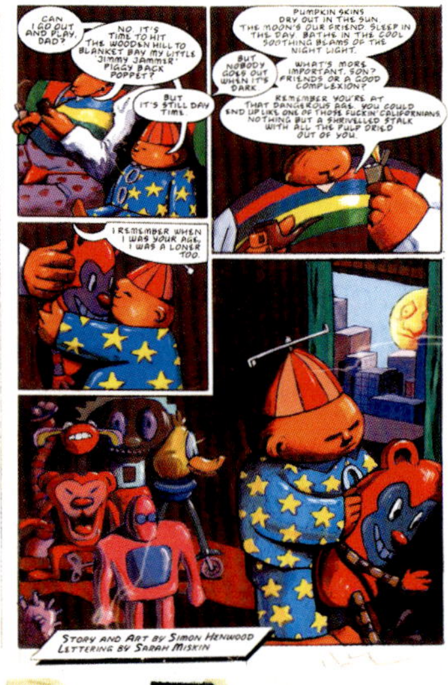

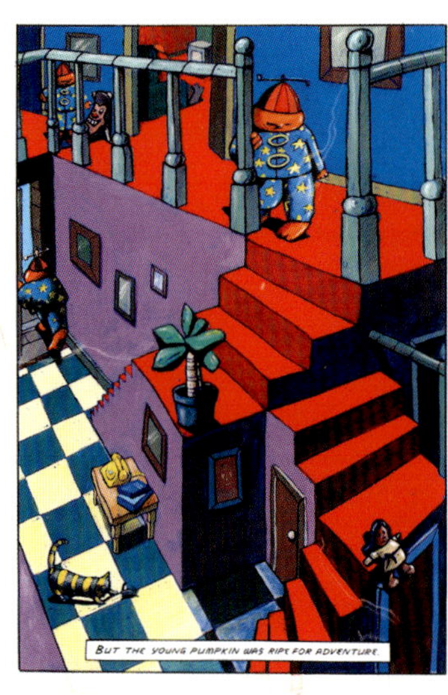

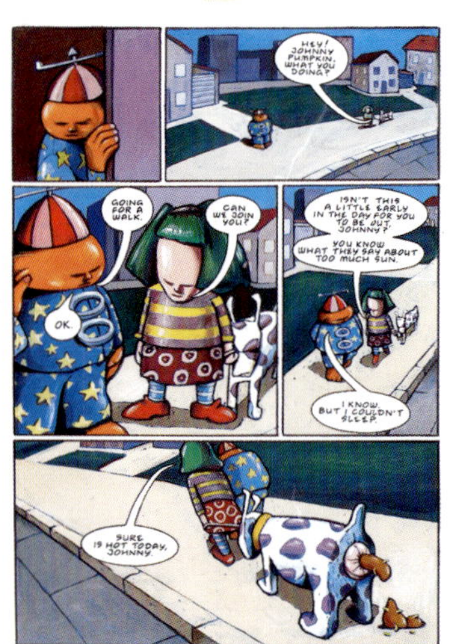

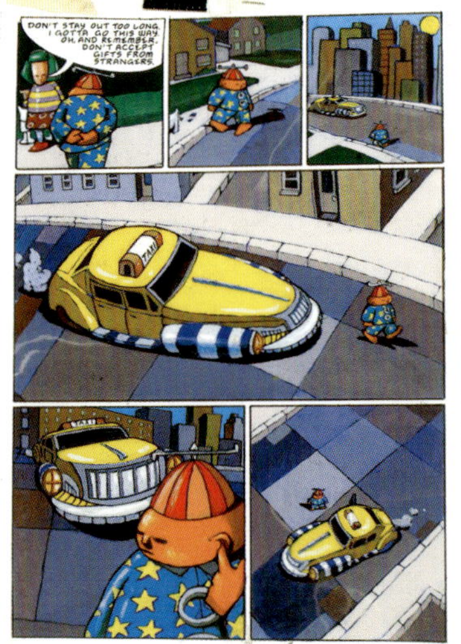

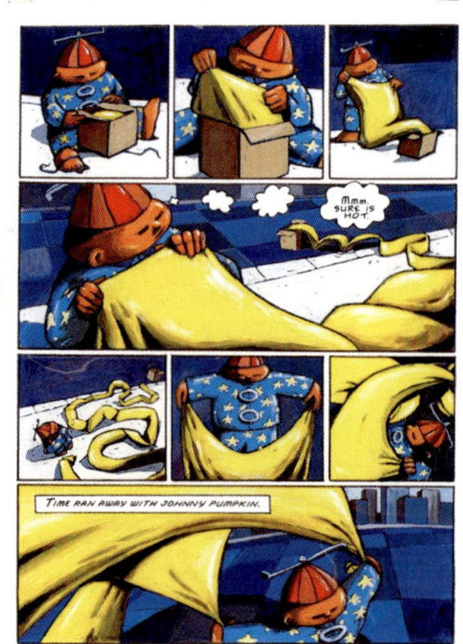

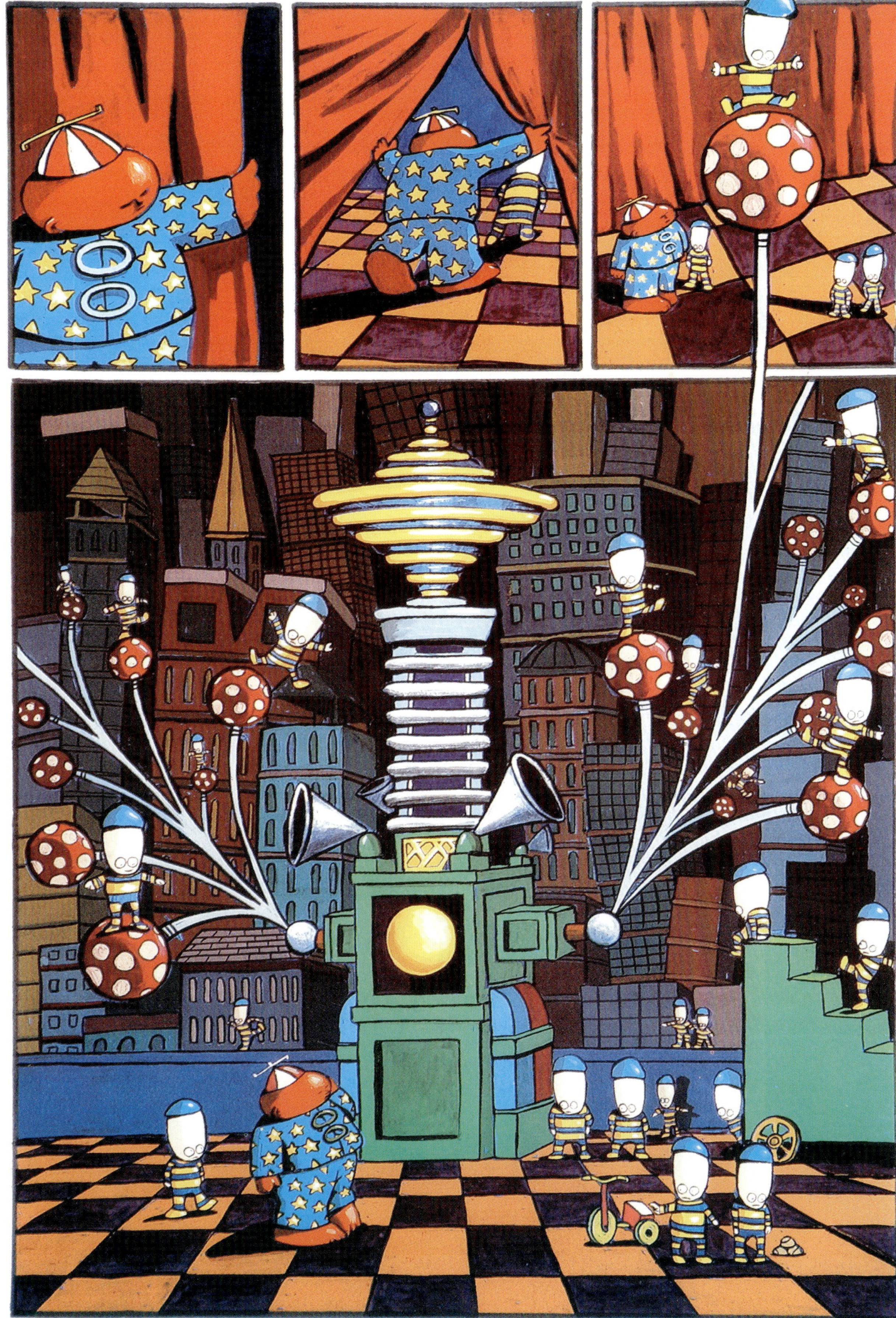

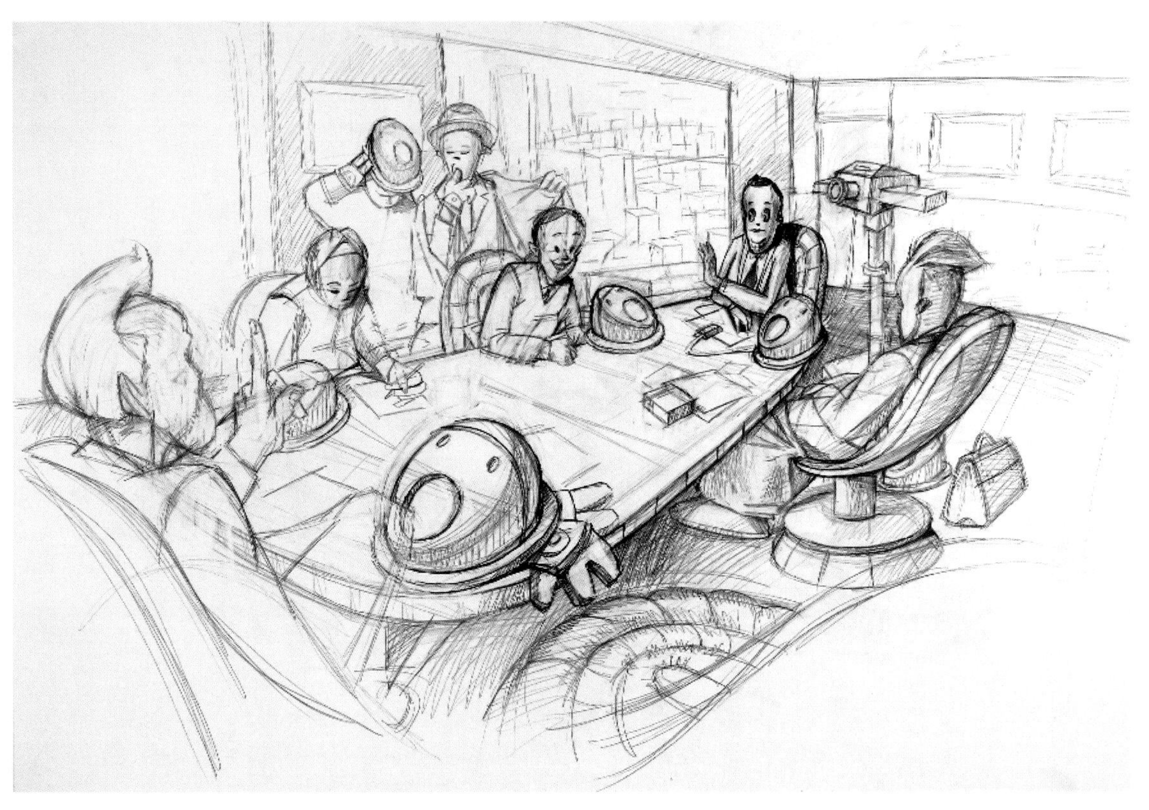

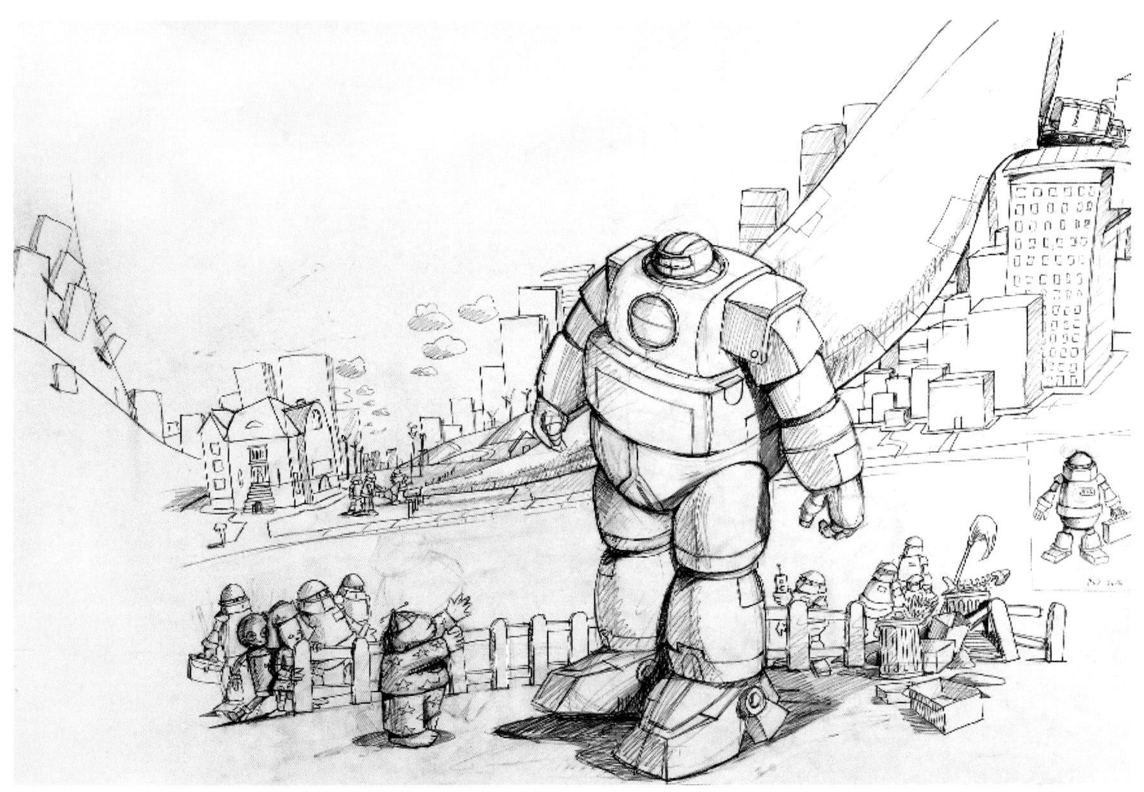

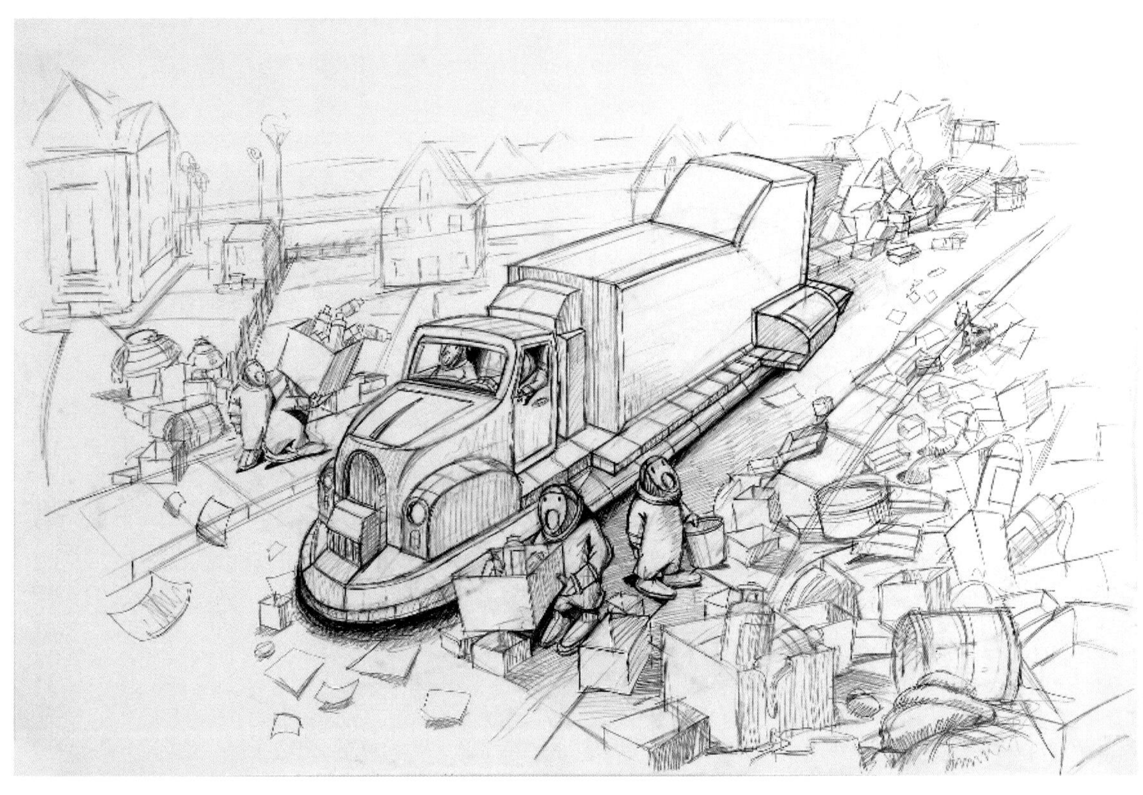

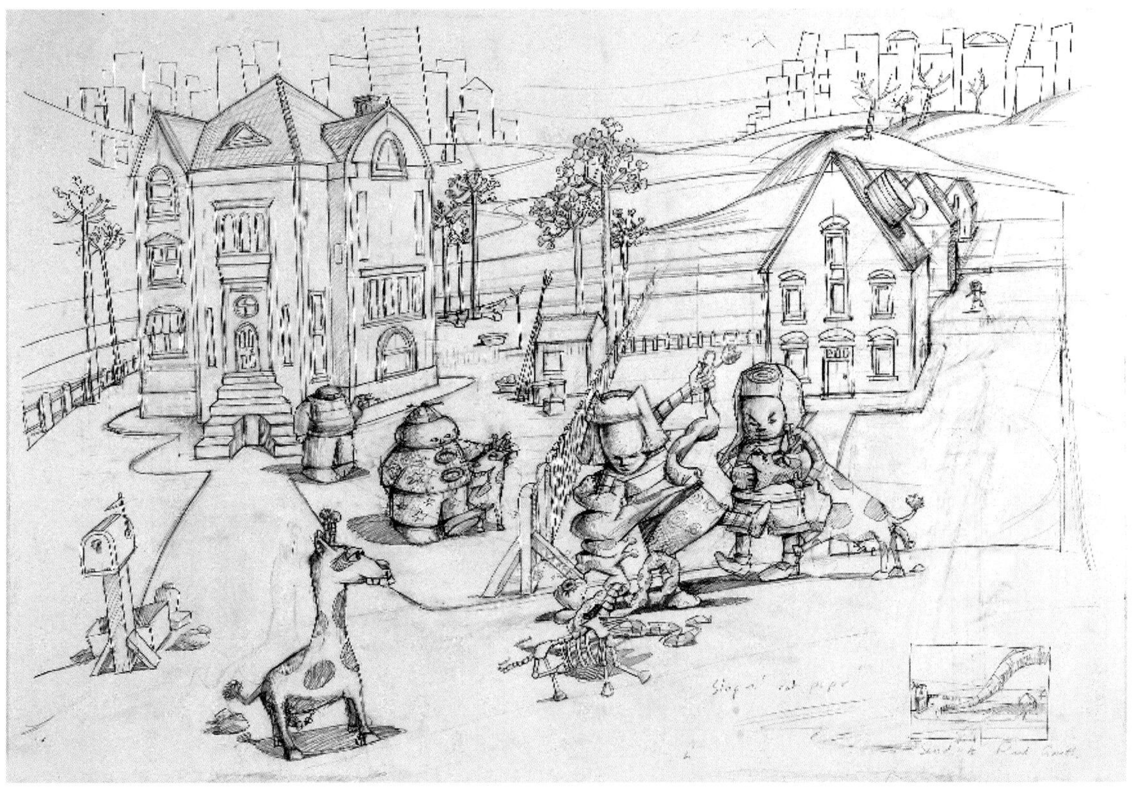

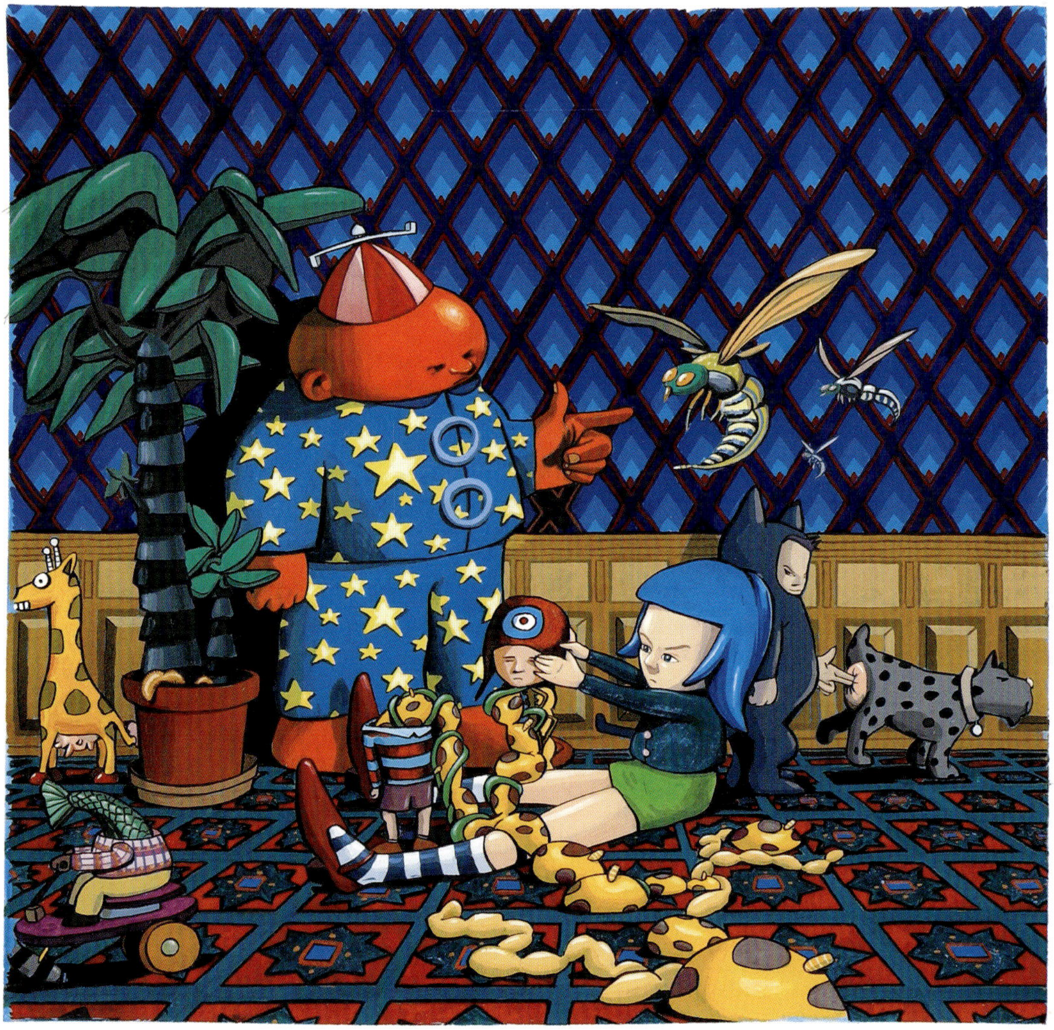

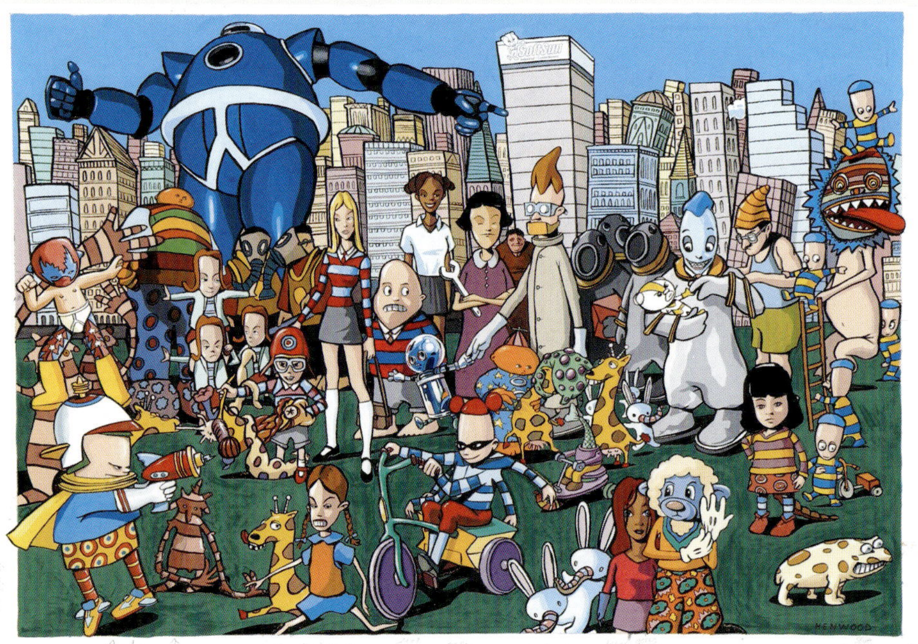

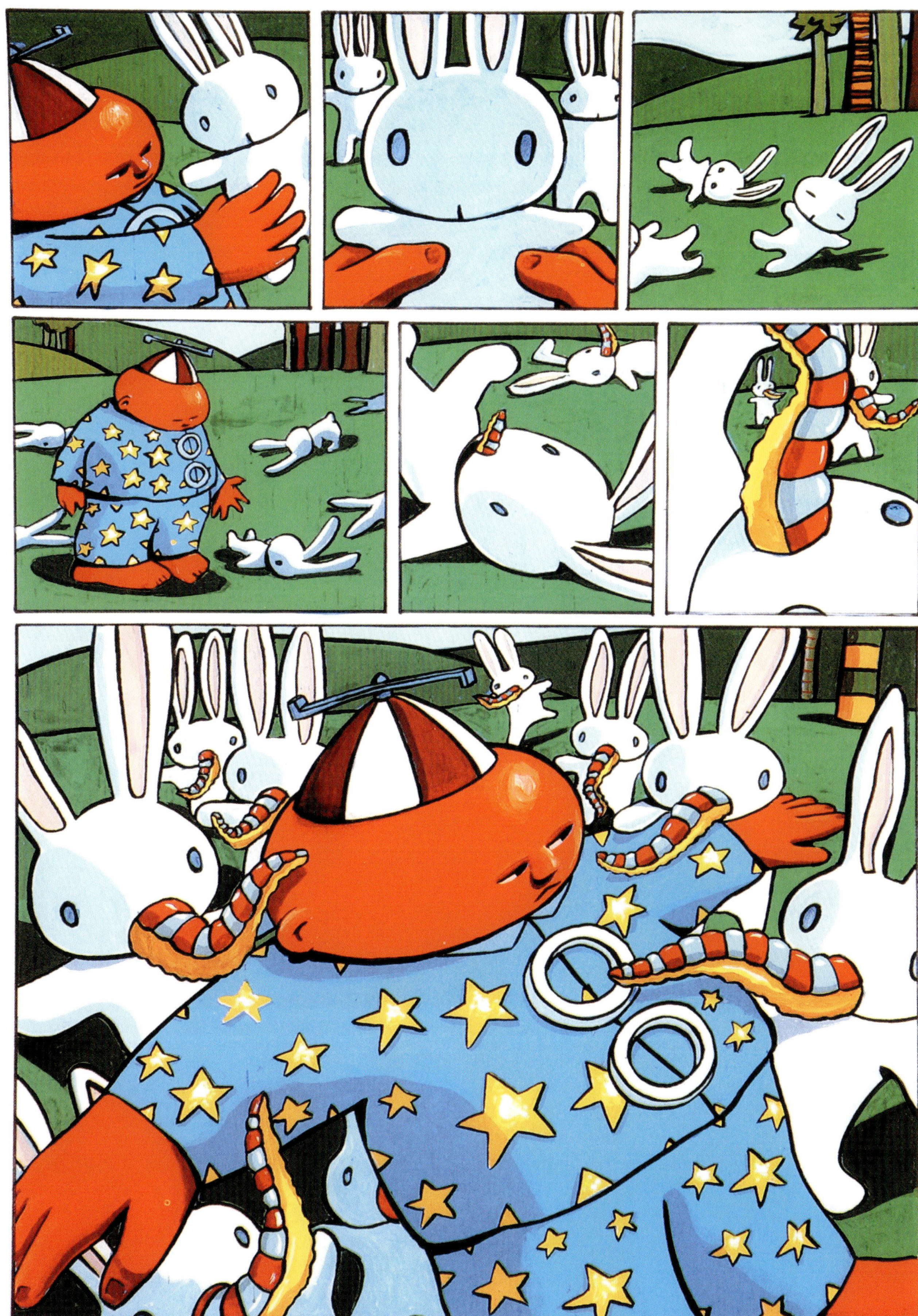

Interview with the Artist
Julian Fuller

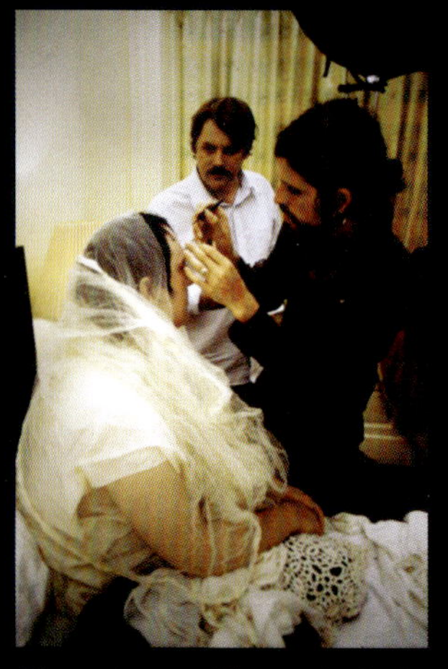

*Henwood on set with Devendra Banhart
and Anthony Hegarty at the Chelsea
Hotel, New York, 2005.*

Opposite Page: *On set Photograph
from The Fallen Eye, London 2007.*

Interview with the artist by Julian Fuller June 2008

The photographs used to illustrate this section, date from the last twenty years. Some are screen grabs from film and videos directed by the artist. The majority of photographs are taken on set or session.

Julian Fuller Before we begin to delve into your history I wanted to talk a little about these photographs. You have never published them before, is that right?

Simon Henwood **Well no. Some have been published, but itís fair to say this is the first time I have attempted to edit a selection of this work though.**

Fuller How long have you been taking pictures? What are the earliest photographs in the book?

Henwood **I've taken photos since I was 16, when my father gave me an SLR camera on my birthday. I still use the same model. I have a few more lenses, but it's the same basic Pentax. The earliest pictures are from the Alice short film and painting series. I think they are from 1992. There is a big archive.**

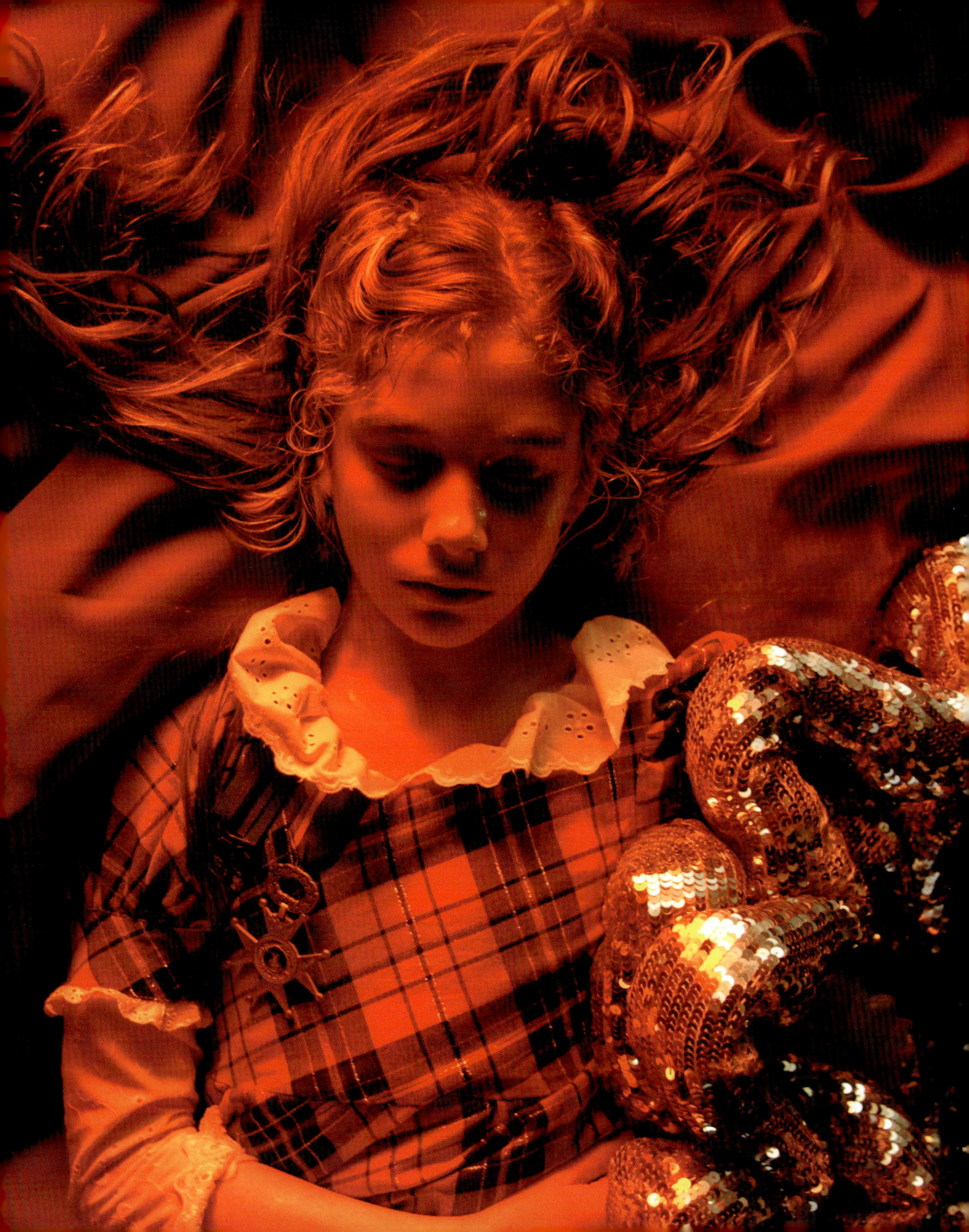

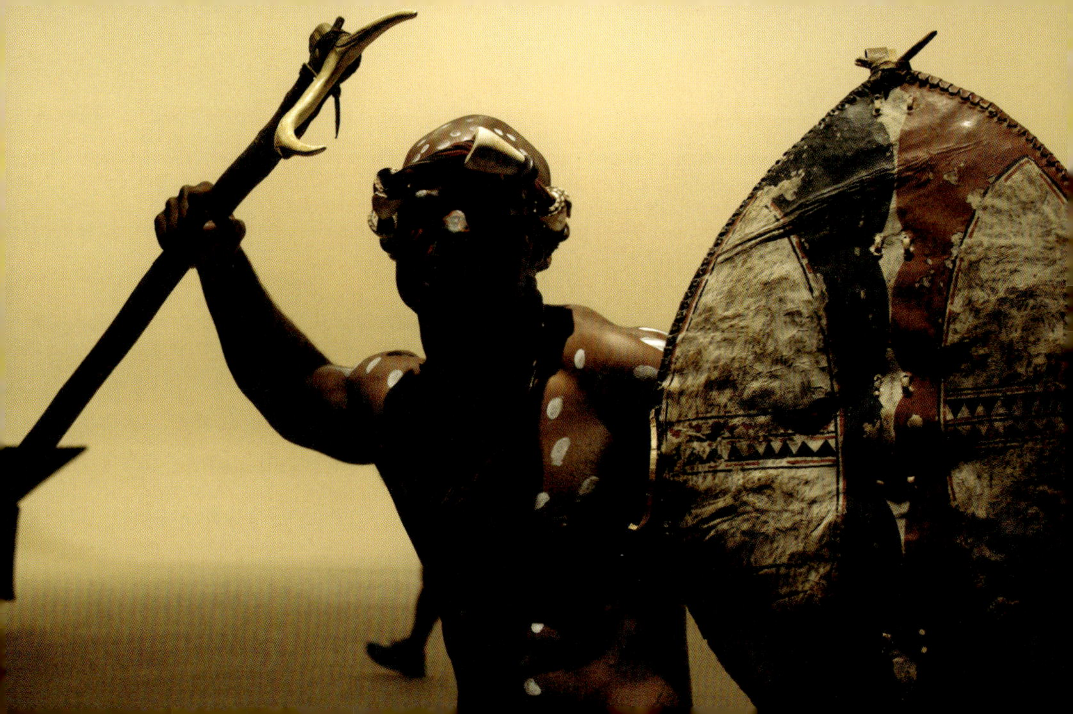

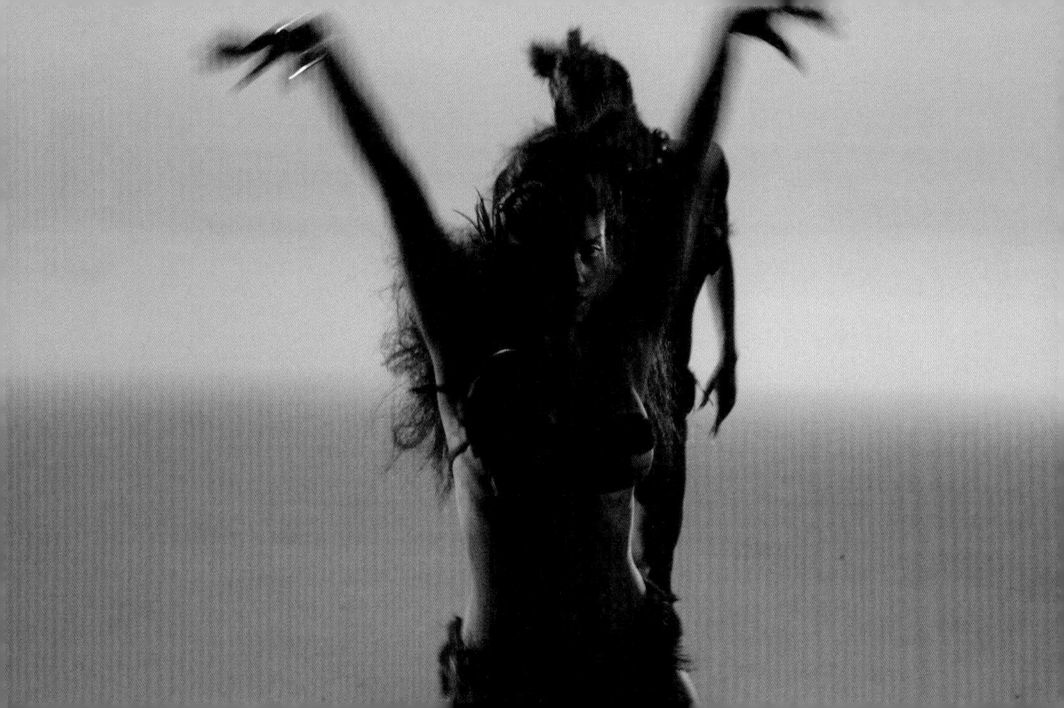

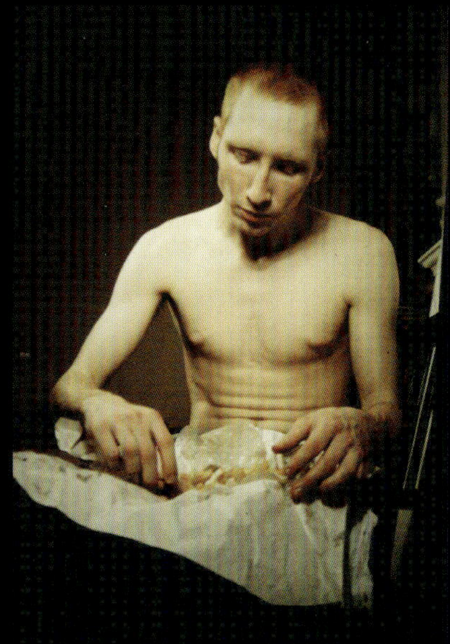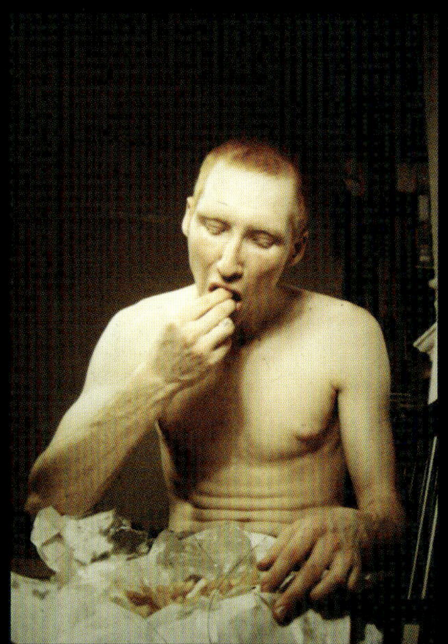

Fuller What made you select these pictures in particular?

Henwood **Well they were the first I got to. (Laughs) I mean I don't have them well catalogued at the moment, so I just started pulling out sessions that I thought told a story. Actually they don't really connect completely, but now at least there is a starting point to expand from.**

Fuller Charlotte Mullins touched on some of the photographic influences shown in the video and film work. How about the subjects of these portraits? Are they all subjects you have painted as well?

Henwood **Some are, but I made a conscious effort to select different subjects. Well at least to show a different approach I have, compared to the portrait.**

Fuller More narrative perhaps?

Henwood **Yes, there is more of a story or setting in the background. A lot of the reference photos I take for painting are totally about the subject and capturing something in the expression. These photographs are definitely more about a combination of subject, setting, light and atmosphere.**

Fuller How much set up is involved in taking the pictures?

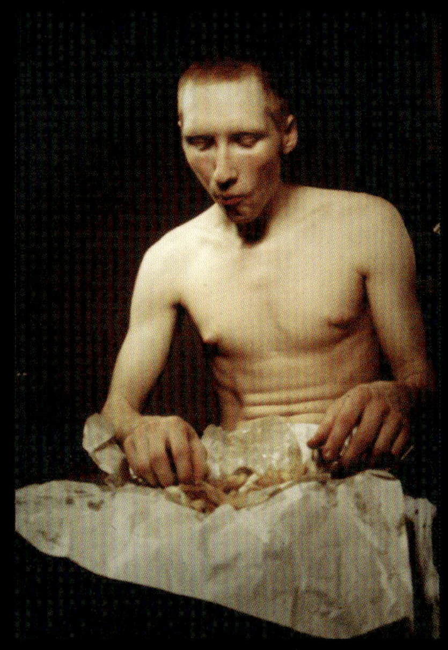 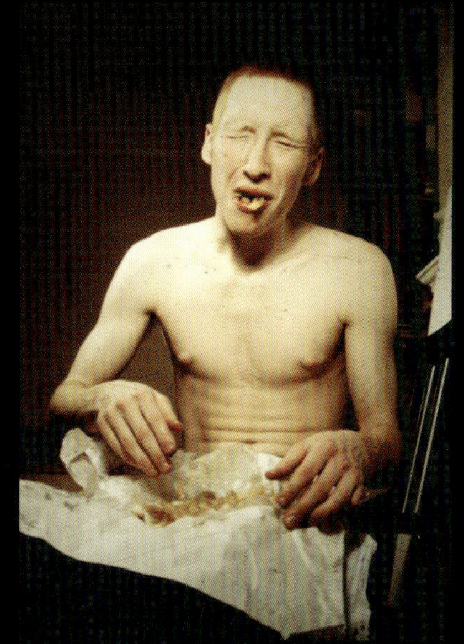

Henwood **None. Well, if I'm on set, there is a lot. (Laughs) But this is not the case for the photographs. I use what's already there, available light, etc.**

Fuller So, lets begin with where you were brought up.

Henwood **I was born in Portsmouth. My father was a meteorologist and was posted every few years. We lived in Germany, all over England and Scotland. I had about eleven schools, always the new kid in class. I finally finished my schooling in Scotland and was to study painting in Glasgow.**

Fuller You studied in Exeter though didn't you?

Henwood **Yes I decided to move south again. I had just turned 17 and was offered a couple of places in London but opted for Devon.**

Fuller What was the college like then? What was the emphasis and focus?

Henwood **Well there were a lot of different departments. I worked between all of them at some point. (Laughs). Painting, design, animation, typography. There was a strong focus on life drawing, everything was based around it. It was compulsory - at least one day a week for four years.**

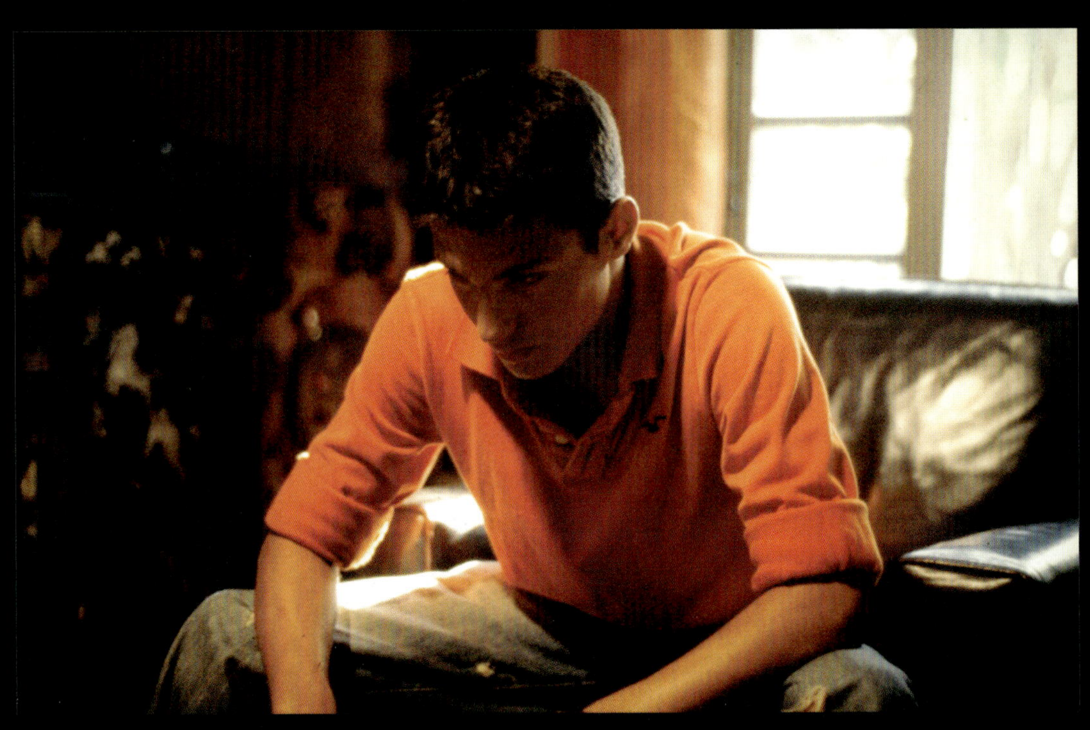

Miami, 2006

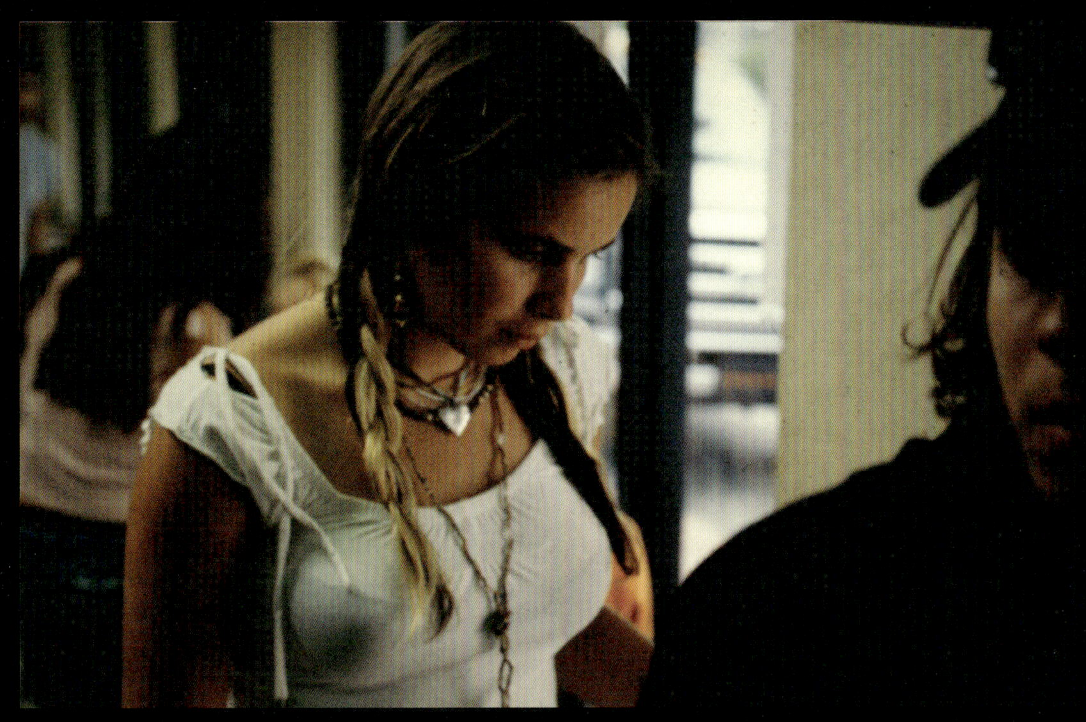

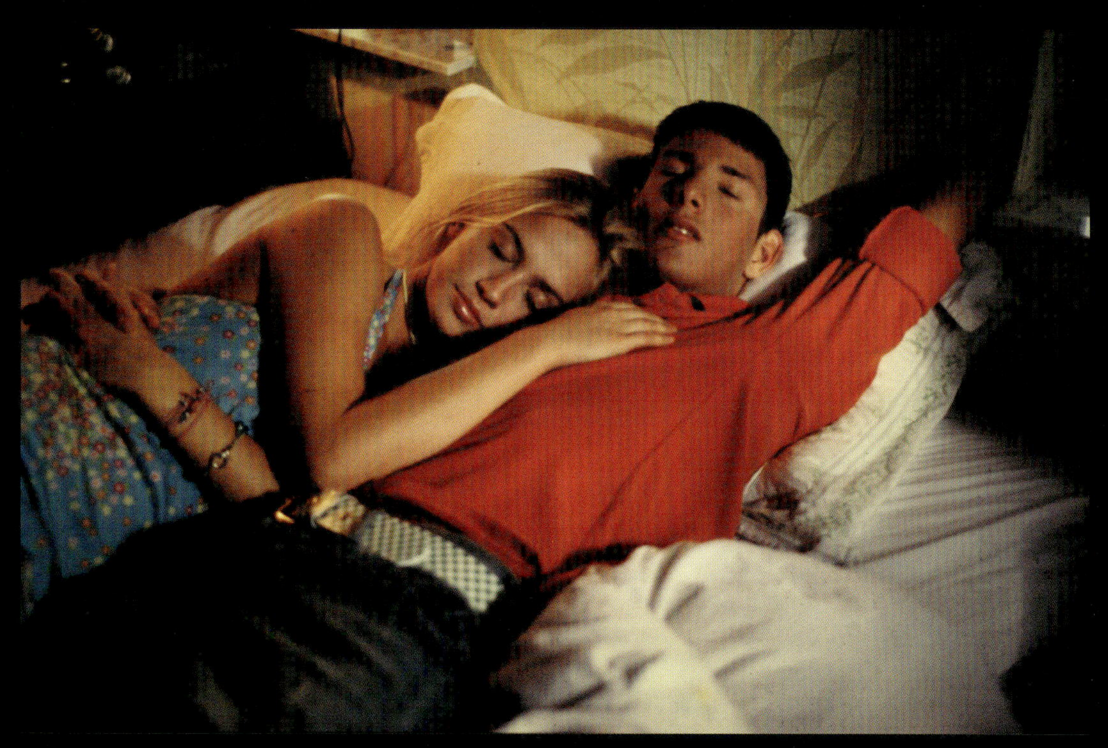

Miami, 2006

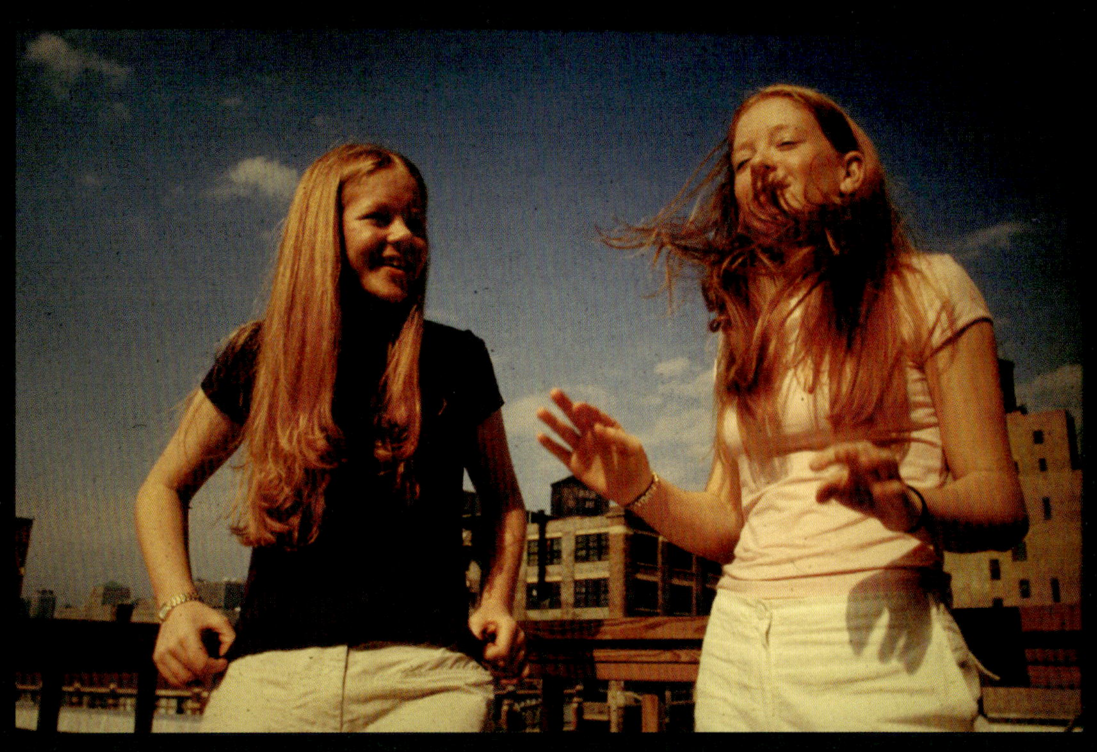

Chicago, 2002

Fuller What painters / artists were you interested in then?

Henwood I studied a lot of Victorian artists and illustrators as the head of the History of Art department was obsessed with Beardsley, Rickets, and Sidney Sime. I made a five minute animated film based on Christina Rosetti's epic poem Goblin Market, hand drawing every frame myself. I also loved the American Underground Comic scene. I found reprinted copies from the 60s and 70s in a shop in Glasgow when I was at school. I remember going to the Peter Blake exhibition and The Pre Raphaelites both at the Tate. There was no young artists movement at that time, just Bacon. I remember meeting Ralph Steadman and he made a drawing of me. Everyone was into something completely different but very conservative.

Fuller What year did you move to London?

Henwood I moved here in 1987. It was initially a very exciting time. I met Francis Bacon in the Coach and Horses pub that year. I idolised him.

Fuller You were working as an illustrator the time?

Henwood Yes, I spent about 3 years working mainly in children's books. I wrote and illustrated approximately a dozen books in that time for publishers in the UK and USA. They were cautionary tales that appealed to adults too.

Fuller You then moved to New York. Why?

Henwood The thing about London at the time was that there was the attitude that you had to stay in your field. I wanted to move on and try new things. There were some younger artists, figurative painters, emerging. I saw the early shows of Rita Ackermann, and John Currin. I started to paint again. The paintings were terrible, but I freed myself forever from having a label, I think.

Fuller How did you survive while you were there?

Henwood I freelanced for the New York Times. You know blagged it, by being British. (Laughs) I lived in the Chelsea Hotel for a while, then got lucky and landed a great apartment round the corner. A sub-let from (the environmental artist) Betsy Damon. She had a huge studio on site, which I used to paint large-scale atrocities. My painter friends must have scoffed at the luxurious studio surroundings I had for such piss weak work.

Fuller What other artists interested you at the time?

Henwood **Well I was interested in everything I suppose. I just wanted to absorb as much as possible. Understand things. I was equally intrigued by the legend or reputation/lifestyle of artists as much as their work. I could never understand why some of my friends seemed to be able to exist on thin air in such an expensive city. I was working ten jobs just to pay the rent and they were just making work, but never selling it.**

Fuller TRUSTAFARIANS?

Henwood **Exactly. (Laughs) I was very naive about it all. However, I did meet a lot of serious artists of the moment, such as Julian Schnabel.**

Fuller Didn't I hear you used to wear Julian Schnabel's cast off shoes?

Henwood **Well that sums it up doesn't it. Yes, my girlfriend at the time introduced me to him. He was throwing out these expensive hand made shoes. They were a few sizes too big for me, but I padded them out somehow. (Laughs)**

Fuller Do you have many photographs from this time?

Henwood **Yes, lots of boring skyscraper photos. One thing I used to do was ride a bike down through the financial district on a Sunday. It was like a trip through the mountains. No people, just these huge concrete and steel monoliths. I always think of Richard Sera's work when I remember that time.**

Fuller What made you return to London?

Henwood **New York energised me with a new sense of purpose. I felt ready to go back and start work seriously. I had had a lot of work published in a very few years, which gave me a lot of confidence that I could self publish something new and create a platform for my self and other artists I liked.**

Fuller This was Purr magazine.

Henwood **Yes. The strap line was "A gun to the head in print". The magazine was perfectly bound and full colour. The first couple of issues were put together as cut and paste artwork. Computer graphics was still out of my reach then.**

Interview Continues on Page 201

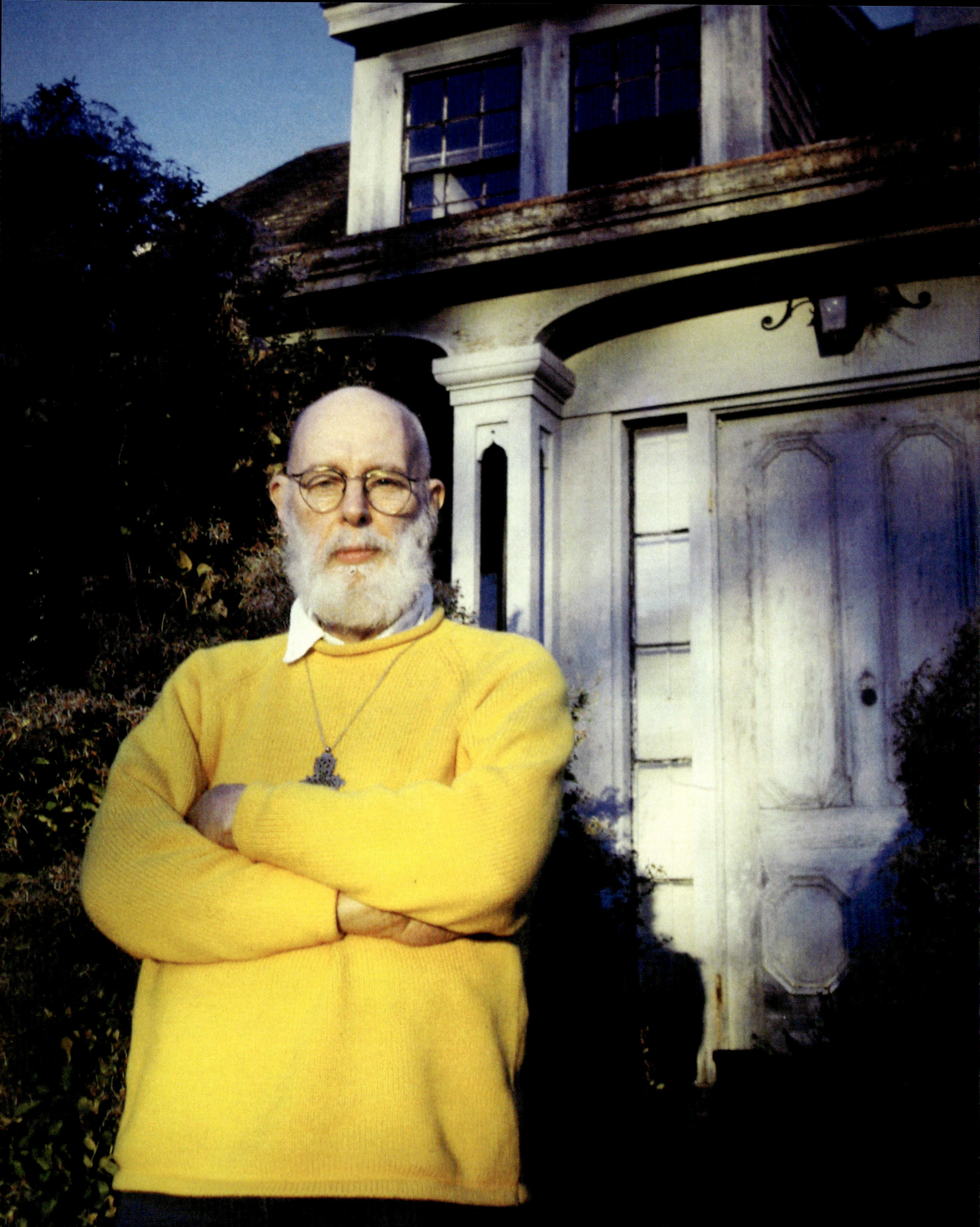

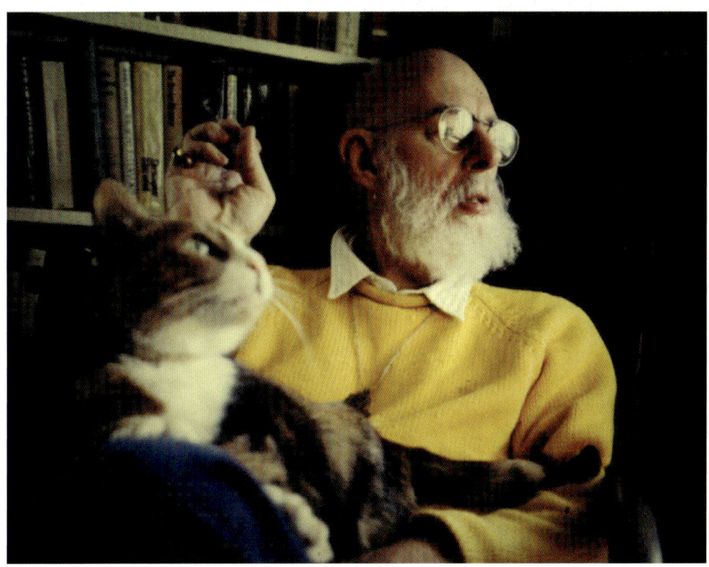

"They always said that Edward Gorey must be dead. At least for about 20 years before he actually died. There are not many interviews with him and even less photographs. For an American icon with over 100 books to his name - this is pretty incredible. In 1994, my Swiss agent (Anne Elizabeth Suter) managed to arrange a meeting for me. So I flew to Boston from New York and got a pond hopper to Cape Cod. I sat up front with the pilot, as I was his only passenger. I remember seeing Edward from the plane standing by the small airstrip waiting for me. First we went to a local restaurant/diner that he visited every day. He took me straight into the kitchen to see what was cooking. Later, his house, as you can see from the pictures, (and as legend also tells) was one large library, patrolled by a small army of cats. Their numbers had dwindled to around five I think, when I was there.

His favourite was Jane. (Sitting on his lap). We talked about the ballet, Star Trek, The Golden Girls, Japan and England. Despite his huge passion for Victoriana, and Dickens, he had never visited here. I think he said, "I'm afraid I might be disappointed. I took many photographs while I was there; including Polaroid's of his many collections. We just sort of did a tour of the house and he showed me snippets of projects and unfinished books. Demonstrated toys and puppets he had made. I remember thinking as I left, out of anyone alive that I would want to meet, it had to be Mr. Gorey. He maintained my vision of him perfectly. For years after, people pestered me to publish more pictures. The Guardian even wrote a full-page story about my visit. I always kept the pictures to myself to maintain the illusion"- *Quote from the artist*

Both Photographs
Edward Gorey at home, Cape Cod, 1995.

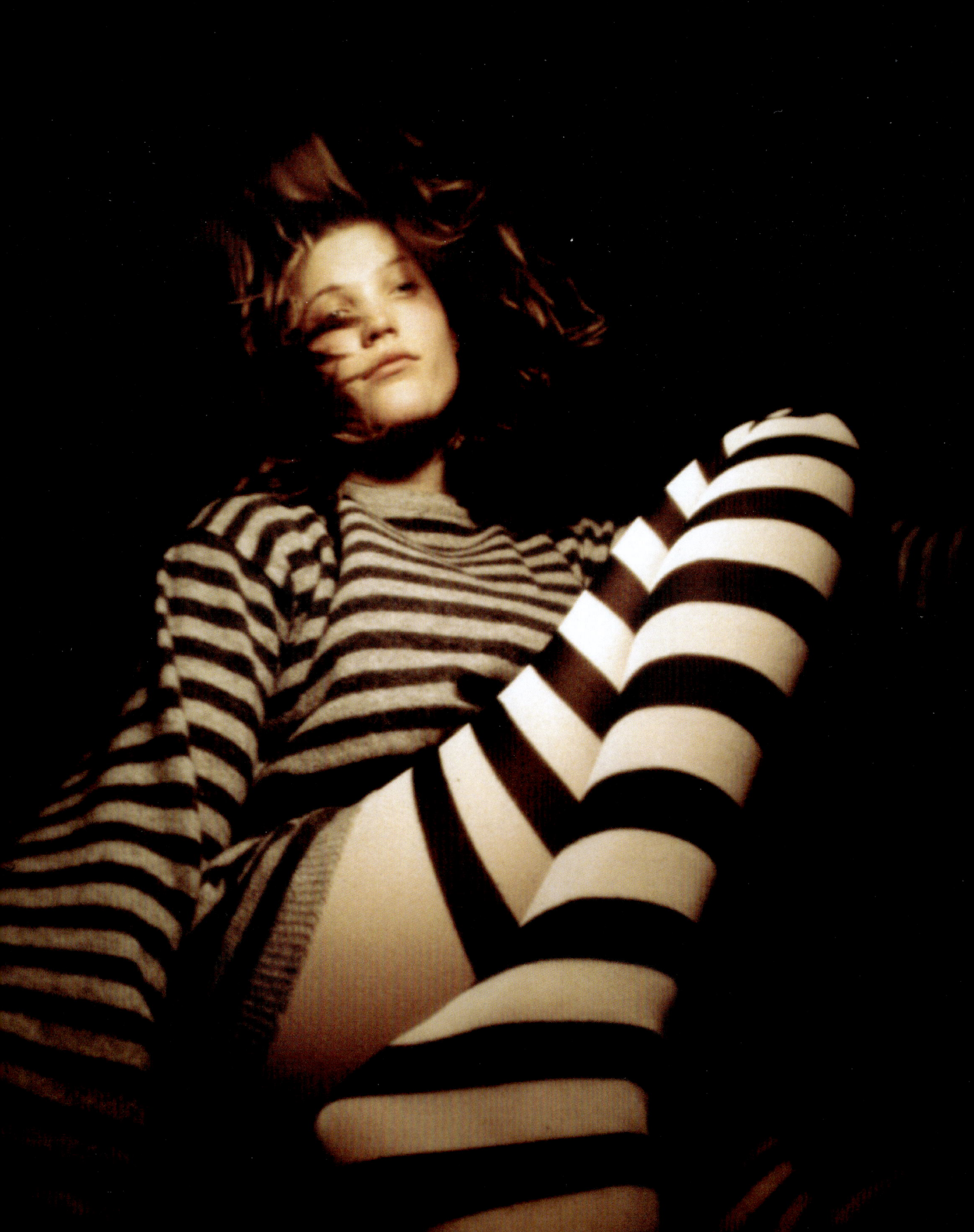

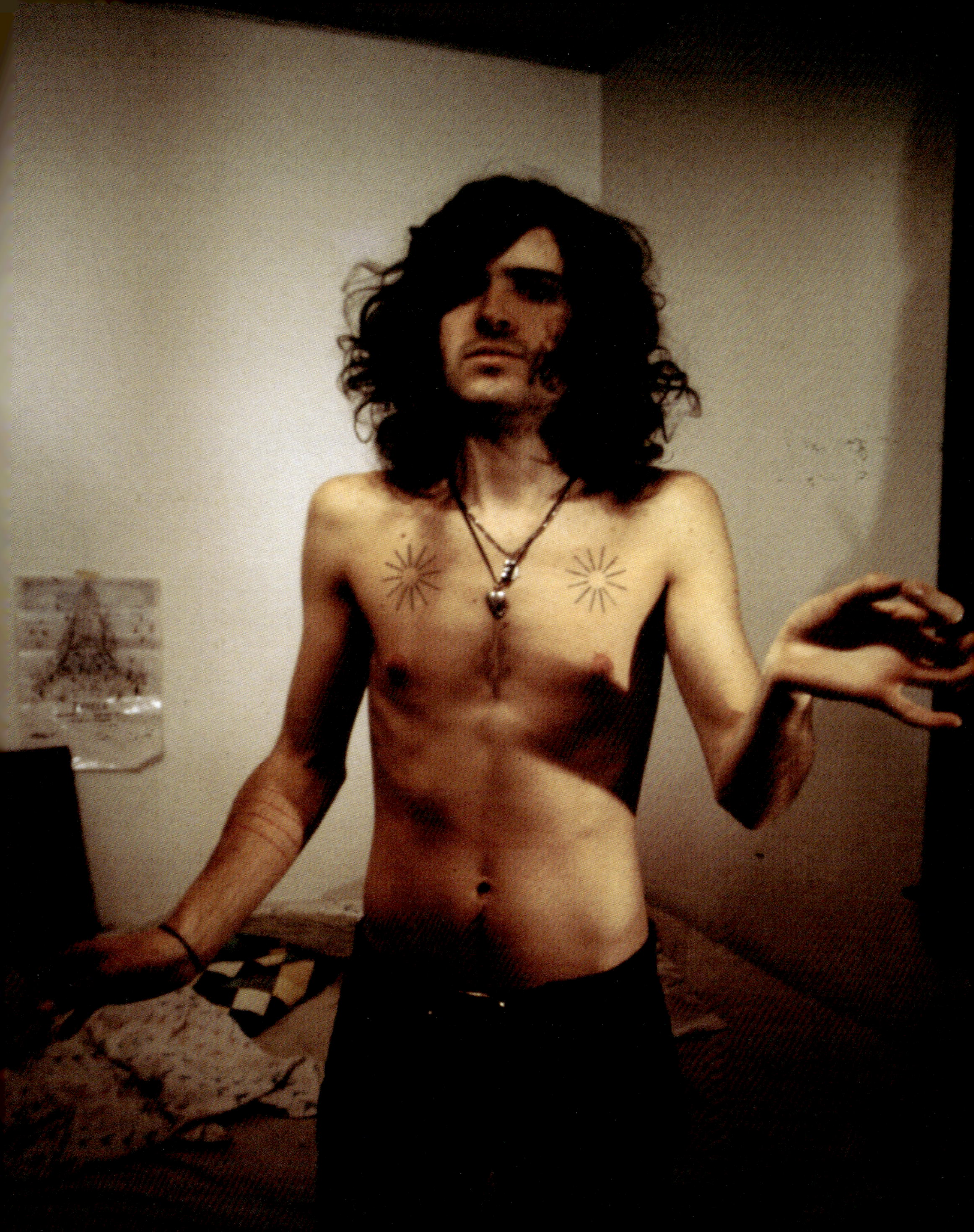

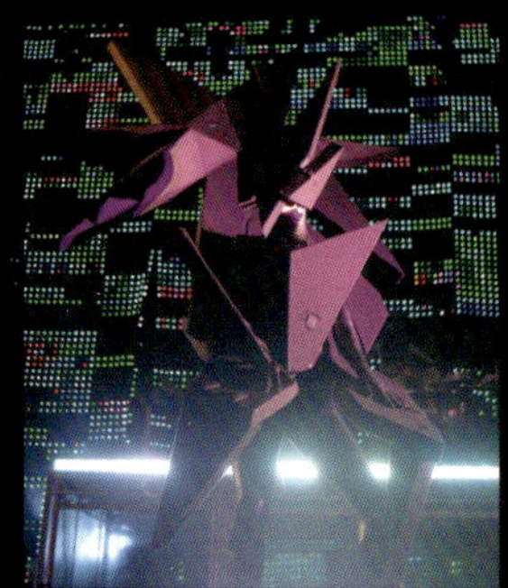

Dancers, Costume design for Kanye West - Glow In The Dark tour, 2007.

Fuller What did you publish?

Henwood **It was a combination of painting, comics, writing, and film. A very common mix these days, but quite new then. The contributors were as different as you can imagine really, stories by Hubert Selby jnr, drawings by HR Giger, and artist interviews were a big part of it.**

Fuller So you published and edited the magazine. What other contribution did you make?

Henwood **I wrote and drew comics (Johnny Pumpkin first appeared in Purr) and interviewed some of the artists and took photographs.**

Fuller Anyone memorable?

Henwood **I think Edward Gorey was the most important piece. It was one of very few interviews he ever did.**

Fuller Did you meet him?

Henwood **Yes, see artist's commentary. I went to his home in the Cape, met his cats and rummaged though his library. (Laughs)**

Fuller How long did the magazine run and why did you stop publishing it?

Henwood **We published five issues. The company I started rather ambitiously also incorporated a record label, publishing arm and eventually a gallery next to the Lisson on Bell Street. At first it was a small operation, which I funded by raising some small investment plus subsidy from other work I was taking on. When a bigger investor became involved it soon collapsed under the weight of - lets say all the shuffling egos. I had also spent less time on my own work and more time fire fighting the business.**

Fuller This was around 1995.

Henwood **Yes**

Fuller What next?

Previous Page
Film still from Short Film Alice, 1993.
Devendra Banhart, Brooklyn, NYC 2004.

Henwood **I started to paint again. I think as a reaction to publishing I began to work on a large scale. Somehow it sort of compensated for the enigmatic engine of publishing or something. (Laughs) I don't know. The early paintings were quite graphic, and I began to join some dots.**

Fuller This is your interest in childhood.

Henwood **That had always been there and these paintings were a reaction against the early children's books and a culmination of exposure to darker themes explored in the magazine. I also met Paula Rego around this time and her Nursery Rhyme series was another key for me. In a way, that led me to the Red Riding Hood theme, exploring a more adult approach in the under current of the story.**

Fuller Where did you first show this work?

Henwood **Well the work has an interesting and evolving history that continues to this day. I didn't exhibit any of these pieces for another four years. I had a show in Tokyo in 1999, which was the first place they were seen. Over the years the work has been re-published in magazines – as recently as 2005 it was used as a cover feature in the Czech Republic. Next year (2009) one of the original pieces is going to be featured in a Riflemaker group show called Voodoo alongside Francis Bacon, and Bellmer.**

Fuller Why do you think it has such resonance?

Henwood **Well it's funny because people read a lot into the work. I think that's probably why. When the paintings first appeared in Alice (Henwood's second magazine venture) particularly the cover image – there was quite a lot of controversy. The woman's section of the Guardian was on a paedophile hunt. I had a strange conversation with a journalist from that section over the phone. She had taken the work completely out of context and not even bothered to read the accompanying text. I remember her being quite disappointed when she found out that there was no story.**

Fuller You had quite a lot of attention over Alice magazine. More so than Purr?

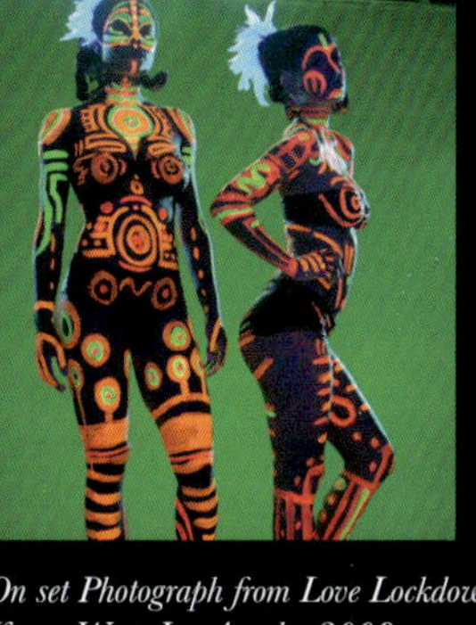

*On set Photograph from Love Lockdown
Kanye West, Los Angeles 2008.*

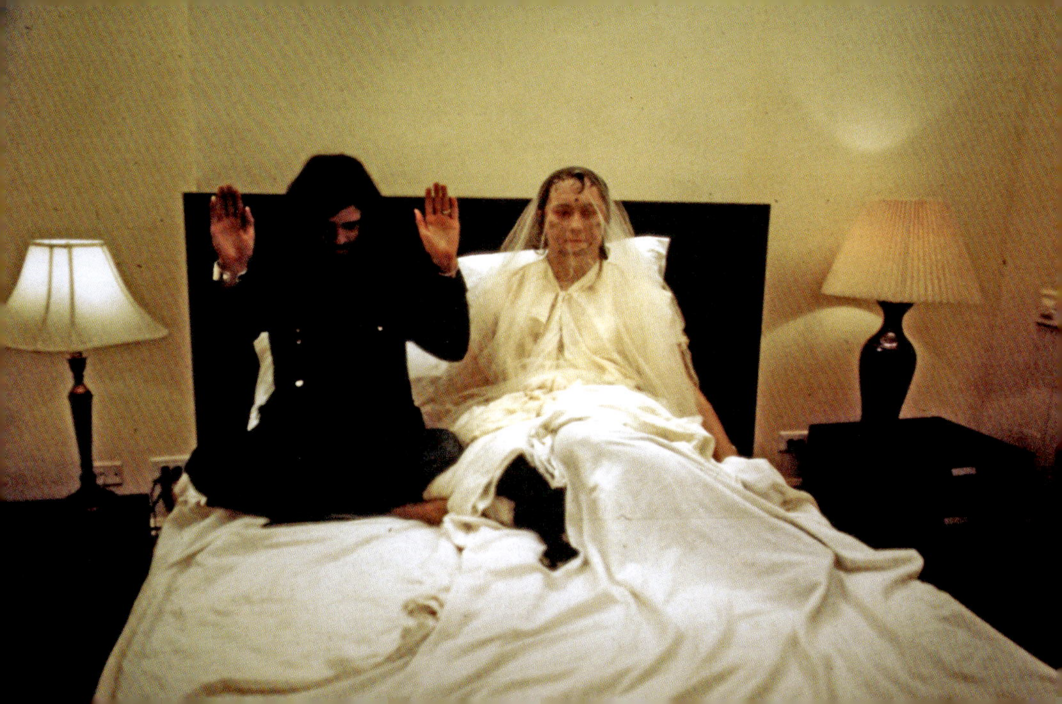

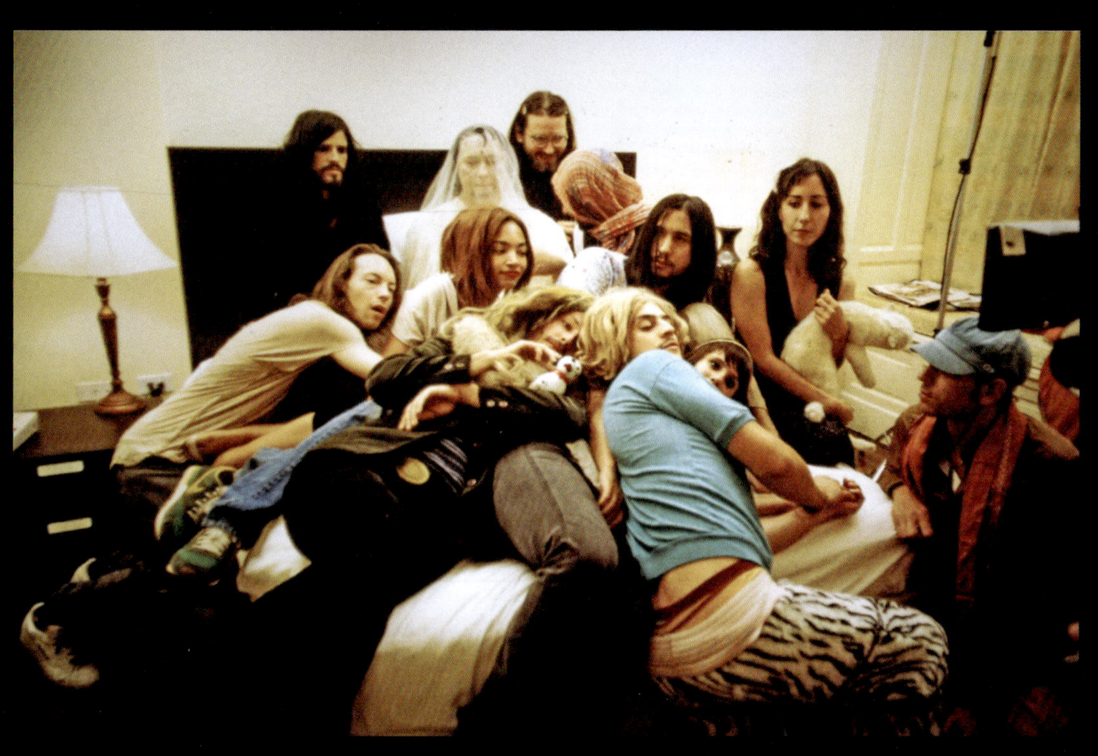

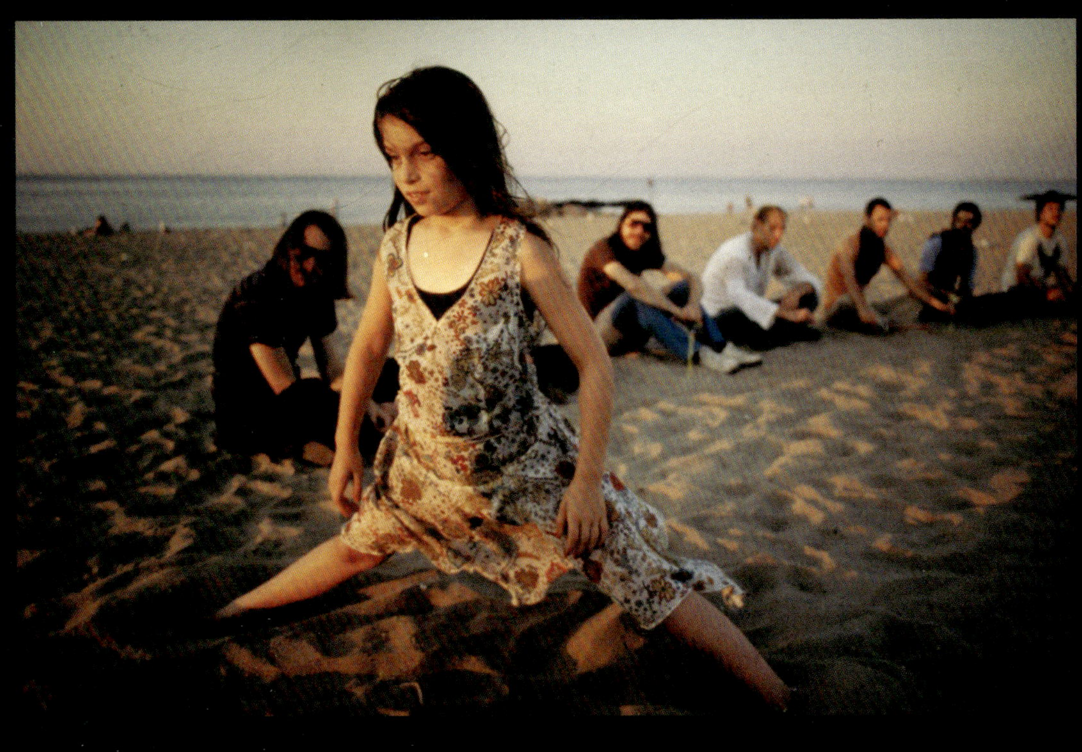

Coney Island, 2005.

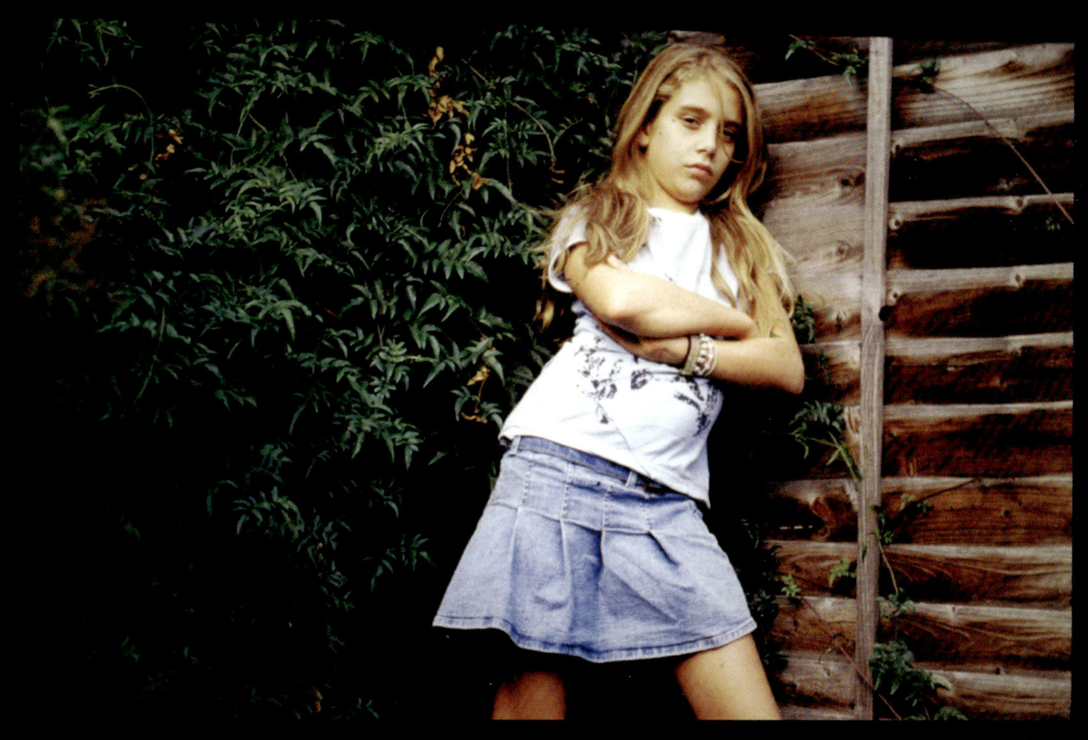

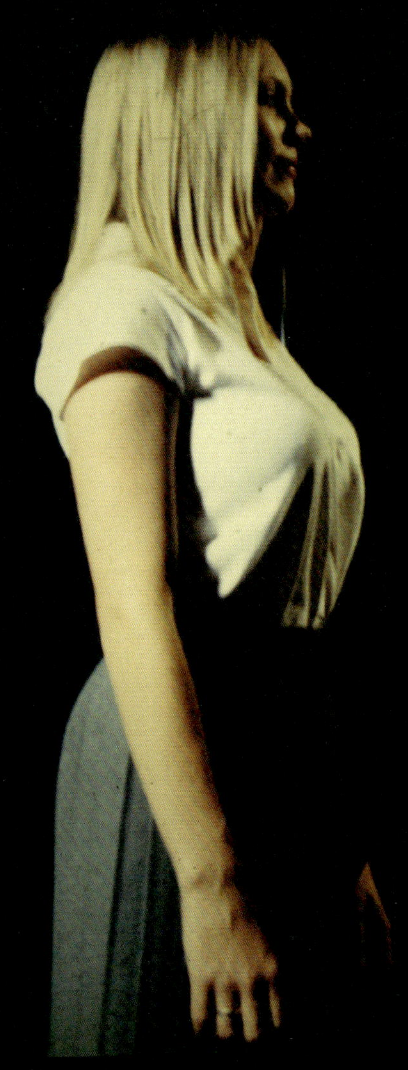

London, 2002.

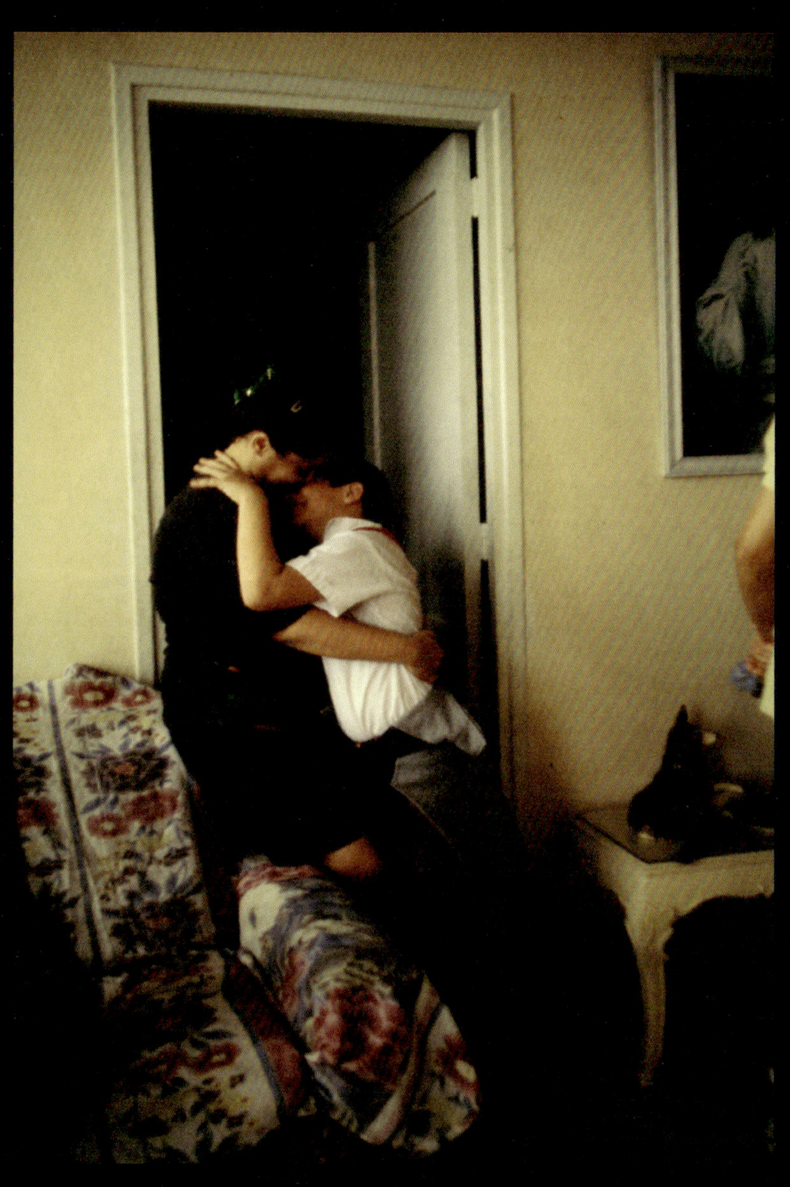

Havana, Cuba, 2004.

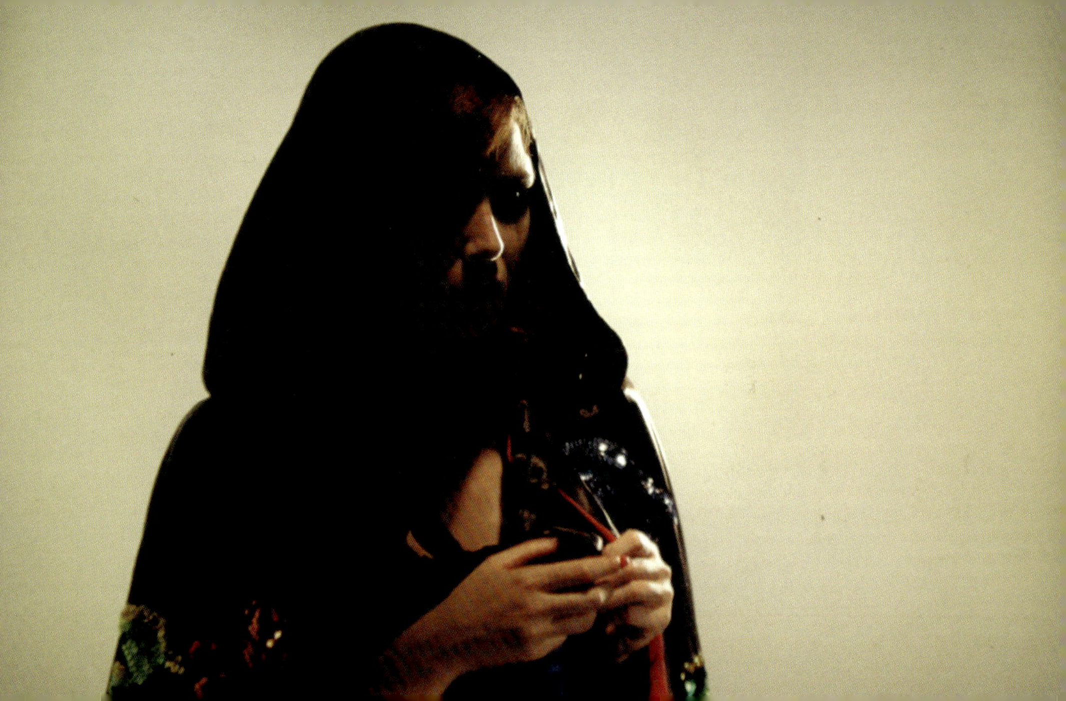

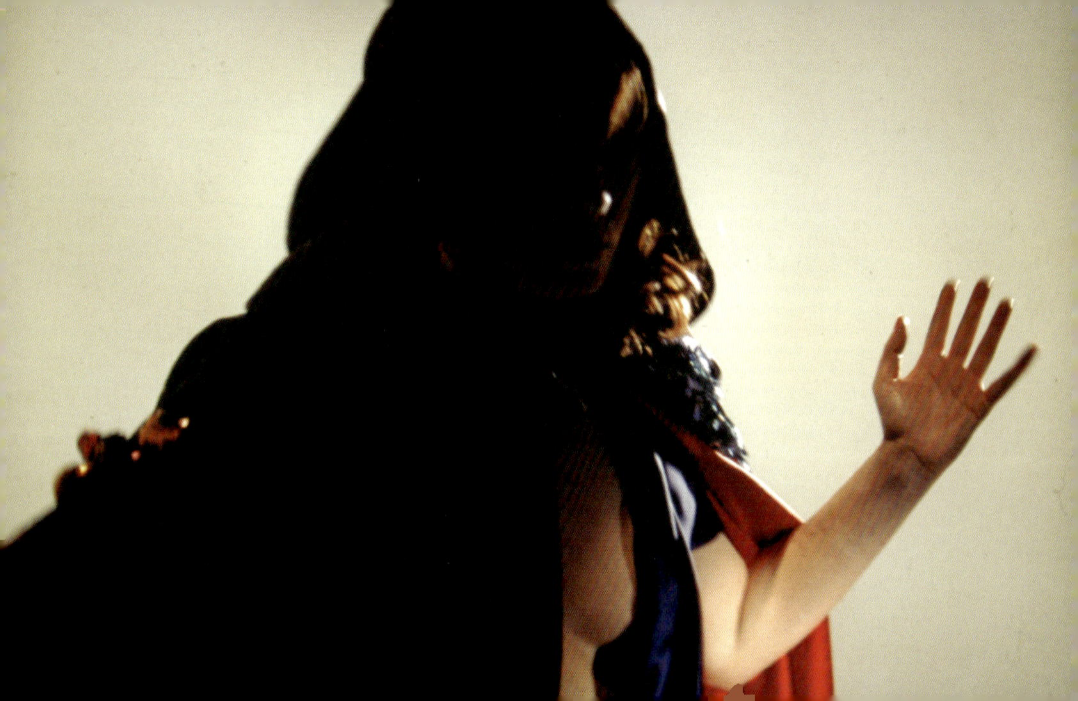

Henwood **Well it was more controversial and it was more focused. I wanted to look at the representation of childhood/children in the arts and media. It definitely got peoples attention. This was a magazine I entirely produced and funded myself. Except for the designer (Colin Higgs) I did everything. The opening party attracted about 2,000 people it was an incredible reception.**

Fuller This was in 1998? Around the same time of your ICA show.

Henwood **It was all linked yes. I showed the first large scale gouache portraits of teenagers there. It was part of the "Spoilt Children" conference. This led to my first shows in New York and Tokyo.**

Fuller This must have been a very busy period for you then, as you were also involved in the computer animation project Johnny Pumpkin. This was something you carried over from Purr magazine?

Henwood **Johnny Pumpkin first appeared on the cover of the launch issue of Purr. His character / identity only evolved by the 3rd issue and became a regular strip in the magazine. I had always been interested in animation and made several short films at college. 3D (CGI) was very new at this time. Toy Story was just about to come out so it was really pioneering times. I met some people who were looking to develop a studio and we began to work together on the project. It was a very slow progression and the software still quite limited. Over a three-year period I was able to raise quite a lot of money (Nearly one million pounds) also the technology got faster and we made a 45-minute film.**

Fuller Was this for broadcast?

Henwood **Yes, initially it was aimed at an adult market, but jumped around the networks before getting stuck in endless legal mud. In 2000 it was selected by the Hammer museum for a show and ran for three months as an installation with my original drawings and designs. It later got picked up by MOMA and toured a couple of other museums as part of Animations.**

Fuller So you were showing painting and animation at the same time

Henwood **It was a very good moment for my work. All the things I had worked on in the past that seemed somehow disparate or at odds with each other were finally being embraced together**

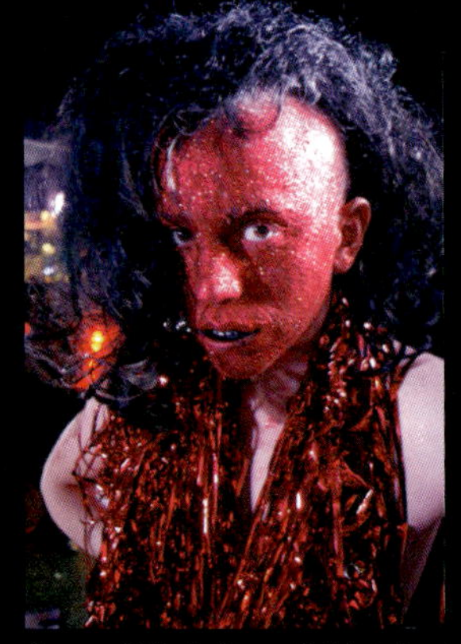

On set of Movie Star - Roisin Murphy, London 2008.

by the art world. There were a lot of Japanese artists emerging with similar criteria, which helped. Murakami, and Nara. I went to Nara's opening and he came to mine. I had these strange new contemporaries out of nowhere. Marcel Dzama to an extent as well.

Fuller Why at this point did you retreat from the gallery circuit?

Henwood **I have always worked across different disciplines. It makes perfect sense for me to change my direction if things are getting stale or predictable or less than challenging. Animation had led me to think about film more and I wanted to learn about it technically. I started making videos, something I had done years ago on a very small scale. First I combined animation and live action ideas. The first attempts were pretty misguided, but they got better. I did continue to paint and had several shows over the next three years. I mainly sold work out of the studio. At this time I was lucky enough to have a big place so could accommodate all my interests.**

Fuller When did your main focus return to painting?

Henwood **Well I'd say I still split my time between painting and film, and also recently some stage design. (Henwood was commissioned to design the set, costumes and back projections for Kanye West's recent European tour). If I'm working on a painting show though, that's all I do.**

Fuller You have recently started working in oil. The work is much more layered than the Gouache paintings. Also the subjects appear to be from found photo references as appose to your own pictures.

Henwood **The Gouache paintings are very immediate. You have to work fast and what you put down stays down. It's more like drawing in away. You can build the layers to a point, but the depth of colour and light is much more surface and graphic. I got to the point where I had to think of ways to create an illusion of depth, and with oil you have more possibilities and the process requires more foundation. Well, that's the way I'm approaching it.**

Fuller The first paintings were in colour and now you are working with a monochrome palette

Henwood **Yes. Well I call it Mono-Prismic. The under painting is in colour, so this bleeds through the final surface.**

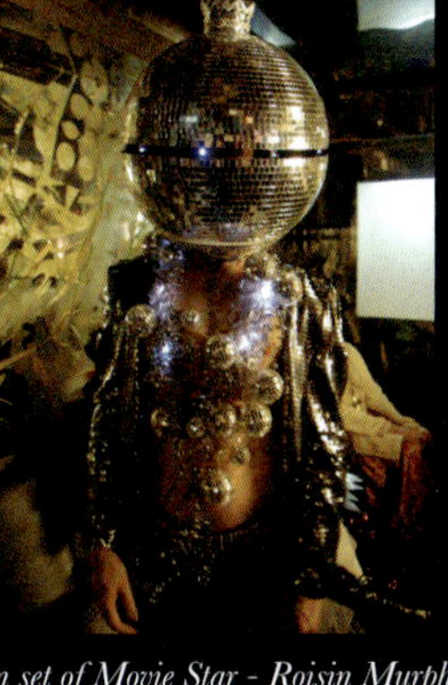

On set of Movie Star - Roisin Murphy, London 2008.

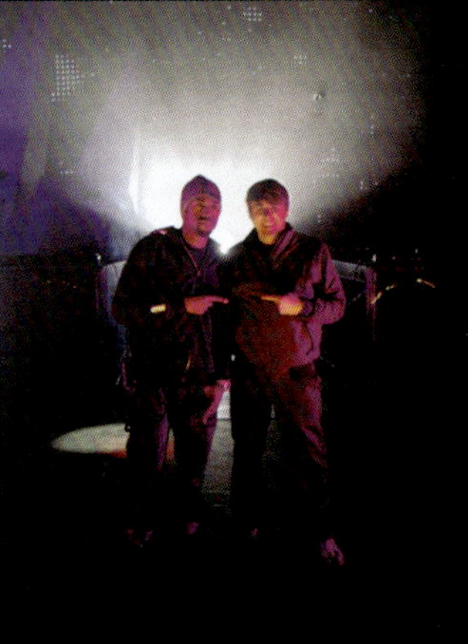

Henwood and Kanye West on the set build of the Glow in the Dark tour, Sheffield, England, 2007.

Fuller So how about the subjects, are they taken from black and white photographs?

Henwood **Yes. I have collected photos from fairs and markets for many years. Sometimes I will buy negative sets and make my own prints. Some of the pictures are taken for publicity, others are amateur set ups. From America, Russia, Romania, Cuba, all the subjects are unknown or aspiring actors or performers. I like the fact that maybe the act of painting them – turning these people into sort of icons – recognises failure as an option.**

Fuller This is an ongoing project isn't it? Where are you taking it?

Henwood **I'm imagining a story or a relationship. I guess I'm directing them, in a way.**

Fuller Last year (2007) you worked with Kanye West. How did that come about? What was the project?

Henwood **A producer of Kanye's contacted me saying he wanted to meet me. I didn't know what about. I presumed it was a video or something. I had a show opening in New York that September and got on the phone with him the night of the opening, actually. After the first meeting it was still not clear what we might work on together. A week later he called and asked me to direct and design his live tour.**

Fuller Have you ever worked on this type of project before?

Henwood **No (laughs) Although it was all very new to me I quickly figured ways around it all. The most challenging thing was the construction of the set from drawings and getting my head around the real scale of things.**

Fuller So you were the set designer?

Henwood **I worked on all aspects of it. I designed the sets with him, costumes and back drop animations.**

Fuller How long did the project last?

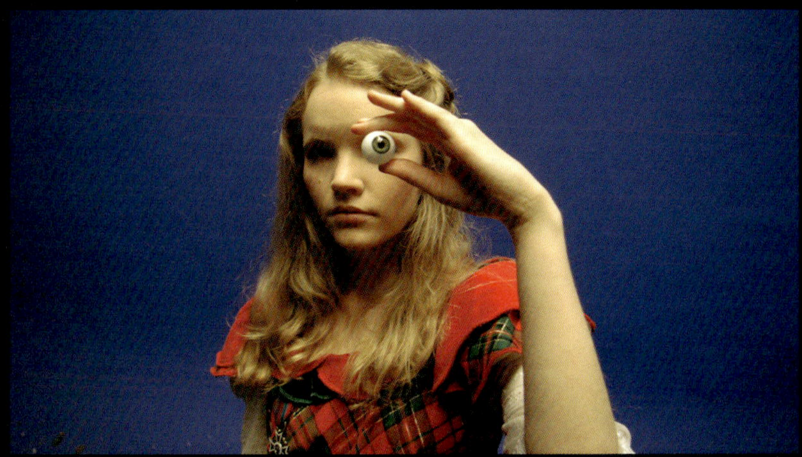

Henwood **I think I worked on it - including going on tour – for about three months. I had meetings back and forth to New York and LA. We worked through dozens of ideas. The actual production week was the most intensive. Kanye's mother died. He had just landed in the UK and got the message. He decided to carry on with the tour and came straight to me. It was a extraordinary week. He has unbelievable focus and stamina and was fascinating to work with.**

Fuller Are you still in contact with him?

Henwood **Oh Yes. (laughs) We are still working of various projects together!**

Fuller How about film? Any future plans?

Henwood **I have shot a short film on 35mm. It's called The Fallen Eye and stars Tamzin Merchant, who was in Pride and Prejudice. It has a period feel, a sort of fantasy costume drama. (Laughs) For a short film it's quite a big production and there is a lot of post, some of which I am still designing.**

Fuller When is it planned for release?

Henwood **Ah, the eternal question.**

Selected Excibitions

Solo Exhibitions

2008 Gallant company, Torch gallery, Amsterdam

2008 Inside, all summer long , Stephane Simoens gallery, Knokke, Belgium

2007 There For The Grace of God, Envoy gallery, New York

2006 Cricklewood, Envoy gallery, New York

2005 The Compact Kido Show, Cano (estudio), Madrid, Spain

2005 Simon Henwood, Colette, Paris, France

2005 Simon Henwood, The Hospital, London, England

2003 Kido, The Gallery at Pentagram, London, England

2000 Simon Henwood, Vedanta Gallery, Chicago, Illinois

2000 Simon Henwood, Hammer Project, UCLA Hammer Museum

2000 Simon Henwood, Richard Heller Gallery, Santa Monica, California

1999 White Kitten, Bronwyn Keenan Gallery, New York

1999 Simon Henwood: New Painitngs, Gallery Speak For, Tokyo, Japan

1998 Taught, ICA, London, England

Group Exhibitions

2009 Voodoo, Riflemaker, London

2008 Face forward, Leroy Neiman gallery, New York

2008 The appearance and the thing itself!, Gallerie Griesmar & Tamer, Paris

2007 Dress Code, Gallerie AAA gallery, Paris

2002 Animations, Kunstvert, Berlin

2001 Animations, PS1, New York including: William Kentridge,
Angus Fairhurst, Christina Mackie

2001 Slice of Life, De Chiara Gallery, New York including:
Diego Gravinese, Laura Mosquera, Suzy Spence

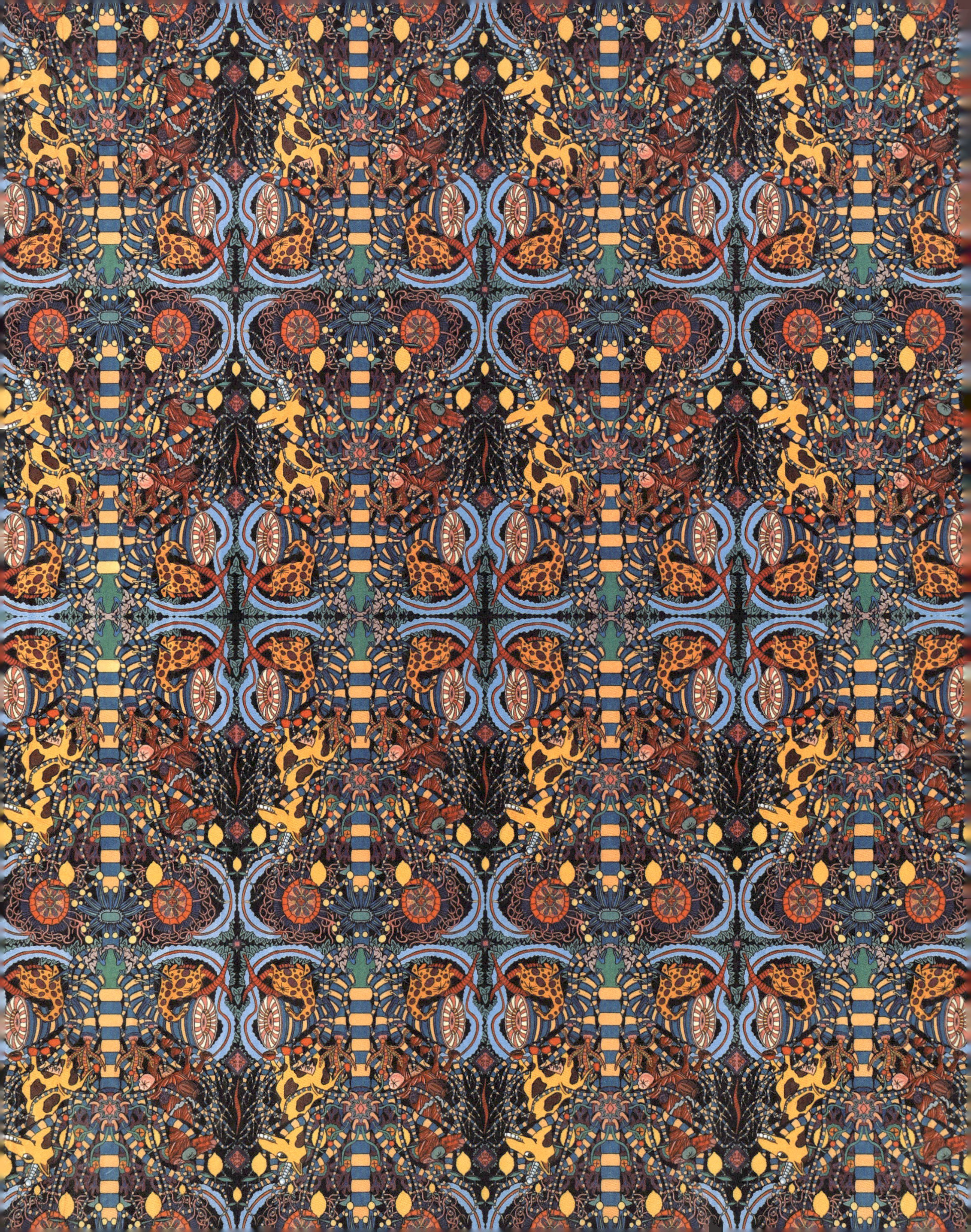